Research and Documentation in the Electronic Age

Fourth Edition

Research and Documentation in the Electronic Age

Fourth Edition

Diana Hacker

With research sources by

Barbara Fister

Gustavus Adolphus College

Bedford / St. Martin's
Boston ◆ New York

0   9   8   7
g   f   e

For information, write: Bedford/St. Martin's, 75 Arlington Street,
Boston, MA 02116 (617-399-4000)

ISBN-10: 0–312–44339–0
ISBN-13: 978–0–312–44339–9

Acknowledgments

Screen shot of database search results Blackwell Synergy Web site, www.blackwell-synergy.com. Reprinted with the permission of Blackwell Publishers, Ltd.

Boston Globe Archives, screen shot. Copyright © 2004 Boston Globe Archives.

Columbia University Library. Library Web pages. Copyright © Columbia University Libraries. www.columbia.edu. Reprinted by permission.

EBSCO Information Services, various screen shots. Reprinted with the permission of EBSCO Information Services.

Caroline M. Hoxby, "The Power of Peers." *Education Next,* Summer 2002. Reprinted by permission.

Henry Jenkins. Excerpted data from "Bearings." Copyright © 2002. Posted online within the *MIT Communications Forum.* Reprinted with permission.

Jill D. Jenson, excerpt from "It's the Information Age, So Where's the Information?" from *College Teaching* (Summer 2004). Copyright © 2004. Reprinted with the permission of the Helen Dwight Reed Educational Foundation. Published by Heldref Publications, 1319 18th Street NW, Washington, DC 20036.

Harvey A. Levenstein. Reprint of the title and copyright pages from *Revolution at the Table: The Transformation of the American Diet* by Harvey A. Levenstein. Copyright © 2003 by the Regents of the University of California Press. Reprinted with permission.

Chan Lowe, "Yep, got my cell" cartoon. Copyright © Tribune Media Services. All rights reserved. Reprinted with permission.

Anne McGrath, "A loss of foreign talent" from *U.S. News & World Report* (November 27, 2004). Copyright © 2004 by U.S. News & World Report, LP. Reprinted with permission.

"The Minnesota Annual Summary" or "Minnesota Health Statistics" report. Copyright © 2005 by the Minnesota Department of Health. www.health.state.mn.us.

L. M. Poupart. Page from "Crime and Justice in American Indian Communities." Copyright © 2002 ProQuest Information and Learning. Reprinted with permission.

Beth Shulman. Reprint of title and copyright pages from *Betrayal of Work* by Beth Shulman. Copyright © 2003 by Beth Shulman. Reprinted by permission of The New Press.

University of Minnesota Libraries, screen shots. Reprinted with permission.

Contents

Introduction

This inexpensive booklet supplements any of Diana Hacker's handbooks. It can be consulted for quick reference as you research and document sources in any college course. For advice about writing a research paper, consult *The Bedford Handbook, A Writer's Reference, Rules for Writers,* or *A Pocket Style Manual,* all by Diana Hacker.

Part I of this booklet offers guidelines on posing an appropriate research question and mapping out a search strategy. Part II gives general guidelines on finding and evaluating sources. Part III describes research practices in a variety of disciplines and lists specialized library and Web resources in many fields. Part IV includes four documentation styles — MLA, APA, *Chicago,* and CSE — and ends with a list of style manuals. Documentation models are provided for both print and electronic sources. Part V is a glossary of research terms.

An online version of this booklet entitled *Research and Documentation Online* is available at <http://dianahacker .com/resdoc>.

PART I. RESEARCH QUESTIONS AND SEARCH STRATEGIES

College research assignments ask you to pose a question worth exploring, to read widely in search of possible answers, to interpret what you read, to draw reasoned conclusions, and to support those conclusions with valid and well-documented evidence. Such assignments may at first seem overwhelming, but if you pose a question that intrigues you and approach it like a detective, with genuine curiosity, you will soon learn how rewarding research can be.

Your search strategies — whether you search your library's databases or catalog, explore the Web, or gather information in the field — will vary depending on the research questions you have posed.

Posing a research question

Working within the guidelines of your assignment, pose a few questions that seem worth researching. Here, for example, are some preliminary questions jotted down by students enrolled in a variety of classes in different disciplines.

- Should the FCC broaden its definition of indecent programming to include violence?
- Which geological formations are the safest repositories for nuclear waste?
- Will a ban on stem cell research threaten important medical advancements?
- What was Marcus Garvey's contribution to the fight for racial equality?
- How can governments and zoos help preserve China's endangered panda?
- Why was amateur archaeologist Heinrich Schliemann such a controversial figure in his own time?

As you formulate possible questions, make sure that they are appropriate lines of inquiry for a research paper. Choose questions that are narrow (not too broad), challenging (not too bland), and grounded (not too speculative).

Choosing a narrow question

If your initial question is too broad, given the length of the paper you plan to write, look for ways to restrict your focus. Here, for example, is how some students narrowed their initial questions.

TOO BROAD

What are the hazards of fad diets?

Is the United States seriously addressing the problem of prisoner abuse?

What causes depression?

NARROWER

What are the hazards of low-carbohydrate diets?

To what extent has the US military addressed the problem of prisoner abuse since the Abu Ghraib discoveries?

How has the widespread use of antidepressant drugs affected teenage suicide rates?

Choosing a challenging question

Your research paper will be more interesting to both you and your audience if you base it on an intellectually challenging line of inquiry. Avoid bland questions that fail to provoke thought or engage readers in a debate.

TOO BLAND

What is obsessive-compulsive disorder?

Where is wind energy being used?

How does DNA testing work?

CHALLENGING

What treatments for obsessive-compulsive disorder show the most promise?

Does investing in wind energy make economic sense?

How reliable is DNA testing?

You may well need to address a bland question in the course of answering a more challenging one. For example, if you were writing about promising treatments for obsessive-compulsive disorder, you would no doubt answer the question "What is obsessive-compulsive disorder?" at some point in your paper. It would be a mistake, however, to use the bland question as the focus for the whole paper.

Choosing a grounded question

Finally, you will want to make sure that your research question is grounded, not too speculative. Although speculative questions — such as those that address philosophical, ethical, or religious issues — are worth asking and may receive some attention in a research paper, they are inappropriate central questions. The central argument of a research paper should be grounded in facts; it should not be based entirely on beliefs.

TOO SPECULATIVE

Is it wrong to share music files on the Internet?

Do medical scientists have the right to experiment on animals?

Are youth sports too dangerous?

GROUNDED

How has Internet file sharing affected the earning potential of musicians?

How have technical breakthroughs made medical experiments on animals increasingly unnecessary?

How should coaches respond to angry parents at youth sporting events?

Mapping out a search strategy

A search strategy is a systematic plan for tracking down sources. To create a search strategy appropriate for your research question, consult a reference librarian and take a look at your library's Web site, which will give you an overview of available resources.

Getting started

Reference librarians are information specialists who can save you time by steering you toward relevant and reliable sources. With the help of an expert, you can make the best use of electronic databases, Web search engines, and other reference tools.

When you ask a reference librarian for help, be prepared to answer a number of questions:

- What is your assignment?
- In which academic discipline are you writing?
- What is your tentative research question?
- How long will the paper be?
- How much time can you spend on the project?

It's a good idea to bring a copy of the assignment with you.

In addition to speaking with a reference librarian, take some time to explore your library's Web site. You will typically find links to the library's catalog and to a variety of databases and electronic sources that you can access from any networked computer. In addition, you may find resources listed by subject, research guides, information about interlibrary loans, and links to Web sites selected by librarians for their quality. What's more, many libraries offer online reference assistance to help you locate information and refine your search strategy.

NOTE: If you connect to the library's Web site from off campus, you may have to set up a remote account to access subscription databases such as *InfoTrac;* ask a librarian for help.

Including the library in your plan

Resist the temptation to do all of your work on the Internet. Even though it may seem tedious at first, becoming familiar with your library's print and electronic resources will save you time and money in the end. Libraries offer a wider range of quality materials than the Web does. The Web is not the best place to find literary criticism, historical analysis, or reports of scientific research, for example; all of these are more likely to be published in traditional ways.

Most college assignments will require using at least some formally published sources, such as books and journal articles. Although you can locate some newspaper and magazine articles online, you may have to pay a fee or purchase a subscription to access them. Most libraries subscribe to databases that will give you unlimited access to many of these materials as well as to scholarly resources that won't turn up in a Web search. You will be able to do some of your work from any computer that can connect to the campus network. Keep in mind, however, that databases don't always include full-text articles of everything they cite. More often than not, you'll need to track down print copies in your library's stacks or request them through interlibrary loan.

Choosing an appropriate search strategy

No single search strategy works for every topic. For some topics, it may be appropriate to search for information in

LIBRARY HOME PAGE

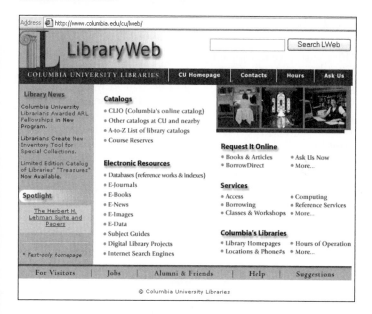

newspapers, magazines, and Web sites. For others, the best sources might be found in scholarly journals and books and specialized reference works. Still other topics might be enhanced by field research — interviews, surveys, or direct observation.

When in doubt about the kinds of sources appropriate for your topic, check with your instructor or a reference librarian.

PART II. FINDING AND EVALUATING SOURCES

Once you have discussed your topic with a reference librarian and sketched out your research strategy, you are ready to begin finding the sources you need. You will use a variety of research tools — such as databases and print indexes, your library's catalog, and the Web — to find sources appropriate for the research question you have posed.

Finding Sources

Finding articles using a database or print index

Libraries subscribe to a variety of electronic databases (sometimes called *periodical databases*) that give students access to articles and other materials without charge. Many databases are limited to works published in the last ten to twenty years. To find older articles, you may need to consult a print index such as the *New York Times Index* or *Readers' Guide to Periodical Literature.*

NOTE: There is a difference between Web-based databases a library pays for through a subscription and those that are free to the public at large. Subscription sites provide edited material that has been scrutinized before being published. That isn't always the case with sites that are free.

What databases offer

Your library has access to databases that can lead you to articles in periodicals such as newspapers, magazines, and scholarly or technical journals. Some databases cover several subjects; others cover one subject in depth. Though each library is unique, your library might subscribe to some of the following databases and collections of databases.

GENERAL DATABASES

EBSCOhost. A portal to more than one hundred databases that include periodical articles, government documents, pamphlets, and other types of documents, many available in full text. Through *EBSCOhost,* your library may also subscribe to a wide variety of subject-specific databases.

InfoTrac. A collection of databases. Some of them index periodical articles, many available in full text. Through *InfoTrac,* your library may also subscribe to specialized databases in business, health, and other fields.

LexisNexis. A set of databases that are particularly strong in coverage of news, business, legal, and political topics. Nearly all of the material is available in full text.

ProQuest. A database of periodical articles, many available in full text. Through *ProQuest,* your library may also subscribe to databases in subjects such as nursing, biology, and psychology.

SUBJECT-SPECIFIC DATABASES

ERIC. An education database offering abstracts of articles published in education journals and other education-related documents.

MEDLINE. A database offering millions of abstracts of medical research studies.

MLA Bibliography. A database of literary criticism, with references to articles, books, and dissertations.

PsycINFO. The most complete database of psychology research, including abstracts to articles in journals and books.

Many databases include the full text of at least some articles; others list only citations or citations with short summaries called *abstracts.* In the case of full-text articles,

Refining keyword searches in databases and search engines

Although command terms and characters vary among electronic databases and Web search engines, some of the most commonly used functions are listed here.

- Use quotation marks around words that are part of a phrase: "Broadway musicals".

- Use AND to connect words that must appear in a document: Ireland AND peace. In some search engines — *Google*, for example — *and* is assumed, so typing it is unnecessary. Other search engines require a plus sign instead: Ireland +peace.

- Use NOT in front of words that must not appear in a document: Titanic NOT movie. Some search engines require a minus sign (hyphen) instead: Titanic -movie.

- Use OR if only one of the terms must appear in a document: "mountain lion" OR cougar.

- Use an asterisk as a substitute for letters that might vary: "marine biolog*" (to find *marine biology* or *marine biologist*, for example).

- Use parentheses to group a search expression and combine it with another: (cigarettes OR tobacco OR smok*) AND lawsuits.

NOTE: Many search engines and databases offer an advanced search option that makes it easy to refine your search.

you may have the option to print an article, save it to a disk, or e-mail it to yourself.

When full text is not available, the citation will give you enough information to track down an article. Check your library's catalog to find out if the library owns the periodical or book in which the article appears and, if so, where it is shelved. If the library does not own the item you want, you can usually request a copy through interlibrary loan;

check with a librarian to find out how long the source will take to arrive.

How to search a database

To find articles on your topic in a database, start with a keyword search. If the first keyword you try results in no matches, don't give up; experiment with synonyms or ask a librarian for suggestions. If your keyword search results in too many matches, narrow your search. The most common way to narrow a search is to connect two search terms with AND: *childhood obesity AND treatments.* These and other strategies for narrowing or broadening a search are included in the chart on page 10.

When to use a print index

If you want to search for articles published before the 1980s, you may need to turn to a print index. For example, if you are looking for a newspaper article written in the 1850s, you might consult the *New York Times Index,* an index that began coverage in 1851. To find older magazine articles, consult the *Readers' Guide to Periodical Literature* or *Poole's Index to Periodical Literature.*

Finding books in the library's catalog

The books your library owns are listed in its computer catalog, along with other resources such as videos. You can search the catalog by author, title, or topic keywords. The screens on pages 12 and 13 illustrate a search of a library catalog.

Don't be surprised if your first search calls up too few or too many results. If you have too few results, try different keywords or search for books on broader topics. If those strategies don't work, ask a librarian for suggestions.

**LIBRARY CATALOG SCREEN 1:
ADVANCED SEARCH**

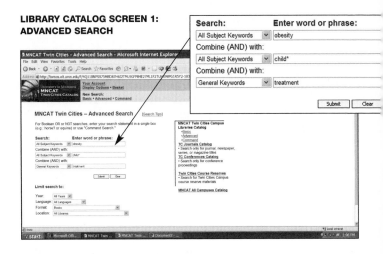

LIBRARY CATALOG SCREEN 2: SEARCH RESULTS

MNCAT Twin Cities
Results for : All Subjects KW= (obesity) AND All Subjects KW= (child*) AND General Key
Sort options : •Author/Year(d)• Year(d)/Author •Author/Title •Title/Year(d) •Year(d)/Title

Records 1 - 7 of 7

#	Title	Author
1 ☐	Treatment of overweight children and adolescents : a needs assessment of health practitioners.	
2 ☐	Body image, eating disorders, and obesity in youth : assessment, prevention, and treatment /	Thompson, J. Kevin.
3 ☐	Childhood and adolescent obesity /	Styne, Dennis M.
4 ☐	Obesity : impact on cardiovascular disease /	Fletcher, Gerald F., 1935-
5 ☐	Obesity in childhood and adolescence : assessment, prevention and treatment : papers emanating from a conference held in Minneapolis, Minnesota, USA, May, 1997 /	Himes, J. H. (John H.)
6 ☐	Prevention and treatment of childhood obesity /	Williams, Christine L., 1943-
7 ☐	Treating childhood and adolescent obesity /	Kirschenbaum, Daniel S.,

LIBRARY CATALOG SCREEN 3: COMPLETE RECORD FOR A BOOK

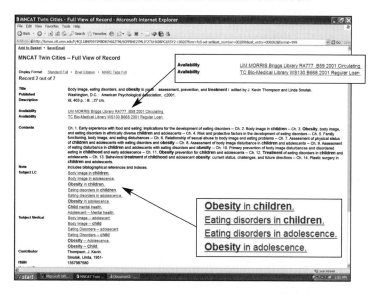

Sometimes catalogers don't use the words you would expect — for example, *motion pictures* might be used as a subject heading instead of *movies* or *films*.

If a search gives you too many results, you will need to narrow your search. Many catalogs offer an advanced search tool that will help you combine concepts and limit your results. For example, a search for the term *obesity* might turn up more than fifty hits, an unmanageable number. An advanced search could significantly limit your results, as shown in screens 1 and 2.

Once you have narrowed your search to a list of relevant sources, you can display or print the complete record for each source, which includes its bibliographic information (author, title, publication data) and a call number.

Screen 3 shows the complete record for the second title on the list generated by the search shown in screens 1 and 2. The call number, listed beside *Availability,* is the book's address on the library shelf. When you're retrieving a book from the shelf, take the time to scan other books in the area since they are likely to be on the same topic.

LIBRARIAN'S TIP: The record for a book lists related subject headings. These headings are a good way to locate other books on your subject. For example, the record on page 13 lists the terms *Obesity in children* and *Obesity in adolescence* as related subject headings. Clicking on these new terms, would provide more books on the subject.

Finding a wide variety of sources on the Web

For some — but not all — topics, the Web is an excellent resource. For example, most government agencies post information on the Web, and federal and state governments use Web sites to communicate with citizens. The sites of many private organizations, such as the American Cancer Society and the Sierra Club, contain useful information about current issues. Even if your subject is not current, you may find the Web useful. Museums and libraries often post digital versions of primary sources, such as photographs, political speeches, and classic literary texts.

Although the Web may be a rich source of information, some of which can't be found anywhere else, it lacks quality control. Anyone can publish on the Web, so you'll need to evaluate online sources with special care (see pp. 31–33).

This section describes the following Web resources: search engines, directories, digital archives, government and news sites, and discussion forums. For lists of library and Web resources in a variety of academic disciplines, see Part III.

Search engines

Search engines take your search terms and seek matches among millions of Web pages. Some search engines go into more depth than others, but none can search the entire Web.

For information about search engines, visit *Search Engine Showdown* at <http://www.searchengineshow down.com>. This site classifies search engines, evaluates them, and provides updates on new search features. Following are some popular search engines:

> *Google* <http://www.google.com>
> *MSN Search* <http://search.msn.com>
> *Teoma* <http://www.teoma.com>
> *Yahoo!* <http://www.yahoo.com>

In using a search engine, focus your search as narrowly as possible. You can sharpen your search by using many of the tips listed in the chart on page 10 or by using the search engine's advanced search form. For example, typing *cell phones* and *driving* into a search engine, you might retrieve thousands of matches. To narrow your search to a more manageable number, you might try *cell phones while driving* AND *accidents.* If your search still turns up an unmanageable number of hits, you can click on Advanced Search. On the advanced search screen, you can restrict your search to government-sponsored sites with URLs ending in *.gov.* The resulting list will be even briefer and may include promising sources for your paper.

Directories

Unlike search engines, which hunt for Web pages automatically, directories are put together by information specialists who choose reputable sites and arrange them by topic: education, health, politics, and so on.

Some directories are more selective and therefore more useful for scholarly research than the directories that typically accompany a search engine. For example, the directory for the *Internet Scout Project* was created for a research audience; it includes annotations that are both descriptive and evaluative. The following list includes directories especially useful for scholarly research:

Internet Scout Project <http://scout.wisc.edu/Archives>

Librarian's Index to the Internet <http://www.lii.org>

Open Directory Project <http://www.dmoz.org>

World Wide Web Virtual Library <http://www.vlib.org>

Digital archives

Archives contain the texts of poems, books, speeches, political cartoons, and historically significant documents such as the Declaration of Independence and the Emancipation Proclamation. The materials in these sites are usually limited to official documents and older works because of copyright laws. The following online archives are impressive collections:

American Memory <http://memory.loc.gov>

Archival Research Catalog <http://www.archives.gov/research_room/arc/>

Avalon Project <http://www.yale.edu/lawweb/avalon/avalon.htm>

Electronic Text Center <http://etext.lib.virginia.edu>

Eurodocs <http://library.byu.edu/~rdh/eurodocs>

Internet History Sourcebooks <http://www.fordham.edu/halsall/index.html>

Online Books Page <http://digital.library.upenn.edu/books>

Government and news sites

For current topics, both government and news sites can prove useful. Many government agencies at every level provide online information. Government-maintained sites include resources such as legal texts, facts and statistics, government reports, and searchable reference databases. Here are just a few government sites:

Census Bureau <http://www.census.gov>

Fedstats <http://www.fedstats.gov>

FirstGov <http://www.firstgov.gov>

GPO Access <http://www.gpoaccess.gov>

United Nations <http://www.un.org>

NOTE: You can access a state's Web site by putting the two-letter state abbreviation into a standard URL: <http://www.state.ca.us>. Substitute any state's two-letter abbreviation for the letters *ca*, which in this case stand for California.

Many popular newsletters, magazines, and television networks offer up-to-date information on the Web. These online services often allow nonsubscribers to read current stories for free. Some allow users to log on as guests and search archives without cost, but to read actual articles users typically must pay a fee. The following are some free news sites:

Google News <http://news.google.com>

Kidon Media-Link <http://www.kidon.com/media-link>

NewsLink <http://newslink.org>

NOTE: Your library may subscribe to *LexisNexis* or other online databases with more full-text news sources than are available for free on the Web (see pp. 8–11).

Discussion forums

The Web offers ways of communicating with experts and others who have an interest in your topic. You might join an online mailing list, for example, to send and receive e-mail messages relevant to your topic. Or you may wish to search a newsgroup's postings. Newsgroups resemble bulletin boards on which messages are posted and connected through "threads" as others respond. To find mailing lists and newsgroups, check a subject directory (see p. 15) to see if any are listed for the discipline you are interested in, or try one of these sites:

> *CataList* <http://www.lsoft.com/catalist.html>
>
> *Google Groups* <http://groups.google.com>
>
> *Tile.net* <http://tile.net>

In addition to mailing lists and newsgroups, you might log on to real-time discussion forums such as chats.

TIP: Be aware that many of the people you contact in discussion forums will not be experts on your topic. Although you are more likely to find serious and worthwhile commentary in moderated mailing lists and scholarly discussion forums than in more freewheeling newsgroups, it is difficult to guarantee the credibility of anyone you meet online.

Considering other search tools

In addition to articles, books, and Web sources, you may want to consult reference works such as encyclopedias and almanacs. Bibliographies (lists of works written on a topic) and citations in scholarly works can lead you to additional sources.

Reference works

The reference section of the library holds both general and specialized encyclopedias, dictionaries, almanacs, atlases, and biographical references. Some are available in electronic format. Reference works provide information in easily digested nuggets; they often serve as a good overview of your subject and include references to the most significant works on a topic. Check with a reference librarian to see which works are most appropriate for your project.

NOTE: See Part III for descriptions of reference works and other resources likely to be useful in a variety of disciplines.

GENERAL REFERENCE WORKS   General reference works are good places to check facts and get basic information. Here are a few frequently used general references:

> *American National Biography*
> *National Geographic Atlas of the World*
> *The New Encyclopaedia Britannica*
> *The Oxford English Dictionary*
> *Statistical Abstract of the United States*
> *World Almanac and Book of Facts*

NOTE: Although general reference works are often a good place to find background about your topic, you should rarely use them in your final paper. Most instructors expect you to rely on more specialized sources.

SPECIALIZED REFERENCE WORKS   Specialized reference works often go into a topic in depth, sometimes in the form of articles written by leading authorities. Many specialized works are available, including these:

> *Contemporary Authors*
> *Encyclopedia of Applied Ethics*

Encyclopedia of Crime and Justice
Encyclopedia of Psychology
McGraw-Hill Encyclopedia of Science and Technology

Check with a reference librarian to see what specialized references are available in your library.

Bibliographies and scholarly citations

Bibliographies are lists of works written on a particular topic. They include enough information about each work (author's name, title, and publication data) so that you can locate the book or article.

Many bibliographies are annotated: They contain abstracts giving a brief overview of each work's contents. You can find book-length bibliographies by adding the term *bibliography* to a catalog search. For example, if you typed the search term "*Civil War*" AND *bibliography*, you would find books that list and describe publications about all aspects of the Civil War.

In addition to book-length bibliographies, scholarly books and articles list the works the author has cited, usually at the end. These lists of sources are tremendously useful shortcuts: Often the author of the work has done some of your research for you. Through these citations, you can quickly locate additional relevant sources on your topic. (For help tracking down works cited in a bibliography or a scholarly work, see the chart on p. 21.)

Tracking down a source cited in a reference or scholarly work

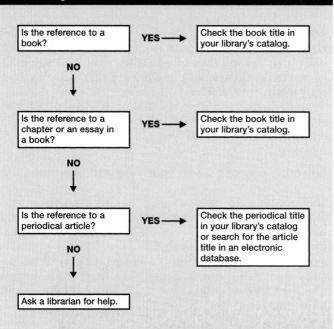

If the work you need is not listed in the library catalog, ask a reference librarian about interlibrary loan service.

Evaluating Sources

With electronic search tools, you can often locate dozens or even hundreds of potential sources for your topic — far more than you will have time to read. Your challenge will be to zero in on a reasonable number of quality sources, those truly worth your time and attention.

Later, once you have decided on some sources worth consulting, your challenge will be to read them with an open mind and a critical eye.

Selecting sources worth your time and attention

The previous sections showed you how to refine your searches in the library's book catalog, in databases, and in search engines. This section shows you how to scan through the results looking for those sources that seem most promising. It also gives you tips on previewing possible sources — without actually reading them — to see whether they are likely to live up to your expectations and meet your needs.

Scanning search results

As you scan through a list of search results, be alert for any clues indicating whether a source might be useful for your purposes or not worth pursuing. You will need to use somewhat different scanning strategies when looking at lists of hits from a book catalog, a database, and a Web search engine.

BOOK CATALOGS   The library's book catalog will usually give a fairly short list of hits (see p. 12 for an example). A book's title and date of publication will often be your first clues as to whether the book is worth consulting. If a title looks interesting, you can click on it for further information: the book's subject matter and its length, for example. The table of contents may also be available, offering a glimpse of what's inside.

DATABASES   Most databases, such as *ProQuest* and *LexisNexis,* list at least the following information, which can help you decide if a source is relevant, current, scholarly enough, and a suitable length for your purposes.

Title and brief description (How relevant?)

Date (How current?)

Name of periodical (How scholarly?)

Length (How extensive in coverage?)

WEB SEARCH ENGINES   Anyone can publish on the Web, and unreliable sites often masquerade as legitimate sources of information. As you scan through search results, look for the following clues about the probable relevance, currency, and reliability of a site — but be aware that the clues are by no means foolproof.

Title, keywords, and lead-in text (How relevant?)

A date (How current?)

An indication of the site's sponsor or purpose (How reliable?)

The URL, especially the domain name (How relevant? How reliable?)

Previewing sources

Once you have decided that a source looks promising, preview it quickly to see whether it lives up to its promise. If you can reject irrelevant or unreliable sources before actually reading them, you will save yourself time. Techniques for previewing a book or an article are relatively simple; strategies for investigating the likely worth of a Web site are more complicated.

PREVIEWING A BOOK   As you preview a book, keep in mind that even if the entire book is not worth your time, parts of it may prove useful. As you preview a book, try any or all of the following techniques:

- Glance through the table of contents, keeping your research question in mind.
- Skim the preface in search of a statement of the author's purposes.
- Use the index to look up a few words related to your topic.
- If a chapter looks useful, read its opening and closing paragraphs and skim any headings.
- Consider the author's style and approach. Does the style suggest enough intellectual depth, or is the book too specialized for your purposes? Does the author present ideas in an unbiased way?

PREVIEWING AN ARTICLE   As with books, the techniques for previewing an article are fairly straightforward. Here are a few strategies:

- Consider the publication in which the article is printed. Is it a scholarly journal? A popular magazine? A newspaper with a national reputation?
- For a magazine or journal article, look for an abstract or a statement of purpose at the beginning; also look for a summary at the end.

- For a newspaper article, focus on the headline and the opening, known as the *lead.*

- Skim any headings and take a look at any visuals — charts, graphs, diagrams, or illustrations — that might indicate the article's focus and scope.

PREVIEWING A WEB SITE It is a fairly quick and easy job to track down numerous potentially useful sources on the Web, but evaluating those sources can require some detective work. Web sites can be created by anyone, and their authors and purposes are not always readily apparent. In addition, there are no set standards for the design of Web sites, so you may need to do a fair amount of clicking and scrolling before locating clues about a site's reliability.

As you preview a Web site, check for relevance, reliability, and currency:

- Browse the home page. Do its contents and links seem relevant to your research question? What is the site trying to do: Sell a product? Promote an idea? Inform the public? Provide Web versions of print sources (such as newspaper stories or government reports)? Is the site's purpose consistent with your research?

- Look for the name of an author or a Webmaster, and if possible assess his or her credibility. Often a site's author is named at the bottom of the home page. If you have landed on an internal page of a site and no author is evident, try linking to the home page.

- Check for a sponsor name, and consider possible motives the organization might have in sponsoring the site. Is the group likely to look at only one side of an issue?

- Find out when the site was created or last updated. Is it current enough for your purposes?

Determining if a source is scholarly

For many college assignments, you will be asked to use scholarly sources. These are written by experts for a knowledgeable audience and usually go into more depth than books and articles written for a general audience. (Scholarly sources are sometimes called *refereed* or *peer-reviewed* because the work is evaluated by experts in the field before publication.) To determine if a source is scholarly, look for the following:

- Formal language and presentation
- Authors who are academics or scientists, not journalists
- Footnotes or a bibliography documenting the works cited in the source
- Original research and interpretation (rather than a summary of other people's work)
- Quotations from and analysis of primary sources (in humanities disciplines such as literature, history, and philosophy)
- A description of research methods or a review of related research (in the sciences and social sciences)

NOTE: In some databases, searches can be limited to refereed or peer-reviewed journals.

NOTE: If a site gives very little information about its authors or sponsors, be suspicious. Do not rely on such sites when conducting academic research.

Distinguishing between primary and secondary sources

As you begin assessing evidence in a source, determine whether you are reading a primary or a secondary source. Primary sources are original documents such as letters, diaries, legislative bills, laboratory studies, field research reports, and eyewitness accounts. Secondary sources are commentaries on primary sources.

Although a primary source is not necessarily more reliable than a secondary source, it has the advantage of being a firsthand account. Naturally, you can better evaluate what a secondary source says if you have first read any primary sources it discusses.

Selecting appropriate versions of electronic sources

An electronic source may appear as an abstract, an excerpt, or a full-text article or book. It is important to distinguish among these versions of sources and to use a complete version of a source, preferably one with page numbers, for your research.

Abstracts and excerpts are shortened versions of complete articles or books. An abstract typically appears in a database record for a periodical article (see p. 28). It is a summary of the article's contents. An abstract can also appear in a catalog listing for a book. An abstract can give you clues about the usefulness of a source for your paper. But because an abstract is so brief (usually fewer than five hundred words), by itself it does not contain enough information to cite in your paper. To understand the author's argument and use it in your own paper, you must read the complete article. When you determine that the full article is worth reading, scroll through the record to find a link to the complete article. If you cannot access the complete article from the database, you may be able to obtain a copy of the periodical from the library stacks; if you are unsure whether your library keeps the periodical, ask a librarian for assistance.

An excerpt is the first few sentences or paragraphs (the *lead*) of a newspaper or magazine article and usually appears in a list of hits in an online search (see the top of p. 29). From an excerpt you can sometimes determine whether the complete article is useful for your paper. Sometimes, however, the thesis or topic sentence of the arti-

DATABASE RECORD WITH AN ABSTRACT

 LINCC, Library Information Network for Community Colleges
Expanded Academic ASAP

—— Article 1 of 2 —— ▶

□
Mark *Civil War History*, June 1996 v42 n2 p116(17)

> **"These devils are not fit to live on God's earth": war crimes and the Committee on the Conduct of the War, 1864-1865.** *Bruce Tap.*

Abstract: The Committee on the Conduct of the War's report on the April 1864 Fort Pillow massacre of black Union soldiers by Confederate forces influenced public opinion against the atrocities of the Confederate troops and accelerated the reconstruction program. Hostility against blacks and abolition in the South prompted the Confederates to target black troops and deny them prisoner of war status. Investigation exposed the barbaric act and the Northern prisoners' suffering in Southern prisons. The report helped the inclusion of black troops in the prisoner exchange program.

    Article A18749078

cle is buried deeper in the article than the excerpt reveals. In these cases, the headline might be a clue to the usefulness of the complete article. You may find that you are required to pay a fee to access the complete article. Before paying a fee, try searching your library's electronic databases for the article. Or your library may have a subscription to the online publication or may keep a copy of the periodical in its stacks.

A full-text work may appear online as a PDF (for *portable document format*) file or as an HTML file (sometimes called a *text file*). (See the database record at the bottom of p. 29.) A PDF file is usually an exact copy of the pages of a periodical article as they appeared in print, including the page numbers. Some corporate and government reports are presented

SEARCH RESULT WITH AN EXCERPT

▾ BOSTON GLOBE ARCHIVES

Your search for **((fort AND pillow AND massacre))** returned **1** article(s) matching your terms.
To purchase the full-text of an article, follow the link that says "Click for complete article."

| Perform a new search |

Your search results:

TALES OF BLACKS IN THE CIVIL WAR, FOR ALL AGES
Published on March 23, 1998
Author(s):   Scott Alarik, Globe Correspondent

For African Americans, the Civil War was always two wars. It was, of course, the war to save the
union and destroy slavery, but for the nearly 180,000 black soldiers who served in the Union
Army, it was also a war to establish their rights as citizens and human beings in the United
States. Their role in defeating the Confederacy is grandly chronicled in two new books, the
massively complete "Like Men of War" and the superbly readable children's book "Black, Blue
and
Click for complete article *(782 words)*

DATABASE RECORD SHOWING HTML (TEXT) AND PDF OPTIONS

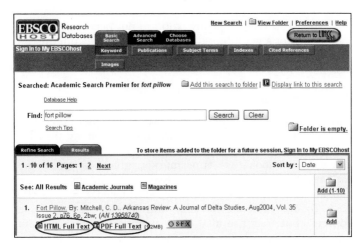

online as PDF files, and these too are usually paginated. A full-text document that appears as an HTML or a text file is not paginated. If your source is available in both formats, use the PDF file in your paper because you will be able to cite specific page numbers.

Reading with an open mind and a critical eye

As you begin reading the sources you have chosen, keep an open mind. Do not let your personal beliefs prevent you from listening to new ideas and opposing viewpoints. Your research question — not a snap judgment about the question — should guide your reading.

TIP: When researching on the Web, it is easy to ignore views different from your own. Web pages that appeal to you will often link to other pages that support the same viewpoint. If your sources all seem to agree with you — and with one another — seek out opposing views and evaluate them with an open mind.

When you read critically, you are not necessarily judging an author's work harshly; you are simply examining its assumptions, assessing its evidence, and weighing its conclsions.

Being alert for signs of bias

Both in print and online, some sources are more objective than others. If you were exploring the conspiracy theories surrounding John F. Kennedy's assassination, for example, you wouldn't look to a supermarket tabloid, such as the *National Enquirer*, for answers. Even publications that are considered reputable can be editorially biased. For example, *USA Today, National Review,* and *Ms.* are all credible sources, but they are also likely to interpret events quite differently from one another. If you are uncertain about a periodical's special interests, consult *Magazines for Libraries.* To check for bias in a book, see *Book Review Digest.* A reference librarian can help you locate these resources.

Like publishers, some authors are more objective than others. If you have reason to believe that a writer is particularly biased, you will want to assess his or her arguments with special care. For a list of questions worth asking, see the chart on page 32.

Assessing the author's argument

In nearly all subjects worth writing about, there is some element of argument, so don't be surprised to encounter experts who disagree. When you find areas of disagreement, you will want to read each source's arguments with special care, testing them with your own critical intelligence. Questions such as those in the chart on page 32 can help you weigh the strengths and weaknesses of each author's arguments.

Assessing Web sources with special care

As you may have discovered, Web sources can be deceptive. Sophisticated-looking sites can be full of dubious information, and the identities of those who created a site are often hidden, along with their motives for having created it. Even hate sites may be cleverly disguised to look legitimate. In contrast, sites with reliable information can stand up to careful scrutiny. For a checklist on evaluating Web sources, see page 33.

Evaluating all sources

CHECKING FOR SIGNS OF BIAS

- Does the author or publisher have political leanings or religious views that could affect objectivity?
- Is the author or publisher associated with a special-interest group, such as Greenpeace or the National Rifle Association, that might promote one side of an issue?
- Are alternative views presented and addressed? How fairly does the author treat opposing views?
- Does the author's language show signs of bias?

ASSESSING AN ARGUMENT

- What is the author's central claim or thesis?
- How does the author support this claim — with relevant and sufficient evidence or with just a few anecdotes or emotional examples?
- Are statistics consistent with those you encounter in other sources? Have they been used fairly? Does the author explain where the statistics come from? (It is possible to "lie" with statistics by using them selectively or by omitting mathematical details.)
- Are any of the author's assumptions questionable?
- Does the author consider opposing arguments and refute them persuasively?
- Does the author fall prey to any logical fallacies?

Evaluating Web sources

TIP: If the sponsorship and the authorship of a site are both unclear, think twice about using the site for your research.

AUTHORSHIP

- Is there an author? You may need to do some clicking and scrolling to find the author's name. If you are on an internal page of a site, for example, you may need to go to the home page or click on an "about this site" link to learn the name of the author.
- If there is an author, can you tell whether he or she is knowledgeable and credible? When the author's qualifications aren't listed on the site itself, look for links to the author's home page, which may provide evidence of his or her interests and expertise.

SPONSORSHIP

- Who, if anyone, sponsors the site? The sponsor of a site is often named and described on the home page.
- What does the URL ending tell you? The URL often specifies the type of group hosting the site: commercial (.com), educational (.edu), nonprofit (.org), governmental (.gov), military (.mil), or network (.net). URLs may also indicate a country of origin: uk (United Kingdom) or jp (Japan), for instance.

PURPOSE AND AUDIENCE

- Why was the site created: To argue a position? To sell a product? To inform readers?
- Who is the site's intended audience? If you do not fit the audience profile, is information on the site still relevant to your topic?

CURRENCY

- How current is the site? Check for the date of publication or the latest update.
- How current are the site's links? If many of the links no longer work, the site may be too dated for your purposes.

PART III. SPECIALIZED LIBRARY AND WEB RESOURCES

Researching in the Humanities

Research in the humanities generally involves interpreting a text or a work of art within a historical and cultural context, making connections, exploring meaning, uncovering contradictions. Scholars in the humanities typically use library resources in at least three ways:

- to obtain primary sources to be interpreted or analyzed
- to find secondary sources to put primary sources in a critical context
- to seek answers to specific questions that arise during research

Research in the humanities is often interdisciplinary, crossing boundaries between literature and history, philosophy and art, or music and religion. Because the subject areas are harder to categorize, the terminology used in humanities research may be less solid and agreed upon than in other fields. Researchers in the humanities are more likely to draw material from texts and artifacts than from original data gathering and experimentation. They must be prepared to be

- flexible, both in search terminology and in search strategy
- tolerant of multiple perspectives on the same object of study

- prepared to use citations in relevant texts to locate other material and clarify connections among works
- willing to return to the library as new questions arise

Fortunately, there are many fine research tools to help. Those listed here are not available in every library, but they give you some ideas to start with. Always bear in mind, too, that librarians are a particularly user-friendly research tool. Plan to ask a librarian for recommended resources as you begin your research, and use the librarian's expertise as your research progresses and your questions grow more specific.

General resources in the humanities

Databases and indexes in the humanities

Arts and Humanities Citation Index. Philadelphia: Institute for Scientific Information, 1978–. An interdisciplinary index to articles in more than 1,100 periodicals, searchable by author, keyword, and cited work. Providing citations and descriptive abstracts, this index is available in print and electronic formats. It may be available at your library as *AHSearch* (through the *FirstSearch* database collection) or as part of the *Web of Science* database.

Humanities Index. New York: Wilson, 1974–. An interdisciplinary index to about 400 of the most prominent English-language journals in the humanities, including art, music, history, and literature. Searchable by author or subject, the index includes many cross-references and subheadings that break large topics into components. This index is available in print and electronic formats; in some libraries, the database includes full text of selected articles.

Web resources in the humanities

Electronic Text Center <http://etext.lib.virginia.edu>. A vast collection of electronic texts, in 12 languages, digitized by the University of Virginia Library. It is possible to search hundreds of texts at once by keyword and to download texts to your computer. The site includes links to other electronic text collections on the Web. (Some texts are available only to University of Virginia students and staff.)

The Online Books Page <http://digital.library.upenn.edu/books>. Provides links to over 20,000 full-text books and journals in English and allows searching by author and title. The site includes special exhibits on women writers, banned books, and prize winners. It is edited by John Mark Ockerbloom at the University of Pennsylvania.

Voice of the Shuttle <http://vos.ucsb.edu>. A wide-ranging index to sites of interest to researchers in humanities disciplines — art, literature, philosophy, religion, and cultural studies — with links to higher education and publishing sites. The site is maintained by Allen Liu and others in the English Department at the University of California, Santa Barbara.

Reference books in the humanities

The Humanities: A Selective Guide to Information Sources. By Ron Blazek and Elizabeth Smith Aversa. 4th ed. Englewood: Libraries Unlimited, 2000. A guide to research tools in the humanities, including the arts, philosophy, religion, and language and literature. A critical annotation is provided for each source listed.

New Dictionary of the History of Ideas: Studies of Selected Pivotal Ideas. 6 vols. New York: Scribner, 2004. Covers concepts in intellectual history, with long, scholarly discussions of important ideas. An update of a 1974 classic, this revised work includes global perspectives in over 750 articles and is available in electronic format.

Art and architecture

Databases and indexes in art and architecture

Amico Library. New York: Art Museum Image Consortium, 1999–. A searchable database of artworks owned by contributing museums and available for educational uses. Includes quality images of paintings, sculpture, prints, watercolors, decorative arts, photographs, and other media from all periods and regions.

ARTbibliographies Modern. Bethesda: Cambridge Scientific Abstracts, 1974–. An electronic index containing citations to and descriptive abstracts of articles, books, catalogs, and essays on modern art and photography from the late nineteenth century to the present.

Art Index. New York: Wilson, 1930–. An author and subject index to more than 400 art periodicals, covering all periods and media, including film and photography. The work is particularly helpful for locating reproductions in periodicals, for research studies, and for news of sales and exhibitions. It is available in print and electronic formats; in some libraries, full text of some articles is also available.

Bibliography of the History of Art (*BHA*). Santa Monica: John Paul Getty Trust, 1991–. Comprehensive and up-to-date coverage of art in Europe and the Americas from antiquity to the present. This index provides citations and abstracts for books, articles, dissertations, and exhibit catalogs published since 1973. Current volumes are available only in electronic format.

Web resources in art and architecture

Artcyclopedia <http://www.artcyclopedia.com>. Provides links to art images on the Web. The site is searchable by artist, work, and museum and browsable by subject, medium, or nationality. It includes information about art movements with examples of relevant artworks and a section on women artists. The site was created and is maintained by John Maylon.

Art History Resources on the Web <http://witcombe.sbc.edu/ ARTHLinks.html>. Provides links to hundreds of sites related to all periods of art history, from prehistoric to twenty-first century, arranged by period and region. Many links are to museums and galleries or to artists' pages that provide biographical information and images. The site is maintained by Christopher Whitcombe, professor of art history at Sweet Briar College.

Great Buildings Collection <http://www.greatbuildings.com>. Offers information on about 1,000 works of architecture and hundreds of architects from all periods and regions. Searchable by building, architect, and place, the site provides biographical information about architects, basic information on works, extensive images, and links to articles published in *Architecture Week.* The site also provides selected 3-D images and listings of buildings by chronology, building type, and architectural style.

Timeline of Art History <http://www.metmuseum.org/toah/splash.htm>. A chronology of art from the Metropolitan Museum of Art in New York, with links to images primarily in the museum's collections. The site is organized both thematically and geographically and includes an alphabetical index and a search engine.

Virtual Library Museums Pages: A Distributed Directory of Online Museums <http://icom.museum/vlmp>. A searchable geographic directory of museums worldwide, many of which are art museums. The site is supported by the International Council of Museums.

World Wide Arts Resources <http://wwar.com>. A commercial site particularly strong in studio arts and the business side of the art professions. The site also includes databases of artists, works, locations, and arts news.

Reference books in art and architecture

Contemporary Artists. Ed. Sarah Pendergast et al. 5th ed. Detroit: Gale Group, 2002. Provides biographies of more than 800 twentieth-century artists from around the world, including information on their work, lists of their exhibits, and bibliographies for further research.

The Dictionary of Art. Ed. Jane Turner. 34 vols. New York: Grove's Dictionaries, 1996. An exhaustive encyclopedia of world art containing scholarly articles on artists, movements, works, and subjects, with bibliographical references and an index.

Encyclopedia of Aesthetics. Ed. Michael Kelly. 4 vols. New York: Oxford University Press, 1998. Includes 600 substantial articles on philosophical concepts relating to art and aesthetics, including overviews of movements, major theorists, national and regional aesthetics, and subjects such as cyberspace, law and art, cultural property, and politics and aesthetics. Each article is followed by an up-to-date bibliography.

Encyclopedia of Twentieth-Century Architecture. Ed. R. Stephen Sennott. 3 vols. New York: Fitzroy Dearborn, 2003. Offers over 700 illustrated articles on architects and buildings as well as styles, building types, and movements worldwide. The work includes coverage of architecture's roles in communities and regions.

Encyclopedia of World Art. 16 vols. New York: McGraw-Hill, 1959–. With supplements. Offers thorough, scholarly articles on artists, movements, media, periods, national traditions, and so on. Each volume has text in the front and a section of plates in the back. There is an index to the entire set, and supplementary volumes present newer information. Though dated, this set remains valuable for its erudite overview articles and well-indexed plates.

The Oxford Companion to Western Art. Ed. Hugh Brigstocke. Oxford: Oxford University Press, 2001. Provides basic information on artists, movements, forms, materials, and techniques, covering the Western world from classical times to the present.

Special resources in art and architecture

Many institutions have collections of art images, on slides or in digital format, typically organized by period, country, or medium. Such collections can provide visual resources for study and presentations. However, many image collections are maintained by the art department rather than the library and may have restricted use. To locate sources for art images, consult the *Image Buyer's Guide*, 7th ed. (Englewood: Libraries Unlimited, 1999).

Classics

Databases and indexes in classics

L'Année philologique: bibliographie critique et analytique de l'antiquité Gréco-Latine. Paris: Société Internationale de Bibliographie Classique (SIBC), 1924/26–. The most thorough index available for classics, covering books and articles on all aspects of Greek and Latin cultures, including archaeology, literature, and philosophy. The index is international in scope and includes works in all languages. It offers citations with brief abstracts and is available electronically as *APh Online.*

TOCS-IN: Tables of Contents of Journals of Interest to Classicists <http://www.chass.utoronto.ca/amphoras/tocs.html>. A Web-based index of the contents of 185 classics journals and collections of essays compiled by a team of classics scholars. Though most of the references date only to the early 1990s, when the project was started, some older material is included. The entries provide basic bibliographic information, with a few including abstracts and/or links to full text.

Web resources in classics

The Ancient World Web <http://www.julen.net/ancient>. A selective guide to classics-oriented Web sites covering art and archaeology, law, science, history, literature, and everyday life. Though less com-prehensive than other classics directories, it is kept up-to-date and offers lively commentary by Julia Hayden.

Diotima: Materials for the Study of Women and Gender in the Ancient World <http://www.stoa.org/diotima>. Includes primary sources from classical texts dealing with women as well as course materials, translations, essays, a searchable bibliography, and links to articles, books, databases, and images. The site is an affiliate of the Stoa Consortium.

Electronic Resources for Classicists: The Second Generation <http://www.tlg.uci.edu/index/resources.html>. Offers a thorough list of sites of interest to classicists, including databases, collections of images, author-specific sites, classics departments, and electronic journals and discussion groups. The site is maintained by Maria C. Pantelia of the University of California, Davis.

External Gateway to Classics Resources on the Web <http://www.classics.cam.ac.uk/everyone/links/links.html>. A database-driven listing of classics sites, organized in six main categories: literature, art history and archaeology, history, philosophy and science, linguistics and philology, and general information. The list is maintained by the Cambridge University Faculty of Classics.

Metis <http://www.stoa.org/metis>. Though little textual information is provided, links lead to animated panoramas of Greek archaeological sites, with options to scan a site or zoom in on specific areas. The site, a project of the Stoa Consortium, includes links to related materials on the Perseus site.

The Perseus Project <http://www.perseus.tufts.edu>. A digital library of resources for students researching the ancient world. Constructed and maintained by the Classics Department at Tufts University, the site focuses on ancient Greece and Rome and includes information on everything from lexicons to images, maps, art, and ancient texts and translations.

Reference books in classics

Ancient Writers: Greece and Rome. Ed. T. James Luce. 2 vols. New York: Macmillan Library Reference, 1982. Offers lengthy critiques and overviews of the works of classical writers. Each essay is written by an expert and is followed by a selected bibliography of editions, translations, commentaries, and criticism.

The Cambridge Ancient History. Ed. I. E. S. Edwards et al. 3rd ed. 14 vols. Cambridge: Cambridge University Press, 1970–. Covers the ancient world chronologically, with chapters written by experts in particular eras. Individual volumes are updated periodically; some volumes are still in their second edition. There is a separate volume of plates for the first two volumes.

Civilization of the Ancient Mediterranean. Ed. Michael Grant and Rachel Kitzinger. 3 vols. New York: Scribner, 1988. Provides lengthy articles on such topics as language and dialects, farming and animal husbandry, myths and cosmologies, women in the ancient world, and building techniques.

Illustrated Encyclopaedia of the Classical World. Ed. Michael Avi Yonah and Israel Shatzman. New York: Harper and Row, 1975. Provides brief definitions and discussions of classical people, places, institutions, and culture. One of the work's strengths is the number of illustrations accompanying the entries.

Oxford Classical Dictionary. Ed. Simon Hornblower and Anthony Spawforth. 3rd ed. New York: Oxford University Press, 1996. Provides concise and informative articles on people, places, events, works of art, and figures in mythology. It is a well-regarded classic in the field.

Oxford Companion to Classical Literature. Ed. M. C. Howatson. 2nd ed. New York: Oxford University Press, 1989. A handy guide to writers and works from classical times, with concise discussions of the social and cultural context of the literature.

Oxford Encyclopedia of Archaeology in the Near East. Ed. Eric M. Meyers. 5 vols. New York: Oxford University Press, 1997. Covers archaeological sites, regions, countries, and peoples in the Near East, from prehistoric times through the Crusades. The work also covers specific areas of archaeology, such as ethics, history, and underwater archaeology.

The Oxford Guide to Classical Mythology in the Arts, 1300–1990s. Ed. Jane Davidson Reid. 2 vols. New York: Oxford University Press, 1993. Lists examples of Western art from medieval to modern times that use figures and subjects from classical mythology as themes. Paintings, sculptures, musical compositions, ballets, and literary works are included.

Place-Names in Classical Mythology: Greece. By Robert E. Bell. Santa Barbara: ABC-CLIO, 1989. Provides descriptions of places referred to in classical mythology and literature. The entries contain many references to literature in which the place is significant.

Princeton Encyclopedia of Classical Sites. Ed. Richard Stillwell et al. Princeton: Princeton University Press, 1976. Offers descriptions of classical sites in Europe, North Africa, and the Middle East and includes references to relevant classical texts.

Literature

Databases and indexes in literature

Literature Resource Center. Detroit: Gale Group, 1998–. An online portal to a number of literature resources including the text of *Contemporary Authors, Contemporary Literary Criticism, Dictionary of Literary Biography, Twayne's Author Series, Scribner's Writers Series*, and the full text of other reference works. Many libraries have some of the contents of this database in print form (see Reference Books in Literature for descriptions).

MLA International Bibliography of Books and Articles on the Modern Languages and Literatures. New York: Modern Language Association, 1921–. The most important ongoing index of scholarship in literature and linguistics, published by the Modern Language Association. The bibliography lists citations to books, book chapters, articles, and dissertations in all languages on literature, linguistics, folklore, and some film criticism. It covers literary criticism in depth, but book reviews and articles appearing in popular magazines are not included. Available in many libraries as an electronic database, it is also published in print format. Since 1980, the print edition is published annually in two volumes. One volume is an alphabetical subject index; the other is arranged by nationality and period.

Web resources in literature

American and English Literature Internet Resources <http://library.scsu.ctstateu.edu/litbib.html>. Includes selective links to online texts and to American and British literature sites by genre as well as to a list of pages devoted to specific writers, with an emphasis on canonical authors of the nineteenth century. Each entry is annotated. The list is maintained by Winnie Shyam at the Buley Library, Southern Connecticut State University.

Internet Public Library Online Literary Criticism Collection <http://www.ipl.org/div/litcrit>. A collection of links, to literary criticism and biographical information, organized by author, title, nationality, and period. The site includes a search engine. Some of the links are out of date, but those that are active tend to be of good quality. The project is part of a large reference site maintained by the School of Information, University of Michigan.

Literary Resources on the Net <http://andromeda.rutgers.edu/~jlynch/Lit>. A selective directory of Web resources of interest to scholars in English and American literature. Arranged by period, it also includes sections on the history of the book, theory, women's literature, ethnicities, and literature of other nationalities. The directory is maintained by Jack Lynch of Rutgers University.

The Online Books Page <http://digital.library.upenn .edu/books>. See this entry in Web Resources in the Humanities, page 36.

Reference books in literature

American Writers. 4 vols. New York: Scribner, 1979–87. With supplements. Offers essays analyzing the life and work of major American writers, arranged chronologically with an alphabetical index. Scribner publishes a similar series for British, Latin American, and European writers. These works are also available in electronic format as part of the *Literature Resource Center* (see Databases and Indexes in Literature).

Bloomsbury Guide to Women's Literature. By Claire Buck. Upper Saddle River: Prentice-Hall, 1992. A thorough compendium of information on women's literature from around the world, from early times to the present. This text provides concise and informative articles and includes lengthy regional surveys. Its coverage of non-Western women writers is particularly good.

Concise Oxford Dictionary of Literary Terms. By Chris Baldick. 2nd ed. New York: Oxford University Press, 2001. Defines and briefly discusses terms used in current critical theory. Notable for its clear and succinct language, this dictionary is also available in electronic format.

Contemporary Authors. Detroit: Gale Group, 1962–. 218 vols. to date. A long-running series that offers profiles of modern authors, including some whose work is not strictly literary. To locate author profiles, consult the most recent index. This work is available online as a separate database or as part of the *Literature Resource Center* (see Databases and Indexes in Literature).

Contemporary Literary Criticism. Detroit: Gale Group, 1973–. 185 vols. to date. A series that offers background on contemporary authors, with excerpts from critical essays and reviews. Citations for original sources are included. Consult the most recent cumulative index, which includes cross-references to other Gale biographical series. This is a good place to get a quick sense of how a writer's work has been received. This work is available online as *Contemporary Literary Criticism Select* or as part of the *Literature Resource Center* (see Databases and Indexes in Literature).

Dictionary of Literary Biography (DLB). Detroit: Gale Group, 1978–. 300 vols. to date. A series that offers lengthy biographies of authors with criticism of their works. Volumes are arranged thematically.

To find an author, consult the index in the most recent volume. Though the *DLB* emphasizes American and British literary authors, it offers substantial coverage of writers from other countries and of journalists and historians. This work is available online as part of the *Literature Resource Center* (see Databases and Indexes in Literature).

Encyclopedia of German Literature. Ed. Matthias Konzett. 2 vols. Chicago: Fitzroy Dearborn, 2000. Covers authors and topics such as literary movements.

Encyclopedia of World Literature in the 20th Century. Ed. Steven R. Serafin. 3rd ed. 4 vols. Farmington Hills: St. James, 1999. Covers twentieth-century authors and movements and provides lengthy surveys of the modern literature of different countries.

European Writers. Ed. William T. H. Jackson and George Stade. 14 vols. New York: Scribner, 1983–91. A chronologically arranged work offering substantial critical essays about writers and their times from the Middle Ages and Renaissance to the present.

Guide to French Literature. Ed. Anthony Levi. 2 vols. Chicago: St. James, 1992. Includes biographical information as well as entries on movements and themes, covering Francophone Africa, the Caribbean, and France.

Literary Research Guide: A Guide to Reference Sources for the Study of Literatures in English and Related Topics. By James L. Harner. 4th ed. New York: Modern Language Association, 2002. A guide to tools and methods of literary scholarship, emphasizing English literature; includes annotated lists of reference sources. Changes and new resources are listed at the author's Web site: <http://www-english.tamu.edu/pubs/lrg/addenda.html>.

Modern Japanese Literature. Ed. Jay Rubin. New York: Scribner, 2000. Offers profiles and analysis of 25 prominent Japanese authors, including the cultural and literary context of their work as well as substantial bibliographies.

The Oxford Companion to English Literature. Ed. Margaret Drabble. 6th ed. New York: Oxford University Press, 2000. Brief descriptions of writers, literary works, schools and movements, and places of literary significance, arranged alphabetically. A number of *Oxford*

*Companion*s cover other national literatures and genres; some are available in electronic format.

The Oxford English Dictionary. Ed. J. A. Simpson and E. S. C. Weiner. 2nd ed. 20 vols. Oxford: Clarendon, 1989. With supplements. An invaluable source for understanding the various meanings of words and their changing definitions. The *OED* provides chronological examples showing how a word has been used throughout history. It is unequaled in its depth of coverage and is available in print and electronic formats.

Music

Databases and indexes in music

Music Index. Detroit: Information Coordinators, 1949–. A subject and author index to more than 600 music periodicals. International in scope, its citations cover both musicology and performance journals. The index is available in print and electronic formats.

RILM Abstracts of Music Literature. New York: RILM, 1967–. Offers abstracts of articles appearing in over 5,000 international journals, books, dissertations, and other materials in the music field. Its coverage is especially strong for music history and musicology. It is available in print and electronic formats.

Web resources in music

The Classical Composer Database <http://www.classical-composers .org>. Offers basic biographical information about composers, both well known and obscure, and links to information about them on the Web. Includes chronologies and a composer's calendar. The list is maintained by Jos Smeets.

The Classical Music Navigator <http://www.wku.edu/~smithch/ music>. Provides information on over 400 composers, with works listed by musical genre, a geographical roster, an index of forms and styles, and a glossary of musical terms. Maintained by Charles H. Smith of Western Kentucky University.

DW3: Classical Music Resources <http://www.lib.duke.edu/dw3>. A comprehensive collection of classical music links, browsable by topic, that includes its own search engine. Each entry has been carefully indexed and includes a brief annotation. Compiled by librarians at the Music Library of Duke University.

Music History 102: A Guide to Western Composers and Their Music from the Middle Ages to the Present <http://www.ipl.org/div/ mushist>. A nicely organized chronological survey of music, with images, audio files, and links to composer profiles. The author of this site is Robert Sherane, a librarian at the Juilliard School of Music; the site is part of the *Internet Public Library*.

Reference books in music

Baker's Biographical Dictionary of Musicians. Ed. Nicolas Slonimsky. 9th ed. 6 vols. New York: Schirmer, 2001. Compact biographies of composers and performers with bibliographies of works by and about them. This reference is good for a quick overview of a musician and his or her impact.

Encyclopedia of Popular Music. Ed. Colin Larkin. 3rd ed. 8 vols. London: Muze, 1998. Offers brief entries on musicians, bands, musicals, and record labels as well as a song title index.

Garland Encyclopedia of World Music. 10 vols. New York: Garland, 1998–2002. Covers the music of peoples of the world in regional volumes that offer regional profiles, the social context of music, and in-depth information on the musical traditions of specific nations and ethnic groups. The work includes musical examples in accompanying CDs.

Music Reference and Research Materials. By Vincent Duckles. 5th ed. rev. New York: Schirmer, 1997. An annotated guide to the literature of music, including histories, bibliographies, discographies, and reference books. The book is arranged by type of source, with subject, title, and author indexes.

New Grove Dictionary of Music and Musicians. Ed. Stanley Sadie. 2nd ed. 29 vols. New York: Grove, 2001. The definitive source on music and music history. The articles in these volumes are carefully researched and documented and provide information on national music traditions, musical forms, composers and musicians, instruments, and more. Libraries may offer the online version of this work, which is available by subscription.

New Oxford History of Music. 11 vols. New York: Oxford University Press, 1957–1990. An excellent chronological exploration of all aspects of music. Each volume covers a different musical period. Some have been published in newer editions. The final volume includes chronologies, bibliographies, and an index to the set.

Oxford Companion to Music. Ed. Alison Latham. Oxford: Oxford University Press, 2002. Covers primarily Western classical music, offering brief entries on musicians, works, musical terms, and movements, with surveys of musical traditions in various countries.

The Oxford Dictionary of Music. By Michael Kennedy and Joyce Bourne. 2nd ed. rev. Oxford: Oxford University Press, 1999. Offers brief identifications of musical terms and musicians; a handy place to find dates and other facts.

Philosophy

Databases and indexes in philosophy

Philosopher's Index. Bowling Green: Philosophy Documentation Center, 1967–. Provides abstracts of articles from over 400 philosophy journals as well as anthologies and books published from 1940 to the present. The index is available in print and electronic formats.

Web resources in philosophy

BioethicsWeb <http://bioethicsweb.ac.uk>. A guide to reputable Web resources on topics such as genetically modified food, medical ethics, cloning, stem cell research, and animal welfare. Based in the UK, this site is supported by the Wellcome Trust, a nonprofit organization that funds research into human and animal health, and is part of the Resource Discovery Network.

Contemporary Philosophy, Critical Theory, and Postmodern Thought <http://carbon.cudenver.edu/~mryder/itc_data/postmodern .html>. A compilation of Web-based sources on postmodernism, including important philosophers, background information, and primary texts. The site was created by Martin Ryder of the University of Colorado at Denver.

Ethics Update <http://ethics.acusd.edu>. Provides bibliographic essays and links to content on ethics theory, teaching and learning, and applied ethics topics such as euthanasia, animal rights, bioethics, and world hunger. The site includes audio and video files as well as textual information. Edited by Lawrence W. Hinman at the Values Institute, University of San Diego.

Stanford Encyclopedia of Philosophy <http://plato.stanford.edu>. Offers authoritative articles that are updated to reflect changes in the field. Entries are kept current by experts in philosophy and reviewed by an editorial board, based at the Metaphysics Research Lab, Stanford University. Because the project is a work in progress, some topics are not yet covered.

World Wide Web Virtual Library: Philosophy <http://www.bris .ac.uk/Depts/Philosophy/VL>. Maintained at the University of Bristol in the UK, this site offers a database-driven, annotated listing of reputable Web sites in philosophy. Those of special note are marked "Editor's Choice."

Reference books in philosophy

Encyclopedia of Applied Ethics. Ed. Ruth Chadwick. 4 vols. San Diego: Academic Press, 1998. Provides lengthy, scholarly discussions of the ethical aspects of issues such as affirmative action, animal rights, and genetic screening as well as contemporary views on theories of humanism, hedonism, and utilitarianism.

Encyclopedia of Bioethics. Ed. Warren T. Reich. Rev. ed. 5 vols. New York: Macmillan, 1995. Covers issues and controversies in bioethics in lengthy, scholarly articles, each accompanied by a bibliography of key sources. Because bioethics is a rapidly changing field, some of the information may be out of date; be sure to check current sources as well.

Encyclopedia of Philosophy. Ed. Paul Edwards. 8 vols. New York: Macmillan, 1967–. With supplement. Offers articles on movements, concepts, and philosophers. Though dated, this work is both scholarly and accessible, so it provides a good starting place for research, particularly on traditional and classical philosophers. For more contemporary approaches, see the *Routledge Encyclopedia,* at the end of this section.

Oxford Dictionary of Philosophy. By Simon Blackburn. New York: Oxford University Press, 1994. Offers succinct definitions of terms in philosophy, primarily Western, and biographical entries on individual philosophers.

Routledge Encyclopedia of Philosophy. 10 vols. London: Routledge, 1998. The most important current encyclopedia of the field, this work extends the classic *Encyclopedia of Philosophy* by adding both new topics and approaches to philosophy and also by including new approaches and new research on classical philosophy. New areas covered include philosophical approaches based on feminism, postcolonialism, poststructuralism, deconstruction, and postmodernism. Some libraries may subscribe to an online version of this work.

Religion

Databases and indexes in religion

Religion Index One: Periodicals and Religion Index Two: Multi-Author Works and Index to Book Reviews in Religion. Evanston: American Theological Library Association, 1949–. The most thorough index to articles, books, selections in books, and reviews for the field of religion, including theology, biblical studies, church history, comparative religions, archaeology and antiquities, and pastoral work. The online version combines both parts and is called *ATLA.*

Web resources in religion

Christian Classics Ethereal Library <http://www.ccel.org>. A digital archive of key Christian historical texts and other material, such as the Early Church Fathers series; works of Boethius, Erasmus, and Luther; and modern works by G. K. Chesterton and Dorothy L. Sayers. Material can be searched or browsed by author, title, subject, or type of text.

ECanon: Online Search Engine for Canonical Texts <http://rosetta .reltech.org/ECanon/ECanon.html>. A tool for searching four translations of the Bible (King James, Revised Standard Version, New Revised Standard Version, and the Westcott and Hort Greek New Testament) by scriptural reference or by keyword.

The Five Gospel Parallels <http://www.utoronto.ca/religion/synopsis>. A tool for comparing the text of the New Testament Gospels as well as several apocryphal texts, including the Gospel of Thomas, side by side. An interesting feature of this program is that users can locate the passages in different texts that deal with the same parables and events. The site is maintained by John W. Marshall of the Department for the Study of Religion, University of Toronto.

Internet Sacred Texts Archive <http://sacred-texts.com/index.htm>. A varied collection of texts on religion, mythology, folklore, and esoteric topics such as alchemy and UFOs, which can be browsed by world region, religion, or subject.

Judaism and Jewish Resources <http://shamash.org/trb/judaism.html>. A directory listing selected Internet resources related to almost any aspect of Judaism and its history. The site includes annotated links on a variety of academic and social topics, with links to museums, libraries, organizations, and the government and news media of modern Israel. Maintained by Andrew Tannenbaum,

Religion, Religions, Religious Studies: Information Sources for Study and Interpretation of Religions <http://www.clas.ufl.edu/users/gthursby/rel>. Offers selective, annotated links to Web material on religious traditions, contemporary issues, religious experience, religious studies programs, and reference sources. Maintained by Gene R. Thursby of the University of Florida.

Religionwriters.com Reference Library <http://www.religionwriters.com/public/library/library.shtml>. Designed to support the work of journalists covering religion and sponsored by the Religion Newswriters Association, this site is particularly good for contemporary issues related to culture and society, government and public affairs, and faith groups, from mainstream to New Age.

Wabash Center Guide to Internet Resources for Teaching and Learning in Theology and Religion <http://www.wabashcenter.wabash.edu/Internet/front.htm>. A selective, annotated directory of Web sites arranged by subject and type of material. Sites of particular note are highlighted, and the directory covers topics such as the history of Christianity, world religions, social issues, theology, and archaeology. Maintained by Charles K. Bellinger at Wabash College.

Reference books in religion

Anchor Bible Dictionary. Ed. David Noel Freedman et al. 6 vols. New York: Doubleday, 1992. A definitive encyclopedia covering names, places, and events of the Bible as well as cultural history, social institutions, archaeological sites, and other topics of interest to biblical scholars. Also available on CD-ROM.

Contemporary American Religion. Ed. Wade Clark Roof. 2 vols. New York: Macmillan Reference, 2000. Five hundred articles that address the religious pluralism of the United States and provide contemporary analyses of practices, traditions, and trends.

Encyclopaedia Judaica. 16 vols. Jerusalem: Encyclopaedia Judaica; New York: Macmillan, 1971–72. Though dated, this work remains an excellent source of information on the Jewish culture and religion, offering in-depth, scholarly articles and ample illustrations. Also available on CD-ROM.

Encyclopedia of Protestantism. Ed. Hans H. Hillerbrand. 4 vols. New York: Routledge, 2004. Offers articles on traditions and faith groups, creeds and professions, historical events, movements, and people, cultural, and social issues as they relate to Protestantism.

Encyclopedia of Religion. 16 vols. New York: Macmillan, 1987. Covers religions from around the world, including information about their ideas, histories, and cultures. The articles are written by experts in their fields and include excellent bibliographies. Available in electronic format.

Harper's Dictionary of Hinduism: Its Mythology, Folklore, Philosophy, Literature, and History. By Margaret Stutley and James Stutley. New York: Harper and Row, 1977. Features short definitions and identifications of terms, figures, and texts important in Hinduism. Though the articles are not detailed, they are good for quick reference.

Mythologies. Ed. Yves Bonnefoy. 2 vols. Chicago: University of Chicago Press, 1991. An encyclopedia surveying mythologies of the world, with articles on cosmology, cults, and myth traditions arranged in geographical sections. The articles are long and scholarly, and they are accompanied by illustrations and thorough bibliographies.

New Catholic Encyclopedia. Ed. Bernard L. Marthaler. 2nd ed. 15 vols. Detroit: Gale Group, 2002. An authoritative source for Catholic theology, canon law, liturgical matters, and the church's position on social issues such as euthanasia and biomedical research. This encyclopedia also has articles on the history of the church, biographical sketches, and institutions.

Oxford Dictionary of the Christian Church. Ed. F. L. Cross. 3rd ed. New York: Oxford University Press, 1997. A small compendium of a vast amount of information, with short, descriptive entries that run from Aaron to Zwingli. The entries provide very concise starting points for understanding and identifying people, concepts, events, places, and biblical references that are important in Christian church history.

Oxford Encyclopedia of the Modern Islamic World. Ed. John L. Esposito. 4 vols. New York: Oxford University Press, 1995. Covers countries of the Islamic world and topics related to Islamic religion, history, and culture. The articles are long and scholarly as well as up-to-date.

Shambhala Dictionary of Buddhism and Zen. New York: Shambhala, 1991. Offers brief explanations of concepts defined by a team of scholars and includes a bibliography of sources.

Theater, dance, and film

Databases and indexes in theater, dance, and film

Film Literature Index. Albany: Film and Television Documentation Center, SUNY Albany, 1975–. The most complete index to international trade, popular, and scholarly publications about film and television. Very thorough in its coverage of reviews, interviews, criticism, and production information. This index, previously available only in print format, has been converted for online access.

MLA International Bibliography of Books and Articles on the Modern Languages and Literatures. New York: Modern Language

Association, 1921–. Useful for scholarly criticism of dramatic works, this bibliography lists citations to books, book chapters, articles, and dissertations. It offers in-depth coverage of literary analysis of plays, but performance reviews and information about stagecraft and acting technique are not typically included. Available in print and electronic formats.

Web resources in theater, dance, and film

Artslynx International Arts Resources <http://www.artslynx .org>. An index of links to performing arts, including theater, dance, music, and film, as well as sources for arts, management and the arts in personal and community enrichment. The editor is Richard Finkelstein of the University of Colorado, Denver.

The Internet Movie Database <http://us.imdb.com>. The largest and oldest Internet film site. The database includes information on hundreds of thousands of movies from the silents to the latest releases, offering information on the release, script, cast, reviews, and links to further information. Users can search by movie title, cast or crew member, year, genre, country, production company, or combinations. Information is available on upcoming releases, news from the industry, and message boards. Now affiliated with *Amazon.com,* this site retains the flavor of its fan-based origins. Some features designed specifically for professionals in the industry are only available by subscription.

Internet Resources on Theatre and Drama <http://www.indiana .edu/~libhper/DTD/theatre/resources.html>. An extensive directory covering a wide variety of research and performance resources on actors, theaters, dramaturgy, playwrights, lighting, costumes, and more. All of the entries are annotated by staff at the Indiana University Libraries.

Theatre History on the Web <http://www.videoccasions-nw .com/history/jack.html>. Includes links of interest to the student, the researcher, and the dramaturg, organized by period and topic. The site is maintained by Jack Wolcott, a retired professor of drama at the University of Washington.

Reference books in theater, dance, and film

American Playwrights, 1880–1945: A Research and Production Sourcebook. Ed. William W. Demastes. Westport: Greenwood, 1995. Covers the lives, works, critical reception, and impact of 40 American playwrights, some prominent and others little known, including many women and minority writers who have not received much critical attention. Each entry is followed by a detailed bibliography of the playwright's works, criticism, and reviews. Greenwood publishes similar sourcebooks for contemporary British and American dramatists as well as volumes devoted to specific playwrights.

Cambridge Guide to Theatre. Ed. Martin Banham. New ed. Cambridge: Cambridge University Press, 1995. Offers international coverage of major playwrights, actors, directors, works, traditions, theories, companies, venues, and events as well as information on theater history, design, and architecture.

Encyclopedia of the Musical Theatre. By Kurt Ganzl. 2nd ed. 3 vols. New York: Schirmer, 2001. Surveys musical theater, providing detailed background on musicals and profiles of those involved with them.

Film Encyclopedia. By Ephraim Katz. 4th ed. New York: HarperPerennial, 2001. Offers over 7,000 brief entries on terms, topics, and individuals related to the history of film. Though it fits into a single volume, this work contains a great deal of handy information.

Halliwell's Filmgoer's Companion. By Leslie Halliwell. Ed. John Walker. 12th ed. New York: Hill and Wang, 1997. Offers brief entries on major films, actors, directors, and producers as well as definitions of technical terms and subjects such as censorship. The book is particularly useful for identifying films of a certain type, such as trial dramas.

International Encyclopedia of Dance. 6 vols. New York: Oxford University Press, 1998. The most exhaustive reference work on dance, covering the historical evolution of dance in the countries of the world, analysis of dance techniques, theories of aesthetics, individuals, companies, and works.

McGraw-Hill Encyclopedia of World Drama. 2nd ed. 5 vols. New York: McGraw-Hill, 1984. Contains articles on playwrights, periods of theatrical history, and notable figures in theater. Brief critical comments on plays are given under author entries. Though dated, this work is particularly useful in its coverage of past productions and includes many illustrations.

Modern Drama Scholarship and Criticism 1966–1980: An International Bibliography. By Charles A. Carpenter. Toronto: University of Toronto Press, 1986; and *Modern Drama Scholarship and Criticism, 1981–1990: An International Bibliography.* By Charles A. Carpenter. Toronto: University of Toronto Press, 1997. Together, these two works offer a thorough bibliography of critical articles and commentary on world theater from 1850 to the present. For works published since 1990, consult the June issues of the journal *Modern Drama,* which include an annual listing of drama scholarship.

World Encyclopedia of Contemporary Theatre. Ed. Don Rubin. 6 vols. London: Routledge, 2000. An authoritative, up-to-date guide to current theater, with a global perspective and thorough coverage by country.

World languages and linguistics

Databases and indexes in world languages and linguistics

MLA International Bibliography of Books and Articles on the Modern Languages and Literatures. New York: Modern Language Association, 1921–. See this entry in Databases and Indexes in Literature, page 43.

Web resources in world languages and linguistics

Ethnologue <http://www.ethnologue.com>. A database of information on world languages, including information about geographic distribution, dialects, numbers of speakers, and linguistic affiliation. The site includes a bibliography. Maintained by SIL International, an organization that promotes language study for international faith-based work, this database is particularly strong for basic information about lesser-known and endangered languages.

iLoveLanguages <http://www.ilovelanguages.com>. Formerly known as *The Human-Languages Page,* this site offers links to language-related Internet resources. Of particular interest is the languages section, in which links are categorized by language, dictionaries, lessons, and so on. The site is searchable.

Linguistics Resources on the Internet <http://www.sil.org/ linguistics/topical.html>. A directory of reputable Internet sources for linguistics maintained by SIL International. The site provides links for every aspect of linguistics, including grammar and syntax, second-language teaching, language rights, and individual languages.

Reference books in world languages and linguistics

Encyclopedia of Contemporary French Culture. Ed. Alex Hughes and Keith Reader. London: Routledge, 1998. Short articles on a wealth of topics on French and Francophone culture from 1945 to the present. Related volumes cover contemporary German, Spanish, Italian, Japanese, and other cultures.

Encyclopedia of German Literature. Ed. Matthias Konzett. 2 vols. Chicago: Fitzroy Dearborn, 2000. Covers authors and topics such as literary movements.

Encyclopedia of Latin American History and Culture. Ed. Barbara A. Tenenbaum and Georgette M. Dorn. 5 vols. New York: Scribner, 1996. Covers a wide variety of topics in over 5,000 articles that together constitute an overview of current knowledge about Latin America. Entries are organized by country and by topic (such as slavery, art, Asians in Latin America); biographical entries are included.

Guide to French Literature. Ed. Anthony Levi. 2 vols. Chicago: St. James, 1992. Includes biographical information as well as entries on movements and themes, covering Francophone Africa, the Caribbean, and France.

International Encyclopedia of Linguistics. Ed. William J. Frawley. 2nd ed. 4 vols. New York: Oxford University Press, 2003. Includes scholarly articles on all aspects of linguistics along with helpful bibliographies for further research.

Latin American Writers. Ed. Carlos A. Solé. 3 vols. With supplement. New York: Scribner, 1989. Surveys prominent writers from Latin America writing in Spanish and Portuguese, providing substantial biocritical essays and useful bibliographies. Entries are arranged chronologically by birth date; the index is arranged alphabetically.

Modern Japanese Literature. Ed. Jay Rubin. New York: Scribner, 2000. Offers profiles and analysis of 25 prominent Japanese authors, including the cultural and literary context of their work as well as substantial bibliographies.

The Oxford English Dictionary. Ed. J. A. Simpson and E. S. C. Weiner. 2nd ed. 20 vols. Oxford: Clarendon, 1989. With supplements. An invaluable source for understanding the various meanings of words and their changing definitions. Unequaled in its depth of coverage, the *OED* provides chronological examples showing how a word has been used throughout history.

Researching in History

Research in history involves developing an understanding of the past through the examination and interpretation of evidence. Evidence may exist in the form of texts, physical remains of historic sites, recorded data, pictures, maps, artifacts, and so on. The historian's job is to find evidence, analyze its content and biases, corroborate it with other evidence, and use the evidence to develop an interpretation of past events that has some importance for the present. Historians use libraries to

- locate primary sources (firsthand information such as diaries, letters, and original documents) for evidence
- find secondary sources, historians' interpretations and analyses of historical evidence
- verify factual material as inconsistencies arise

Doing historical research is a little like excavating an archaeological site. It requires patience, insight, and imagination as well as diligence and the right tools. As you find and examine primary sources, you need to imagine them in their original context and understand how your present-day point of view may distort your interpretation of them. You need to recognize not only your own biases but the biases that shaped primary materials in their own period. You need to brush away the layers of interpretation that time has imposed on them and imaginatively re-create the complexities of the environment in which they were created. Students doing historical research should be prepared to

- survey historians' interpretations of the past while recognizing how their purposes or backgrounds might influence their interpretations

- understand the context in which primary sources were generated

- identify conflicting evidence and locate factual and interpretive information that can help resolve or illuminate those differences

Many bibliographies can help you identify primary and secondary sources related to a particular topic or historical period. Be sure to examine bibliographies and footnotes in secondary sources as you find them, since they will often lead you to primary sources. Finally, innumerable encyclopedias, dictionaries, handbooks, and chronologies can provide information to round out your interpretations and ground them in fact. Consult a librarian to find out what the reference shelves offer for your topic and whether the library has any special collections of microfilm, archives, manuscripts, or other primary sources especially suited to your research.

General resources in history

Databases and indexes in history

Humanities Index. New York: Wilson, 1974–. An interdisciplinary index to about 400 of the most prominent English-language journals in the humanities, including art, music, history, and literature. Searchable by author or subject, the index includes many cross-references and subheadings that break large topics into components. This index is available in print and electronic formats; in some libraries, the database includes full text of selected articles.

JSTOR. New York: JSTOR, 1995–. A multidisciplinary historical archive of scholarly journals. The complete contents of core journals have been digitized from the first issues. The most current issues (typically from the past three to five years are not included). This archive is useful to historians for two reasons: many prominent history journals are included (such as the *American Historical*

Review) and, because the contents go back to the nineteenth century, full-text searches can reveal the historical development of concepts, words, and phrases in scholarly publications.

Social Sciences Citation Index. Philadelphia: Institute for Scientific Information, 1956–. A multidisciplinary index of social science journals, including history, women's studies, and urban studies. Searchable by author or keyword, the index gives bibliographic citations, 60 percent of which include extracts. It allows searches by cited source, a good way to trace the influence of a particular work. The online version, *Web of Science,* has a "related search" feature for identifying works that cite one or more of the same sources.

Web resources in history

Bedford/St. Martin's HistoryLinks <http://bcs.bedfordstmartins .com/hrel/newhistorylinks>. Provides annotated, selective links relevant to U.S., ancient, and Western history. Categories include chronological periods and regions as well as topics such as immigration, race, the industrial revolution, and women and feminism.

Best of History Websites <http://www.besthistorysites.net/index .shtml>. Though the audience for this site is K–12 history teachers, it is a useful and up-to-date guide to reputable Web sites, arranged by region and period, with links to art history, maps, news, and teaching materials. The site is maintained by Tom Dacord of the Center for Teaching History with Technology.

WWW Virtual Library: History Central Catalogue <http://vlib.iue.it/ history/index.html>. The premier meta-site for history, organized by research methods and materials, historical topics, countries and regions, and eras and epochs.

Reference books in history

American Historical Association Guide to Historical Literature. Ed. Mary Beth Norton and Pamela Gerardi. 3rd ed. 2 vols. New York: Oxford University Press, 1995. Offers citations of important historical publications, arranged in 48 sections covering theory, international history, and regional history. Though it does not include recent publications, it remains an indispensable guide to the best work in the field.

Dictionary of Historical Terms. By Chris Cook. 2nd ed. New York: Peter Bedrick, 1990. Covers a wide variety of terms related to historical events, places, and institutions in a remarkably small package. This is a good place for quick identification of terms used by historians.

Encyclopedia of Historians and Historical Writing. Ed. Kelly Boyd. 2 vols. London: Fitzroy Dearborn, 1999. Provides information on historians, on regions and periods, and on topics in the field such as history of religion, women's and gender history, and art history.

World history

Databases and indexes in world history

Historical Abstracts. Santa Barbara: ABC-CLIO, 1955–. Provides citations and abstracts of articles, book reviews, books, and dissertations from over 2,000 journals in world history from 1450 to the present. North American history is covered in the companion index *America: History and Life.* Both are available in print and electronic formats.

Web resources in world history

ABZU: A Guide to Information Related to the Study of the Ancient Near East on the Web <http://www.etana.org/abzu>. Links to thousands of Web-accessible texts — articles, books, papers, and scholarly editions of the world's earliest texts, searchable or browsable by author or title. A collaborative project undertaken by several organizations, including the Oriental Institute at the University of Chicago, this resource is valuable for archaeologists and historians.

The Scientific Revolution: Readings, Resources, Research <http://www.clas.ufl.edu/users/rhatch/pages/03-Sci-Rev/SCI-REV-Home>. Offers overviews, biographies, chronologies, and a rich selection of primary texts, well annotated and arranged. The site was created by Robert A. Hatch of the University of Florida.

Reference books in world history

Cambridge History of Africa. 8 vols. Cambridge: Cambridge University Press, 1975–86. Covers African history chronologically and in depth. Use the table of contents and indexes for access. Other *Cambridge History* works cover many countries and regions such as China, Japan, Latin America, and Southeast Asia.

Civilization of the Ancient Mediterranean. Ed. Michael Grant. 3 vols. New York: Scribner, 1988. Provides lengthy articles that introduce many facets of the classical world. Each article is followed by a helpful bibliography.

Civilizations of the Ancient Near East. Ed. Jack M. Sasson. 4 vols. New York: Scribner, 1995. A collection of essays on the culture and history of Egypt, Syro-Palestine, Mesopotamia, and Anatolia. The work includes some coverage of Arabian, northeast African, and Aegean cultures as well as extensive bibliographies.

Companion Encyclopedia of the History of Medicine. Ed. W. F. Bynum and Ray Porter. 2 vols. New York: Routledge, 1994. Includes essays on body systems and how they have been perceived through time, theories of illness (including the history of specific diseases and their treatments), clinical history, and medicine in society and culture.

Dictionary of the Middle Ages. Ed. Joseph R. Strayer. 13 vols. New York: Scribner, 1982–89. Supplement, 2004. An encyclopedia covering people, events, ideas, movements, texts, and cultural features of the medieval world. Articles are often illustrated with period artwork and are followed by bibliographies of primary and secondary sources.

Encyclopedia of Asian History. Ed. Robin Lewis and Ainslie Embree. 4 vols. New York: Macmillan Library Reference, 1988. Discusses people, places, events, and topics in detailed and well-documented essays covering central Asia, southern Asia, and the Far East.

Encyclopedia of European Social History from 1350 to 2000. Ed. Peter N. Stearns. 6 vols. New York: Scribner, 2001. Offers substantial, well-documented survey essays on topics such as social change, urban and rural life, gender, popular culture, religion, and everyday life.

Encyclopedia of Latin American History and Culture. Ed. Barbara A. Tennenbaum and Georgette M. Dorn. 5 vols. New York: Scribner, 1996. Presents a wide variety of topics in over 5,000 articles that together constitute an overview of current knowledge about the region. Entries cover countries, topics (such as slavery, art, Asians in Latin America), and biographical sketches.

Encyclopedia of the Enlightenment. Ed. Alan Charles Kors. 4 vols. Oxford: Oxford University Press, 2002. Covers ideas, figures, historical events, and culture in Europe from the 1670s to the early nineteenth century.

Encyclopedia of the Holocaust. Ed. Israel Gutman. 4 vols. New York: Macmillan Library Reference, 1996. Offers lengthy articles on people, places, events, and concepts related to the Holocaust, each followed by a selective bibliography.

Encyclopedia of the Renaissance. Ed. Paul F. Grendler. 6 vols. New York: Scribner, 1999. Offers nearly 1,200 substantial articles on topics related to the culture and history of the period.

Encyclopedia of the Vietnam War: A Political, Social, and Military History. Ed. Spencer C. Tucker. 3 vols. Santa Barbara: ABC-CLIO, 1998. Includes 900 entries covering prominent figures, military events, and war protests. The third volume offers a wealth of primary source documents in English and English translation.

New Cambridge Modern History. 14 vols. Cambridge: Cambridge University Press, 1957–79. Covers world history from 1493 to 1945, chronologically and by topic, providing detailed and lengthy narrative surveys of the times. Similar works published by Cambridge University Press cover ancient and medieval history.

The Oxford Encyclopedia of the Reformation. Ed. Hans J. Hillerbrand. 4 vols. New York: Oxford University Press, 1996. Lengthy, scholarly articles treat people, places, events, documents, and ideas related to the Reformation. Each article reflects current research and interpretation and is followed by a selective bibliography.

Times Atlas of World History. Ed. Geoffrey Barraclough and J. R. Overy. 5th ed. London: Times Books, 1999. Offers more than 600 maps showing historical periods and movements such as the spread of world religions, the industrial revolution, and European expansion. The maps are supplemented by explanations and discussions of each period.

The Timetables of History: A Horizontal Linkage of People and Events. By Bernard Grun. 3rd ed. rev. New York: Simon and

Schuster, 1991. Includes chronological tables that cover, for a given year, worldwide politics, religion, the arts, and science. This work provides an interdisciplinary and global picture of a period.

American history

Databases and indexes in American history

America: History and Life. Santa Barbara: ABC-CLIO, 1964–. Provides citations and abstracts of articles, books, dissertations, and book reviews on U.S. and Canadian history and culture. Searchable by keyword, author, subject, and source, the index offers in-depth coverage of specialist publications in North American history and allows for interdisciplinary examinations of American culture. A companion to *Historical Abstracts,* it is available in print and electronic formats.

Web resources in American history

American Women's History: A Research Guide <http://frank.mtsu.edu/~kmiddlet/history/women.html>. Offers clearly organized information on more than 2,000 print and online resources. Includes a subject guide, a state index, and an introduction to research tools for primary and secondary sources. The site is maintained by Ken Middleton, a reference librarian at Middle Tennessee State University.

WWW Virtual Library: United States History <http://vlib.iue.it/history/USA/index.html>. Organized by period and topic, with links to research tools and associations, this selective directory focuses on history sites of interest to scholars.

Reference books in American history

American National Biography. Ed. John Arthur Garraty and Mark C. Carnes. 24 vols. New York: Oxford University Press, 1999. Compiled under the auspices of the American Council of Learned Societies, this is the most important and comprehensive biographical reference work on American historical figures. Each sketch is a detailed scholarly profile followed by a critical bibliography.

Dictionary of American History. Ed. Stanley I. Kutler. 3rd ed. 10 vols. New York: Scribner, 2003. An encyclopedia of terms, places, and concepts in U.S. history, with maps and illustrations as well as references for further research.

Encyclopedia of African-American Culture and History. Ed. Jack Salzman, David Lionel Smith, and Cornel West. 5 vols. New York: Macmillan, 1996. A wide-ranging encyclopedia covering people, places, events, concepts, and topics of all sorts. Articles are written by specialists and have useful bibliographies.

Encyclopedia of American Cultural and Intellectual History. Ed. Mary Kupiec Cayton and Peter W. Williams. 3 vols. New York: Scribner, 2001. Provides in-depth articles on American thought and culture. Topics include historical approaches, cultural groups, major cultural regions, and political thought.

Encyclopedia of American Social History. Ed. Mary Clayton et al. 3 vols. New York: Scribner, 1993. Fills in the gaps left by conventional political-biographical history sources. The work presents lengthy and well-documented articles covering topics such as religion, class, gender, race, popular culture, regionalism, and everyday life in the United States from pre-Columbian to modern times.

Encyclopedia of the American Civil War. 5 vols. Santa Barbara: ABC-Clio, 2000. Subtitled *A Political, Social, and Military History,* this source offers over 1,600 articles on topics related to the Civil War and its context, including events leading up to the war and its consequences. A special section is devoted to primary sources; photographs, drawings, and maps are included.

Encyclopedia of the Confederacy. Ed. Richard N. Current. 4 vols. New York: Simon and Schuster, 1993. Covers Confederate society, culture, and politics as well as events and people in the Civil War–era South. The articles are arranged alphabetically.

Encyclopedia of the North American Colonies. Ed. Jacob Ernest Cook. 3 vols. New York: Scribner, 1993. A collection of lengthy essays covering government and law, economic life, labor, social issues, families, the arts, education, and religion, arranged thematically. The third volume contains a thorough index.

Encyclopedia of the United States in the Nineteenth Century. Ed. Paul Finkelman. 3 vols. New York: Scribner, 2001. Covers major ideas and issues in American social, political, and military history.

Encyclopedia of the United States in the Twentieth Century. Ed. Stanley I. Kutler. 4 vols. New York: Scribner, 1996. An ambitious survey of U.S. cultural, social, and intellectual history in broad articles arranged topically. Each essay is followed by a thorough bibliography.

United States History: A Multicultural, Interdisciplinary Guide to Information Sources. By Ron Blazek and Anna Perrault. 2nd ed. Westport: Libraries Unlimited, 2003. A selective and descriptive guide to research materials in U.S. history.

Primary sources

There is no simple, foolproof way to find primary sources for historical research; rather, locating such sources tends to be an intuitive and creative process involving guesswork and blind alleys. Potentially useful materials can be found in journals, memoirs, letters, magazines, newspapers, and official documents published during the time you are interested in. Try searching the library catalog, adding the search term *sources* or *documents* to your keyword or using the names of prominent figures as authors. Primary documents may also be available in your library or on the Web, through the following sources.

Databases and indexes: The popular press

American Periodicals Series, 1741–1900. 2,770 microfilm reels. Ann Arbor: University Microfilms International, 1946–79. A large collection of articles from journals published from colonial times through the nineteenth century. This database identifies journals focused on specific topics and offers full-text articles. It is available on microfilm and in electronic format.

The Civil War: A Newspaper Perspective. Wilmington: Accessible Archives, 1995–. Offers selected full-text articles in plain-text format from more than 2,500 issues of newspapers representing both southern and northern perspectives for the years 1860–1865. The database includes eyewitness accounts, hundreds of maps, official reports of battles, and advertisements from the period. It is available in electronic format.

HarpWeek. Norfolk: HarpWeek, 1990–. An electronic edition of the contents of *Harper's Weekly,* a popular, illustrated publication, for the years 1857–1916. Images of the pages have been digitally scanned to retain the original appearance and include both illustrations and full text. Some libraries may have only segments of this database covering the Civil War and/or Reconstruction.

Historical Newspapers Online. Ann Arbor: ProQuest, 1999–. Offers the searchable full text of the *New York Times,* the *Wall Street Journal,* and other newspapers from their first issue on. Users can view both the article in its original format and the entire page on which the article appeared.

New York Times Index. New York: New York Times, 1851–. A valuable print source for finding newspaper coverage on a particular historical topic. Topics are grouped under broad subjects, with individual stories listed chronologically. Each index citation provides the date, section, page, and column of a story. Even without reading the stories themselves, users can get a detailed sequence of events from the index. Though the keyword search capability of *Historical Newspapers Online* offers some advantages, this print index provides a unique chronological record of events.

The Official Index to the Times. London: Times Publishing, 1966–. An excellent source for news on British life and world affairs, from 1790 on. It offers citations for articles from the *London Times* and is available in print and electronic formats. Sections of this index are published as *Palmer's Index to the Times.*

Poole's Index to Periodical Literature, 1802–1881. 6 vols. Boston: Houghton Mifflin, 1892. With supplement covering 1882–1906. Provides citations to American and English periodicals, books, newspapers, and government documents of the nineteenth century. An electronic edition is also available, with 3.8 million citations and enhanced indexing.

Readers' Guide to Periodical Literature. New York: Wilson, 1900–. Indexes popular magazines by subject. This index is a good source for popular reactions to events, literary topics, and popular culture of the twentieth century. It is available in print and electronic formats. A companion index covers 1890–1900.

Web resources: Primary documents

American Memory <http://memory.loc.gov>. A rich source of electronic reproductions of texts, images, sound, and film from the collections of the Library of Congress and collaborating libraries and museums. Materials include motion pictures from as early as 1897, sound recordings from World War I, and more than 300 pamphlets written by African Americans between Reconstruction and World War I. Browse collections using the "collection finder" or search across collections.

The Avalon Project at the Yale Law School: Documents in Law, History, and Diplomacy <http://www.yale.edu/lawweb/avalon/avalon.htm>. A collection of full-text primary source documents particularly rich in legal and diplomatic history and human rights. Organized by period and topic and searchable by keyword, this collection is well edited and of high quality. Documents include internal links to materials referenced in the text.

EuroDocs: Primary Historical Documents from Western Europe <http://www.lib.byu.edu/~rdh/eurodocs>. A wealth of primary source material from 22 countries (plus Vatican City). Sites are sorted by country and listed chronologically. Available sources include letters, facsimiles of paintings and photographs, journals, and official documents. The links are compiled by Richard Hacken at Brigham Young University Library.

Internet History Sourcebooks Project <http://www.fordham.edu/halsall/index.html>. A large collection of online texts and primary documents for the study of history. Three major sourcebooks, edited by Paul Halsall of Fordham University, cover ancient, medieval, and modern history; other collections are focused on history of science, African history, Islamic history, women's history, and more.

Making of America <http://www.hti.umich.edu/m/moagrp>. A digital archive of books and journals from the antebellum period through Reconstruction, extremely useful for the study of American social history, with strengths in education, science and technology, psychology, sociology, and American history. A work in progress, it already includes the full text of over 8,000 books and 50,000 journal articles published in the nineteenth century.

Web resources: Government documents

Foreign Relations of the United States: Diplomatic Papers <http://www.state.gov/www/about_state/history/frusonline.html>. Provides collected correspondence, memoranda, treaties, presidential messages, and other documents related to U.S. foreign policy, arranged chronologically and by region. Online volumes cover the years from the Truman through the Johnson administration. For earlier documents, see the print collection *Foreign Relations of the United States: Diplomatic Papers* (Washington: Government Printing Office, 1861–).

Public Papers of the Presidents of the United States <http://www.gpoaccess.gov/pubpapers/about.html>. A repository of proclamations, speeches, statements, photographs, and other presidential papers. Currently available online are documents from the George H. W. Bush administration on. Papers from Hoover on will eventually be added; for now, see the print version of *Public Papers of the Presidents of the United States* (Washington: Office of the Federal Register, 1957–).

Reprint series

American Culture Series. 643 microfilm reels. Ann Arbor: University Microfilms International, 1941–74. Reproduces over 6,000 American books and pamphlets published between 1493 and 1875. The materials are organized by 12 disciplines. Series I spans 1493–1806; the larger Series II expands the pre-1806 material and extends to 1875.

American Women's Diaries. 90 microfilm reels. New Canaan: Readex, 1980–. Reproduces the diaries of women who lived and traveled in the western, southern, and eastern United States. Available on microfilm only.

Early English Books, 1475–1640. 2,034 microfilm reels. Ann Arbor: University Microfilms International, 1938–67. *Early English Books, 1641–1700.* 2,396 microfilm reels. Ann Arbor: University

Microfilms International, 1961–. A vast collection of books from the first texts printed in England to the Restoration. Full texts are available in microfilm and in electronic format as *Early English Books Online* (*EEBO*).

Early English Text Society Series. 287 vols. London: Early English Text Society and IDC Publisher, 1864–. A long-running scholarly series that republishes Old English and Middle English texts in scholarly editions, bringing unpublished manuscripts, medieval dramas, and historical documents into print. New volumes of the series are being published by the Oxford University Press.

March of America Facsimile Series. 103 vols. Ann Arbor: University Microfilms International, 1966. A reprint series of original editions of early English accounts of travel to the New World. Available in print only.

Oral and local history collections

You may want to undertake an oral history project or track down oral histories that others have compiled by consulting the *Oral History Index* (Westport: Meckler, 1990) or the *Directory of Oral History Collections* (Phoenix: Oryx Press, 1988). Or you can simply search your library's catalog using the term *oral history* or combining *oral history* with a keyword. Also consider getting primary sources from a county or state historical society's collections or even from the archives of your own college or university. You may find yourself working with material no one else has analyzed before.

Researching in the Social Sciences

Social scientists interpret and analyze human behavior, generally using empirical methods of research. Though original data gathering and analysis are central to social sciences research, researchers also use library and Internet resources to

- obtain raw data for model building or analysis
- locate information about a particular model, theory, or methodology to be used in a research project
- review the literature to place new research in context

Subjects of study in the social sciences sometimes cross disciplines and may be difficult to locate using the typical subject headings in indexes and abstracts. In addition, new theories may take some time to circulate in the literature, especially in print sources. Consequently, the researcher should be prepared to

- identify potential search terms by scanning indexes and abstracts in relevant works
- use the references in published articles and books to trace connections among theories and ideas
- work from most recent to older sources

A review of the literature for a social sciences research project not only should identify what research has been done but should compare and contrast the available information and evaluate its significance.

Each of the social sciences has a well-developed set of research tools to help you find relevant material. The tools listed here will give you ideas for beginning your research. Consult a librarian for help in refining your search.

General resources in the social sciences

Databases and indexes in the social sciences

American Statistics Index. Washington: Congressional Information Service, 1974–. A useful index to statistics that are buried within government publications. Providing bibliographic citations and abstracts, it is available in print and electronic formats. The online version, *Statistical Masterfile* or *LexisNexis Statistical,* contains some links to full texts. It is searchable by keyword, subject, author, title, agency, or year and can be limited by demographic, geographic, or other variables.

Social Sciences Citation Index. Philadelphia: Institute for Scientific Information, 1956–. An interdisciplinary index to more than 1,700 journals in the social sciences. Searchable by author or keyword, the index gives bibliographic citations, 60 percent of which include abstracts. It allows searches by cited source, a good way to trace the influence of a particular work. The electronic version, part of the *Web of Science,* also offers a powerful "related records" search, which identifies articles that cite one or more of the same sources.

Social Sciences Index. New York: Wilson, 1974–. An interdisciplinary index to key journals in the social sciences, including anthropology, psychology, sociology, economics, and political science. It is available in print and electronic formats. The electronic version covers 1983 to the present. Your library may also offer the *Social Sciences Index Full Text,* which includes citations, abstracts, and the full texts of selected articles from 1989 to the present.

Web resources in the social sciences

FedStats <http://www.fedstats.gov>. A well-organized portal for statistical information available from over 100 U.S. government agency sites. Statistics can be searched by keyword or browsed by topic or agency. Links to downloadable data sets are included.

Internet Crossroads in Social Science Data <http://dpls.dacc.wisc.edu/newcrossroads/index.asp>. Offers over 700 annotated links to online data sources. Searchable by keyword or browsable by category, the site includes links to government and nongovernment sites concerned with domestic and international economics and labor, health, education, geography and history, politics, sociology, and demography. The site is maintained by the Data and Program Library Service at the University of Wisconsin, Madison.

SOSIG: Social Science Information Gateway <http://sosig.ac.uk>. A selective catalog of thousands of Web sites in the social sciences, hosted in the United Kingdom. Users can browse by topic and region or search by keyword. Each entry has been reviewed and is annotated. The focus is on high-quality sites that provide information directly rather than links to other sites. This site is an excellent resource for international social science data.

U.S. Census Bureau <http://www.census.gov>. Offers access to an astounding amount of demographic, social, and economic data. The search engine can pinpoint relevant statistical tables and reports. The site is updated almost daily with newly released reports.

Reference books in the social sciences

The Gallup Poll. Wilmington: Scholarly Resources, 1972–. An annual print compilation of opinion poll statistics gathered by the Gallup organization from 1935 to the present. The weekly update publication *Gallup Poll Tuesday Briefing* reports summaries of recent opinion polls.

Historical Statistics of the United States, Colonial Times to 1970. 2 vols. Washington: Government Printing Office, 1975. Offers vital statistics, economic figures, and social data for the United States over time; includes a subject index. For more recent figures, consult annual volumes of the *Statistical Abstract of the United States.*

International Encyclopedia of the Social and Behavioral Sciences. Ed. Neil J. Smelser and Paul B. Baltes. 26 vols. Amsterdam: Elsevier, 2001. A vast compendium of scholarly articles on topics in the social sciences. International and interdisciplinary in perspective, this work is particularly useful for the cross-references among related topics.

International Historical Statistics, 1750–2000: Europe. 5th ed. By B. R. Mitchell. New York: Palgrave, 2003. Offers time-series data for

European countries, including figures on population, agriculture, the economy, transportation and communications, and education. Other volumes by the same author cover other regions of the world.

The Social Sciences: A Cross-Disciplinary Guide to Selected Sources. Ed. Nancy L. Herron. 3rd ed. Englewood: Libraries Unlimited, 2003. Provides information about the most important tools for social sciences research, with essays describing the structure of each discipline's literature.

Statistical Abstract of the United States. Washington: Government Printing Office, 1879–. Perhaps the single most useful collection of statistical information available in a small package. It includes hundreds of tables of figures on areas such as population, economics, and social factors, with references to the original sources. An index provides easy access. Statistical abstracts from 1995 to the present are available on the Web at <http://www.census .gov/statab/www>.

Anthropology

Databases and indexes in anthropology

Abstracts in Anthropology. Farmingdale: Baywood, 1970–. Offers abstracts of articles from journals and books and includes conference proceedings in cultural and physical anthropology, archaeology, and linguistics; available in print only.

Anthropology Plus. Mountain View: RLG, 2002–. An online index to anthropology publications from the eighteenth century to the present. This work combines indexes maintained by the British Museum Anthropology Library and Harvard's Tozzer Library.

Human Relations Area Files (*HRAF*). Ann Arbor: University Microfilms International, 1968–. A huge collection of anthropological data, including books, articles, and field reports, arranged into 300 cultural groups. Within each group, information is categorized by subject, such as food production, interpersonal relations, and religion. Because the organization is the same under each culture, it is easy to make cross-cultural comparisons. Material from 1993 is available electronically as eHRAF; material published before 1993 is available on microfiche. The classification system is provided in the *Outline of World Cultures* (OWC), 6th ed. rev. (New Haven: Human Relations Area Files Press, 1983) and *Outline of Cultural Materials* (OCM), 5th ed. rev. (New Haven: Human Relations Area Files Press, 1982).

Web resources in anthropology

Anthropology Glossary <http://www.as.ua.edu/ant/glossary.php>. A searchable glossary of terms used in anthropology and archaeology. Results include definitions as well as a bibliography of articles related to the search term. Maintained by the Department of Anthropology at the University of Alabama.

Anthropology Resources on the Internet <http://www.aaanet.org/resinet.htm>. A selective guide to sites on anthropology, archaeology, and ethnology, as well as organizations, institutions, and online discussion groups. The list is part of the Web site of the American Anthropological Association.

Anthropology Resources on the Internet: WWW Virtual Library: History: Archaeology/Prehistory <http://www.anthropologie.net>. A directory of sites primarily devoted to anthropology, founded in 1995. Includes journals, organizations, institutions, research and data arranged by region, and links to topics such as law and cultural heritage and paleoanthropology. The site is edited by Bernard Olivier Clist.

Reference books in anthropology

Atlas of World Cultures: A Geographic Guide to Ethnographic Literature. By David H. Price. Newbury Park: Sage, 1989. Places bibliographic information about cultures in a geographic context. Forty maps are used to locate 3,500 cultural groups, for which bibliographies are provided.

Cambridge Encyclopedia of Human Evolution. Ed. Steve Jones et al. Cambridge: Cambridge University Press, 1992. A handy source for overviews of the field. The work surveys human evolution in thematic chapters.

Countries and Their Cultures. Ed. Melvin Ember and Carol Ember. 4 vols. New York: Macmillan Reference, 2001. Covers world cultures, including both the national culture held in common by citizens of a country and variations within the country. The work includes demographic, historical, economic, political, and religious information about each culture.

Dictionary of Anthropology. Ed. Thomas Barfield. Oxford: Blackwell, 1997. Defines and explores terms and concepts in social and cultural anthropology. The work includes some biographical sketches and longer articles on theoretical topics.

Encyclopedia of Cultural Anthropology. Ed. David Levinson and Melvin Ember. 4 vols. New York: Holt, 1996. Offers 340 lengthy articles written by specialists on approaches, methods, concepts, and topics related to cultural anthropology. Articles are followed by bibliographies of key research.

Encyclopedia of Prehistory. Ed. Peter N. Peregrine and Melvin Ember. 9 vols. New York: Kluwer, 2001. Provides information on all cultures known through archaeology, arranged by region. Major traditions are surveyed along with specific information about archaeological sites. The work is published in conjunction with the *Human Relations Area Files.*

Encyclopedia of World Cultures. Ed. David Levinson. 10 vols. Boston: G. K. Hall, 1991–. With supplements. Covers more than 1,500 cultural groups, alphabetically arranged within regions. Entries summarize information on the distribution, belief systems, kinship structures, and history of the groups and provide selective bibliographies. The encyclopedia is based on information in the *Human Relations Area Files.*

Business and economics

Databases and indexes in business and economics

ABI/Inform. Ann Arbor: ProQuest, 1971–. Covers industries, management techniques, and business trends as well as profiles of corporations and corporate leaders worldwide.

Accounting and Tax Index. Ann Arbor: University Microfilms International, 1992–. Supersedes the *Accountant's Index Supplement, 1920–1992.* A detailed index of more than 1,000 articles on taxation and accounting, conference papers, reports, and books. It is available in print and electronic formats.

Business and Company Resource Center. Detroit: Gale Group, 2001–. An online database of business magazine articles, company histories, rankings, and industry information. Many of the materials are available in full text.

Business Source Premier. Ipswich: EBSCO, 1990–. A database of journals and magazines in business and economics, with some full-text coverage (for a few titles going as far back as the 1920s). Coverage includes management, finance, accounting, and international business.

EconLit. Nashville: American Economic Association, 1969–. Provides citations (most with abstracts) to articles in scholarly journals in the field, covering all aspects of economics worldwide. Based in part on abstracts published in *The Journal of Economic Literature.*

LexisNexis: Business. Miamisburg: LexisNexis, 1998–. A collection of full-text databases of continuously updated business news sources, industry news, and company and financial data as well as other news and legal sources.

Web resources in business and economics

Bureau of Labor Statistics <http://www.bls.gov>. A mine of current statistical data and reports covering consumer spending, employment, wages, productivity, occupations, international trade, and industries as well as "The U.S. Economy at a Glance." The Bureau is a unit of the U.S. Department of Labor.

Economic Census, 2002 <http://www.census.gov/econ/census02>. Undertaken every five years, the economic census gathers data on retail, wholesale, manufacturing, and other business by state and local subdivision. Results for 2002 will contain more than 16,000 reports.

Economic Report of the President <http://www.gpoaccess.gov/eop/index.html>. Prepared annually by the chair of the Council of Economic Advisers, this publication explains the rationale for the president's budget submitted to Congress. Of particular interest are the tables that cover income, production, and employment in time series. The report is available in PDF format (1995 to the present).

globalEDGE <http://globaledge.msu.edu>. Offers worldwide business information, including methods of comparing country data, country background information, an annual compilation of market potential indicators, breaking news of interest to the business community, and a glossary of international business terms. The site was created by the Center for Business Education and Research at Michigan State University.

NetEc <http://netec.wustl.edu/NetEc.html>. An international project to share information of interest to academics and economists. It offers printed working papers, electronic working papers, home pages on economics, computer programs of use to economists, and two well-organized resource guides to economics Internet sites.

OSU Virtual Finance Library <http://fisher.osu.edu/fin/overview .htm>. Well-organized links on banks, exchanges, and market news, with pages for various audiences: students, researchers, executives, investors, and educators. The site is provided by the Department of Finance, Ohio State University.

SEC Filings and Forms (EDGAR) <http://www.sec.gov/edgar .shtml>. Provides information about publicly held corporations, which are required by federal law to file reports on their activities with the U.S. Securities and Exchange Commission. Most reports filed from 1994 to the present are publicly available through the *EDGAR* (Electronic Data Gathering, Analysis, and Retrieval System) database at this site. Information in company reports includes financial status, chief officers, stock information, company history, pending litigation that might have an economic impact on the company, and more. The site provides a brief tutorial for searching *EDGAR*.

U.S. Congressional Budget Office <http://www.cbo.gov>. Offers material compiled by a nonpartisan office for congressional decision making. The site includes federal budget analysis; the economic outlook; analysis of specific topics on housing, health, education, national security, and telecommunications; and more.

VIBES: Virtual International Business and Economics Resources <http://libweb.uncc.edu/ref-bus/vibehome.htm>. Provides nearly 3,000 links to sites related to international business and economics. Links include free full-text files of recent articles, reports, and statistical tables, organized by topics such as international trade law, patents, emerging markets, and regional and national sites. Compiled by Jeanie M. Welch of the J. Murrey Atkins Library, University of North Carolina at Charlotte.

Reference books in business and economics

Blackwell Encyclopedia of Management: Business Ethics. Ed. Patricia Werhane and R. Edward Freeman. 2nd ed. Cambridge: Blackwell, 2005. Offers substantial entries written by experts in business ethics on such topics as equal opportunity, corporate crime, participatory management, environmental risk, business ethics in different cultures, and electronic surveillance. This work is part of the series *The Blackwell Encyclopedia of Management.*

Encyclopedia of Business and Finance. Ed. Burton S. Kalinski. 2 vols. New York: Macmillan Reference, 2001. Offers over 300 articles on accounting, economics, finance, information systems, ethics, management, and marketing, with a U.S. focus.

Encyclopedia of Political Economy. Ed. Philip Anthony O'Hara. 2 vols. London: Routledge, 1999. Provides analyses of topics related to money and finance, labor, family and gender, political ideologies, development, theoretical schools, and methodology.

New Palgrave: A Dictionary of Economics. Ed. John Eatwell et al. 4 vols. London: Macmillan Reference; New York: Stockton Press, 1987. A revision of the classic *Palgrave's Dictionary of Political Economy,* offering lengthy, scholarly analyses of economic theories and theorists. Consult newer publications for emerging economic theory and analysis.

New Palgrave Dictionary of Economics and the Law. Ed. Peter Newman et al. 3 vols. London: Macmillan Reference; New York: Stockton Press, 1998. Offers international in-depth coverage of such topics as antitrust, cartels, contracts, civil procedure, theories of economics with legal import, taxation, securities regulation, and property rights.

New Palgrave Dictionary of Money and Finance. Ed. Peter Newman et al. 3 vols. London: Macmillan Reference; New York: Stockton Press, 1992. Defines financial terms and provides detailed discussions of concepts related to monetary economics, finance, and banking.

Oxford Encyclopedia of Economic History. Ed. Joel Mokyr. 5 vols. New York: Oxford University Press, 2003. Covers concepts and theories, economic development, background on countries and regions, and the history of specific products such as oil and coffee.

Communication studies

Databases and indexes in communication studies

Communication Abstracts. Beverly Hills: Sage, 1978–. Provides abstracts from more than 150 scholarly journals, books, and research reports in the field; available in both print and electronic formats.

Communication and Mass Media Complete. Ipswich: EBSCO, 2004–. An online database that covers both scholarly articles on communication studies and trade and popular coverage of the media. A substantial portion of the contents is linked to full text, with especially rich historical material in communication theory. This database was formed by a merger of the National Communication Association's *CommSearch* (an index to core journals in the field, sometimes called "Matlon" after its first editor, Ronald J. Matlon) and the *Mass Media Articles Index.*

Speech Index: An Index to Collections of World Famous Orations and Speeches for Various Occasions. 4th ed. Metuchen: Scarecrow, 1966–. With supplements through 1980. A print index to historical speeches included in more than 250 anthologies.

The Year's Work in Cultural and Critical Theory. Oxford: Blackwell, 1994–. An annual roundup of recent research on feminist theory, postcolonial studies, popular culture, virtual culture, film theory, cultural policy, and visual culture, presented as evaluative review essays written by leading scholars. This work is published in conjunction with the English Association (UK).

Web resources in communication studies

Communication Studies Resources <http://www.uiowa.edu/~commstud/resources>. A well-organized directory of Web resources useful for research. The directory covers advertising, culture studies, digital media, film studies, interpersonal and small-group communication, journalism and mass media, media studies, and rhetoric as well as online tools for communication studies researchers. It is maintained by Karla Tonella of the University of Iowa Department of Communication Studies.

First Amendment Handbook <http://www.rcfp.org/handbook/index.html>. Provides detailed analyses of constitutional law issues as they relate to the practice of journalism. Sections cover access to courts, places and people, the Freedom of Information Act, confidentiality, surreptitious recording, libel, invasion of privacy, prior restraint, and copyright. From the Reporters Committee for Freedom of the Press, compiled by Gregg P. Leslie.

Freedom Forum <http://www.freedomforum.org>. The Web site of a nonpartisan foundation devoted to free speech and freedom of the press. Includes online exhibits from the Newseum (a museum of news media), graphic images of front pages from around the world updated daily, and the latest news and analysis of First Amendment issues.

Journalism.org: Research, Resources, and Ideas to Improve Journalism <http://www.journalism.org>. News about the news industry, information for working journalists, background on issues of concern to journalists, and a detailed survey of the state of the news media, including print, broadcast, cable news, magazines, local TV, alternative media, and online news sources. The site is jointly maintained by the Project for Excellence in Journalism and the Committee of Concerned Journalists.

MCS: The Media and Communications Studies Site <http://www.aber.ac.uk/media>. A well-organized, searchable collection of links to Web content on a wide variety of topics—gender and ethnicity, news media, advertising, film studies, visual images, textual analysis, media influence, and more. The site is based at the University of Wales, Aberystwyth.

Reference books in communication studies

ABC-CLIO Companion to the Media in America. By Daniel Webster Hollis. Santa Barbara: ABC-CLIO, 1995. Covers important developments in mass media and significant media organizations and people in concise articles.

American Voices: Significant Speeches from American History, 1640–1945. Ed. James Andrews and David Zarefsky. New York: Longman, 1991. A chronologically arranged anthology of major speeches of historical and oratorical significance. A companion volume covers speeches from 1945 to the end of the 1980s.

Biographical Dictionary of American Journalism. Ed. Joseph P. McKerns. New York: Greenwood, 1989. Provides lengthy biographical sketches of major journalists, each followed by a list of sources.

Encyclopedia of Rhetoric. Ed. Thomas O. Sloane. Oxford: Oxford University Press, 2001. Offers substantial, scholarly overviews of research on such topics as invention, ethos, fallacies, and rhetoric and social movements.

History of the Mass Media in the United States: An Encyclopedia. Ed. Margaret A. Blancard. Chicago: Fitzroy Dearborn, 2000. Covers all forms of mass media from 1690 to 1990, offering short articles on technological, legal, economic, and political developments as well as major organizations and institutions.

International Encyclopedia of Communications. Ed. Erik Barnouw et al. 4 vols. New York: Oxford University Press, 1989. A multidisciplinary compilation of essays on communications, ranging from animal communications to dance as a means of communication. Each essay is followed by a selected bibliography. The encyclopedia is dated, so consult newer sources as well.

Museum of Broadcast Communications Encyclopedia of Television. Ed. Horace Newcomb et al. 3 vols. Chicago: Fitzroy Dearborn, 2000. Covers genres, programs, people, organizations, and topics related to television history. Information on television programs includes casts, producers, programming history, and bibliographies. The same publisher also offers *Encyclopedia of Radio* (2004).

Criminal justice

Databases and indexes in criminal justice

Criminal Justice Abstracts. Thousand Oaks: Sage, 1968–. Provides abstracts of articles, books, reports, and government documents that deal with crime trends, crime prevention and deterrence, juvenile justice, police, courts, punishment, and sentencing. Available in print and electronic formats. Published in conjunction with the Criminal Justice Collection of Rutgers University Libraries.

Web resources in criminal justice

Bureau of Justice Statistics <http://www.ojp.usdoj.gov/bjs>. Provides a wealth of information about crime and victimization, law enforcement, corrections, prosecutions, courts and sentencing, drugs, firearms, and more. This authoritative source for data and analysis of crime in the United States is a unit of the U.S. Department of Justice.

Criminal Justice Links <http://www.criminology.fsu.edu/cjlinks>. A long-running directory of international resources on crime, the courts, forensic sciences, crime in the news and popular culture, and other aspects of the field. The site is maintained by Cecil Greek of the Florida State University School of Criminology.

Internet Resources <http://www.lib.jjay.cuny.edu/links>. Prepared by librarians at one of the premier criminal justice libraries in the world, the Lloyd Jay Sealy Library of the John Jay College of Criminal Justice, this directory has a wealth of material on a variety of topics, with special emphasis on New York City. All links are annotated; the site is updated frequently.

National Criminal Justice Reference Service <http://www.ncjrs.org>. A federal information resource offering a huge amount of information on corrections, juvenile justice, the courts, law enforcement, drug interdiction, victimization, and more. It includes a database of criminal justice articles, some with full text. Provided by the U.S. Department of Justice.

Zeno's Forensic Site <http://forensic.to/forensic.html>. Based in the Netherlands and maintained by Zeno Geradts, this site provides annotated links to information on arson investigation, firearms identification, DNA analysis, fingerprints, toxicology, forensic entomology, forensic psychology, and more.

Reference books in criminal justice

Encyclopedia of Crime and Justice. Ed. Josua Dressler. 2nd ed. 4 vols. New York: Macmillan Reference, 2002. One of the best sources for overall coverage of the field. Includes issues in law, criminology, and sociology and references to classic studies and recent research. Though the focus is on criminal justice in the United States, international perspectives are included.

Encyclopedia of Crime and Punishment. Ed. David Levinson. 4 vols. Thousand Oaks: Sage, 2002. Covers a huge range of topics in an accessible manner, from crimes to policing to corrections.

Encyclopedia of Criminology and Deviant Behavior. Ed. Clifton D. Bryant. 4 vols. Philadelphia: Brunner-Routledge, 2001. Provides substantial, scholarly articles on theory and research on crime, sexual deviance, and self-destructive behaviors. This work is particularly useful for understanding the psychological and sociological context of crime.

Encyclopedia of Forensic Sciences. Ed. Jay A. Siegel. 3 vols. San Diego: Academic Press, 2000. The most comprehensive reference work of its type, this encyclopedia provides information on crime scene processing, handling of evidence and witnesses, forensic medicine, firearms identification, DNA analysis, and more, in detailed, technical articles.

Education

Databases and indexes in education

Education Index. New York: Wilson, 1929–. An author-subject database of articles in education journals, books, and yearbooks, including both research-based studies and material on classroom practice. Online versions of this index may include abstracts and full text of selected journals.

ERIC: Education Resources Information Center. Washington: Institute of Education Sciences, 1966–. Provides descriptive abstracts of over a million journal articles and ERIC documents — research reports, conference papers, curriculum guides, and other materials — that are not otherwise formally published. Some non-journal documents are available in full text. An invaluable tool for educators, this database service is sponsored by the U.S. Department of Education and is available free online at <http://www.eric.ed.gov>.

Web resources in education

Educator's Reference Desk <http://www.eduref.org>. A directory of resource guides and lesson plans, searchable by grade level, as well as a collection of questions and answers about a variety of education topics. The site is a project of the Information Institute of Syracuse.

ENC Online <http://www.enc.org>. The Web site of the Eisenhower National Clearinghouse for Mathematics and Science Education, funded by the U.S. Department of Education. It offers links to math and science curriculum materials, ideas for teachers, news about science education, and professional development tools.

GEM: The Gateway to Educational Materials <http://thegateway.org>. A directory of online classroom materials. The site offers a sophisticated search engine as well as browsing by keyword, subject, grade level, or type of resource. Search results lead to lesson plans, curriculum units, and other Web materials for educators. The site is sponsored by the U.S. Department of Education.

National Center for Education Statistics. <http://nces.ed.gov>. Provides a wealth of statistical data on schools and libraries in the United States, including academic achievement; the condition of schools; comparative information on school districts, colleges, and libraries; dropout rates; enrollment trends; school safety; and more. The center is a unit of the U.S. Department of Education.

Reference books in education

Encyclopedia of Early Childhood Education. Ed. Leslie R. Williams and Doris P. Fromberg. New York: Garland, 1992. Offers articles on historical, political, economic, sociocultural, intellectual, and educational influences on early childhood education.

Encyclopedia of Education. Ed. James W. Guthrie. 2nd ed. 8 vols. New York: Macmillan Reference, 2003. Covers education theory, history of education, education and social forces, and education reform efforts in over 850 articles, emphasizing the U.S. experience but with some international perspectives. Volume 8 includes primary sources and a thematic outline.

Encyclopedia of Educational Research. Ed. Marvin C. Alkin. 6th ed. 4 vols. New York: Macmillan, 1992. Provides surveys of research in the field, ranging from class size to critical thinking. Surveys are followed by bibliographies for further research.

Philosophy of Education: An Encyclopedia. Ed. J. J. Chambliss. New York: Garland, 1996. Offers substantial analyses covering various philosophers and their contributions; philosophical topics such as behaviorism, critical thinking, and epistemology; and concepts such as *school* and *truth* from a philosophical angle.

World Education Encyclopedia: A Survey of Educational Systems Worldwide. Ed. Rebecca Marlow-Ferguson. 2nd ed. 3 vols. Detroit: Gale Group, 2002. Provides overviews of education at all levels throughout the world and some discussion of administration and financing, research, and the state of the profession. The appendix includes comparative statistical tables and maps.

Ethnic and area studies

Databases and indexes in ethnic and area studies

Bibliography of Asian Studies. Ann Arbor: Association for Asian Studies, 1956–. An index to European-language scholarly publications in Asian studies. Organized by country, with subdivisions by topic, the index provides more than 410,000 bibliographic citations. Available in print and electronic formats.

Ethnic NewsWatch. Ann Arbor: ProQuest, 1985–. An electronic full-text database specializing in publications published by ethnic communities in the United States, which are often left out of general news and magazine databases. Providing valuable alternative insights, this work includes many publications in Spanish and can be searched in a Spanish-language interface.

Handbook of Latin American Studies. Austin: University of Texas Press, 1935–. A selective, annotated bibliography of scholarly works on Latin America. This is an excellent source of citations for any topic in Latin American studies, including Hispanic populations in the United States. Now prepared by the Hispanic Division of the Library of Congress, an electronic version of this work, *HLAS Online,* is available at <http://lcweb2.loc.gov/hlas>. The site can be searched by keyword or subject heading in English, Spanish, or Portuguese.

HAPI: Hispanic American Periodical Index. Los Angeles: UCLA Latin American Center, 1970–. An index to articles in over 400 scholarly journals published in Latin America or covering topics relevant to Latin America and Latin Americans living in North America. Available in print and electronic formats.

Web resources in ethnic and area studies

African American Digital Initiatives <http://www.howard.edu/ library/Assist/Guides/Afro-Am_Digital.htm>. A directory of links to high-quality archival material online from libraries and museums around the country. The list is maintained by the Howard University Libraries.

Africa South of the Sahara <http://www-sul.stanford.edu/depts/ ssrg/africa/guide.html>. Selected, annotated sites arranged by country and topic, with sources for current news from Africa. The site is maintained by Karen Fung for the African Studies Association.

Asian American Studies Resources <http://sun3.lib.uci.edu/ ~dtsang/aas2.htm>. A no-frills list of links to bibliographies, publications, research institutes, movements, gay Asian resources, and more. The list was compiled by Daniel C. Tsang at the University of California, Irvine.

Asian Studies WWW Virtual Library <http://coombs.anu.edu.au/ WWWVL-AsianStudies.html>. Covers information on all regions of Asia and the Middle East. The site is comprehensive, frequently updated, and organized by both an alphabetical index and a hierarchical topical index. It is edited by T. Matthew Ciolek of the Australian National University.

Center for World Indigenous Studies <http://www.cwis.org>. Offers information on various indigenous peoples and issues of political and cultural identity and nationhood. Of particular note is the Fourth World Docu-Program, which provides full-text documents related to communities around the world as well as relevant international and multilateral documents.

LANIC: Latin American Network Information Center <http://lanic
.utexas.edu>. Provides over 12,000 links to Web resources for Latin
America, arranged by country or by topic, such as economy, education, and government. The site is affiliated with the Lozano Long
Institute of Latin American Studies, University of Texas at Austin,
one of the premier Latin American Studies programs in the world.

NativeWeb: Resources for Indigenous Cultures around the World
<http://www.nativeweb.org>. A rich site for information on native peo-
ples, particularly on Native North Americans, but global in scope. The
site includes cultural, historical, educational, and current affairs information.

PAIR: Portal to Asian Internet Resources <http://webcat.library
.wisc.edu:3200/PAIR/index.html>. A joint project undertaken by
the libraries of the universities of Minnesota, Wisconsin–Madison,
and Ohio State, this searchable database catalogs reputable Web
resources originating in Asia, including Central, South, Southeast,
and East Asia. Resources are also browsable by country.

Pew Hispanic Center. <http://www.pewhispanic.org/index.jsp>.
Includes the text of several reports as well as information on demographics, economics, labor, immigration, education, health, and
Latinos in the military. The Pew Hispanic Center, a research organization, is a project of the Pew Research Center.

Reference books in ethnic and area studies

*Africana: The Encyclopedia of the African and African American
Experience.* Ed. Kwame Anthony Appiah and Henry Louis Gates Jr.
New York: Basic Civitas, 1999. A one-volume trove of information,
lavishly illustrated and with scholarly essays.

American Immigrant Cultures: Builders of a Nation. Ed. David
Levinson and Melvin Ember. 2 vols. New York: Macmillan Library
Reference, 1997. Offers in-depth profiles of immigrant communities in the United States, including their defining features, patterns
of cultural variation, immigration history, demographics, and cultural characteristics.

Atlas of the North American Indian. By Carl Waldman. Rev. ed.
New York: Facts on File, 2000. Offers maps on tribal locations,

reservations, sites of cultural and archaeological importance, and other significant places. Includes related text and bibliographies.

Dictionary of Native American Mythology. By Sam D. Gill and Irene F. Sullivan. Santa Barbara: ABC-CLIO, 1992. Provides quick access to information about individuals, events, and topics in Native American mythology, from all tribes and periods. Includes a bibliography.

Encyclopedia of African American Civil Rights: From Emancipation to the Twenty-First Century. Ed. Charles D. Lowery and John F. Marszalek. Rev. ed. 2 vols. New York: Greenwood, 2003. A dictionary of terms, events, and prominent people related to the civil rights movement. The work includes selected primary sources.

Encyclopedia of African-American Culture and History. Ed. Jack Salzman, Cornel West, and David L. Smith. 5 vols. New York: Macmillan Library Reference, 1996. With supplement. Offers extensive articles on people, institutions, events, issues, and themes related to African Americans. Includes many illustrations and bibliographies.

Encyclopedia of Africa South of the Sahara. Ed. John Izard Middleton. 4 vols. New York: Scribner, 1997. Covers countries, ethnic groups, and topics in nearly 900 substantial articles.

Encyclopedia of American Immigration. Ed. James Climent. 4 vols. Armonk: Sharpe, 2001. Covers immigration history, demographics, and political, economic, and cultural issues as well as background on specific immigrant groups. Includes the text of several important primary documents.

Encyclopedia of Contemporary French Culture. Ed. Alex Hughes and Keith Reader. London: Routledge, 1998. Short articles on a wealth of topics related to French and Francophone culture from 1945 to the present. Other volumes cover contemporary German, Spanish, Italian, Japanese, and other cultures.

Encyclopedia of Latin American History and Culture. Ed. Barbara A. Tenenbaum and Georgette M. Dorn. 5 vols. New York: Scribner, 1996. Covers a wide variety of topics in over 5,000 articles that together constitute an overview of current knowledge about Latin America. Entries are organized by country and by topic (such as slavery, art, Asians in Latin America); biographical entries are included.

Encyclopedia of the Modern Middle East. Ed. Reeva S. Simon et al. 4 vols. New York: Macmillan Library Reference, 1996. Covers political, historical, social, economic, and cultural topics in substantial, well-documented articles.

Gale Encyclopedia of Multicultural America. Ed. Julie Galens et al. 2nd ed. 3 vols. Detroit: Gale Group, 2000. Offers more than 100 substantial essays on ethnic groups in the United States, covering origins, circumstances of arrival, family, community, culture, economy, politics, and significant contributions. Each essay ends with a bibliography and contacts for further research.

Gale Encyclopedia of Native American Tribes. 4 vols. Detroit: Gale Group, 1998. Offers information on the history and current status of nearly 400 tribes, with historical background, past and current location, religious beliefs, language, means of subsistence, healing practices, customs, oral literature, and current issues facing the tribe.

Handbook of Hispanic Cultures in the United States. 4 vols. Houston: Arte Público, 1993. A survey of art, history, sociology, and anthropology of Hispanic Americans. Chapters within each volume are arranged by topic, and articles are lengthy and well illustrated.

Handbook of North American Indians. 13 vols. to date. Washington: Smithsonian Institution, 1978–. Offers scholarly essays on the history, social situation, politics, religion, economics, and tribal traditions of Native American groups. The work covers aboriginal cultures in North America by region and topics such as white-Indian relations, the arts, and languages.

The Historical and Cultural Atlas of African Americans. By Molefi K. Asante and Mark T. Mattson. New York: Macmillan, 1991. A geographically oriented overview of African American life, experiences, and traditions. Included are maps representing African origins, the slave trade, the Civil War, current social and economic status, and other topics.

Oxford Encyclopedia of the Modern Islamic World. 4 vols. New York: Oxford University Press, 1995. Covers Islamic peoples, movements, and issues throughout the world.

Geography

Databases and indexes in geography

Geographical Abstracts. New York: Elsevier, 1989–. An index to books and articles relevant to human and physical geography. The work provides bibliographic citations along with abstracts of more than 2,000 books and reports and more than 3,000 articles. The electronic version is called *Geobase.*

The Online Geographical Bibliography. Milwaukee: American Geographical Society, 1985–. An electronic index to journal articles, books, and maps from the American Geographical Society collection. This work provides citations to research on topics such as biogeography, climatology, human geography, hydrology, and physical geography as well as regional geography. The most recent additions to this database are listed in *Current Geographical Publications: Additions to the Research Catalogue of the American Geographical Society,* which was first published in 1938 and is now available only online.

Web resources in geography

American FactFinder <http://factfinder.census.gov>. Provides a wealth of information about populations and places in the United States. The powerful search facility can be used to pinpoint tables of data and to create maps based on the variables you supply, with tools that enable creation of thematic maps from national to street level. The site is provided by the U.S. Census Bureau.

Geosource. <http://www.library.uu.nl/geosource>. A directory of Web sources for human geography, physical geography, planning, geoscience, and environmental science. The information is organized by topic, region, and country and by type, such as organizations, journals, and institutions. The site is maintained by Jeroen Bosman of the Central Library, Utrecht University.

Perry Castañeda Library Map Collection <http://www.lib.utexas.edu/maps/index.html>. An excellent and frequently updated list of links to over 2,400 online maps in digital form. Organized primarily by region and country, the site also includes maps of current interest, linked to world events. The site is a service of the General Libraries, University of Texas at Austin.

Places Online <http://www.placesonline.org>. A map-based set of links to "the world's best" sites for visual information about places around the world, chosen to provide a high-quality sense of a specific place. The site is a service of the Association of American Geographers.

TerraFly <http://www.terrafly.com>. Provides aerial satellite images of specific places. Users can zoom in and out or "fly" across an area. Additionally, clicking on a point in any U.S. location opens detailed data in another window, down to census block level. Based at Florida International University, this project combines information from the Census Bureau, NASA, the U.S. Geological Survey, and other public sources into a single, powerful tool.

Reference books in geography

Columbia Gazetteer of the World. Ed. Saul B. Cohen. 3 vols. New York: Columbia University Press, 1998. Provides the exact location of places and geographical features around the world and gives a very brief definition or description. This is the most complete gazetteer available.

Dictionary of Concepts in Human Geography. Ed. Robert P. Larkin and Gary L. Peters. Westport: Greenwood, 1983. Covers the historical development of theories in the field, with references to classic studies. Newer resources should also be consulted.

Dictionary of Human Geography. Ed. Ron Johnson et al. 4th ed. New York: Blackwell, 2000. Defines and discusses terms, topics, and concepts in human geography. Brief bibliographies follow many of the entries.

Encyclopedic Dictionary of Physical Geography. Ed. Andrew Goudie et al. 2nd ed. New York: Blackwell, 1999. Defines and discusses terms and concepts in physical geography and includes brief, selective bibliographies.

Special resources in geography

Maps and atlases are basic tools for the geographer. Atlases, because of their size, are often shelved in special bookcases; maps may be housed in a special collection of their own. Think in terms not only of the familiar sort of world atlas, such as the *Atlas of the World,* 8th ed. (New York: Oxford University Press, 2000), but also of atlases that provide information on population, trade, history, water resources, and so on. Additionally, at some institutions, sophisticated GIS (Geographic Information Systems) software may be available for creating your own maps.

Law

Databases and indexes in law

Index to Legal Periodicals and Books. New York: Wilson, 1994–. Index to legal journals, law reviews and books, government publications, institutions, and bar associations. Also available in electronic format. An earlier version of the index, covering only journal articles, was started in 1908; this retrospective index is available online in some libraries.

LexisNexis: Legal Research. Bethesda: LexisNexis, 1998–. The *LexisNexis* databases include an extensive legal section. Of particular note is the ability to search for the full text of state and federal court decisions (also known as "case law") by keyword, party name, or citation, and the Law Reviews section, which offers the full text of scholarly articles that analyze legal issues in depth.

WestLaw Campus. Eagan: West, 2002–. A database of legal research materials, including laws, cases, legal articles, and reference material as well as analysis of legal issues provided by West and an integrated system that indicates which cases remain precedent-setting.

Web resources in law

Code of Federal Regulations <http://www.gpoaccess.gov/cfr/index.html>. Provides access to federal "administrative law" — regulations set by federal government agencies to spell out how a law passed by Congress will be carried out. The CFR is searchable by keyword, title, or citation information or can be browsed by topic (or "title").

EISIL: Electronic Information System for International Law <http://www.eisil.org>. A directory of information on international legal issues, including international human rights, criminal law, use of force, environmental law, and economic law. Each section includes the text of important international agreements and links to significant organizations. EISIL is a service of the American Society of International Law.

FindLaw U.S. Supreme Court Decisions <http://findlaw.com/casecode/supreme.html>. Provides the full text of Supreme Court decisions from 1893 to present, with handy hotlinks to cited decisions. Searchable by citation, party name, or keyword, the database is part of *FindLaw*, a commercial portal to legal information.

Guide to Law Online: Nations of the World <http://www.loc.gov/law/guide/nations.html>. A country-by-country directory of legal information, including constitutional, executive, legislative, and judicial law, as well as related information such as human rights reports. The links are compiled by the Law Library of Congress.

LII: Legal Information Institute <http://www.law.cornell.edu>. A directory to legal information on the Web, including texts of case law and statutes for state, federal, and international jurisdictions. The site, organized alphabetically by topic, also provides links to court opinions and directories to law organizations and journals. The institute is a project of the Cornell University Law School.

Oyez: Supreme Court Multimedia <http://www.oyez.org/oyez/frontpage>. Offers information about the U.S. Supreme Court, most notably audio files of all oral arguments held before the Supreme Court since 1995, with selected landmark cases as far back as 1955. Oral arguments offer a fascinating glimpse into the background of decisions. The site also provides current Supreme Court news and a link to *On the Docket*, a news feed on Supreme Court matters from the Medill School of Journalism at Northwestern University.

U.S. Code <http://uscode.house.gov/lawrevisioncounsel.shtml>. From the Office of the Law Revision Counsel, U.S. House of Representatives, this site provides the text of federal laws of the United States currently in force, arranged by topic (or "title") and section. The site offers an option to search or browse the code and provides a link to *Thomas*, a site maintained by the Library of Congress that provides the text of bills introduced in Congress. For state laws, consult official state Web sites or the *LII* directory, above.

Reference books in law

Black's Law Dictionary. Ed. Bryan A. Garner and Henry Campbell Black. 8th ed. St. Paul: West, 2004. Offers brief, technical definitions of legal terms, with an emphasis on the U.S. legal system.

Encyclopedia of the American Constitution. Ed. Leonard Williams Levy et al. 2nd ed. 6 vols. New York: Macmillan Library Reference, 2000. Covers essential topics and landmark cases related to constitutional law.

Encyclopedia of the American Judicial System. Ed. Robert J. Janosik. 3 vols. New York: Macmillan Library Reference, 1987. Offers substantial articles covering the workings of the court system and its effects on society.

Historic U.S. Court Cases: An Encyclopedia. Ed. John W. Johnson. 2nd ed. 2 vols. New York: Routledge, 2001. Essays on major cases that have had an impact on American law and society, with sections on civil liberties, minority rights, women, and economics.

West's Encyclopedia of American Law. 12 vols. St. Paul: Gale Group, West Group, 1998. Covers legal issues clearly in articles written for a general audience. This work is supplemented by *The American Law Yearbook.*

Political science

Databases and indexes in political science

CIAO: Columbia International Affairs Online. New York: Columbia University Press, 1997–. A digital library of working papers, journals, books, course materials, and case studies on world affairs.

LexisNexis: Congressional. Bethesda: LexisNexis, 1970–. The most comprehensive database of information on the U.S. Congress. This database provides bibliographic citations, descriptive abstracts, and the full texts of many documents including bills, laws (with legislative histories), committee reports, the *Congressional Record,* and more.

Monthly Catalog of United States Government Publications. Washington: Government Printing Office, 1895–. An index to publications from federal agencies and Congress, arranged by issuing body and indexed by author, title, subject, and series or report number. Current years are available online, with free access to the index from 1995 to present, at <http://www.gpoaccess.gov/cgp/index.html>.

PAIS International. New York: Public Affairs Information Service, 1972–. An index to books, articles, and government documents on public affairs, including politics, social issues, and economics. International in scope, this work combines the *Public Affairs Information Service* (1915–90), a long-running publication that is a good resource for historical analysis of politics, and *PAIS Foreign Language Index* (1972–90). Available in print and online.

Web resources in political science

Country Studies <http://lcweb2.loc.gov/frd/cs/cshome.html>. Online editions of book-length country profiles produced for U.S. diplomats by the Federal Research Division of the Library of Congress. The site includes substantial information on each nation's culture, history, economy, and political system. It is searchable by topic and country. Be sure to note publication dates; some country studies are more than ten years old and may include outdated information. Some libraries may have print versions.

Foreign Affairs Online <http://www.people.virginia.edu/~rjb3v/rjb.html>. A meta-index to sites related to international law, international relations, human rights, NGOs and IGOs, and U.S. foreign policy. Well organized and thoroughly annotated, the site is maintained by Robert J. Beck.

LSU Libraries Federal Agencies Directory <http://www.lib.lsu.edu/gov/fedgov.html>. Offers links to federal agency Web sites, arranged hierarchically and alphabetically, with a search engine.

National Security Archive <http://www.gwu.edu/~nsarchiv>. The Web site of a project based at George Washington University that has collected the world's largest nongovernmental archive of declassified documents, many of them covering controversial issues and obtained through the Freedom of Information Act. Though some of the documents are not accessible through the Web site, large collections of papers called "briefing books" are available on a variety of foreign affairs topics. This site is a rich set of primary source documents on key international issues.

THOMAS: Legislative Information on the Internet <http://thomas .loc.gov>. Provides the text of bills introduced in Congress along with committee action from the 104th Congress (1995) to the present. Users can search the site by bill number or keyword to learn about the legislative process, find a state's members of Congress, and access a comprehensive database on current and past legislation. A service of the Library of Congress, the site also provides a full-text search of the *Congressional Record,* a daily record of activity in Congress, and committee information. Most official state Web sites provide similar bill-tracking information for state legislatures.

United Nations <http://www.un.org>. Offers news releases, virtual tours, documents, and basic information about the United Nations and its bodies. Three different search engines explore a large database and list of links. The site includes a wealth of reports, statistical data, and other information on human rights, international law, peacekeeping missions, and other topics.

University of Michigan Documents Center <http://www .lib.umich.edu/govdocs>. Offers a well-organized and current list of links to local, state, federal, foreign, and international Web sites, with official information as well as links to statistical information sources and a guide to political science material on the Web.

Reference books in political science

Almanac of American Politics. Ed. Michael Barone and Richard E. Cohen. Washington: National Journal, 1972–. Summarizes the state of American politics at both national and state levels, giving voting results on key issues and state-by-state analyses of political concerns. Updated every two years.

America Votes. Ed. Richard M. Scammon. Washington: Congressional Quarterly, 1956–. A biennial summary of state and national election returns; useful for historical as well as current information.

Congressional Quarterly's Guide to Congress. 5th ed. 2 vols. Washington: Congressional Quarterly, 2000. Provides detailed histories and discussions of congressional processes and issues.

Similar guides put out by the same publisher cover the presidency, the Supreme Court, and U.S. elections.

CQ Almanac Plus. Washington: Congressional Quarterly, 2001–. An annual summation of U.S. politics that analyzes key issues, important legislation, voting records of congressional representatives, and major Supreme Court decisions. Continues *Congressional Quarterly Almanac* (1945–2000).

CQ Weekly Report. Washington: Congressional Quarterly, 1967–. A weekly publication covering events in Washington. Includes a detailed index every six months. Another weekly that provides similar coverage is the *National Journal.*

Encyclopedia of American Foreign Policy. 2nd ed. 3 vols. New York: Scribner, 2002. Offers essays on topics related to foreign policy issues and doctrines, such as terrorism, environmental diplomacy, and refugee policies. This work is more theoretical in orientation than the *Encyclopedia of U.S. Foreign Relations,* below.

Encyclopedia of U.S. Foreign Relations. Ed. Bruce W. Jentleson and Thomas G. Paterson. 4 vols. New York: Oxford University Press, 1997. Includes over 1,000 articles covering historical events, relations with countries, biographical sketches of leaders associated with foreign policy, treaties, doctrines, and key concepts. Published under the auspices of the Council on Foreign Relations, the work also provides chronologies and comparative country data.

International Encyclopedia of Public Policy and Administration. Ed. Jay M. Shafrirz. 4 vols. Boulder: Westview, 1998. Covers topics in public administration such as regional development, emergency management, budget reform, cost of living adjustments, and more. This work, with its global scope and interdisciplinary coverage, provides broad perspectives. It also includes coverage of principles, theories, legal concepts, and management topics as well as definitions of terms used in the field of public policy.

Political Handbook of the World. Ed. Arthur S. Banks and Thomas C. Muller. Binghamton: CSA Publications, 1927–. Covers countries of the world, giving basic background information, discussions of political parties and structures, and analyses of current political trends. Updated annually.

United States Government Manual. Washington: Government Printing Office, 1973–. Outlines the organization of federal government agencies, providing organizational charts, contact names and addresses, and descriptions of agencies' missions. Also available online at <http://www.gpoaccess.gov/gmanual>.

Psychology

Databases and indexes in psychology

Psychological Abstracts. Washington: American Psychological Association, 1927–. Provides nearly two million references to journal articles, books, book chapters, and dissertations from journals in psychology and related fields published from 1840 to the present, most of them with abstracts. A thesaurus of the subject descriptors is available to determine the most effective search terms. The electronic version of this index is titled *PsycINFO* and covers publications from 1840 to the present; in some libraries *PsycINFO* provides selected links to full-text articles. Recently added material also includes the sources cited in a work and links to works that have cited a given article.

Web resources in psychology

APA Online <http://www.apa.org>. The site for the American Psychological Association, providing news from the field, a roundup of selected research on topics such as anger, trauma, addictions, and depression, and information about the organization, such as the APA's Code of Ethics. Some of the information at this site is available to members only, though some of it, such as the *PsycINFO* database and APA journals, is probably available through your library.

National Institute of Mental Health <http://www.nimh.nih.gov>. From the federal agency charged with research into mental health and illness, this site offers useful information about health topics and statistics, with links to current research findings and clinical trials.

PsychCrawler <http://www.psychcrawler.com>. A search engine for sites of interest to psychology researchers. Though the number of sites is limited and very selective, the search engine allows for highly focused searches. *PsychCrawler* is a product of the American Psychological Association.

Psychology World Wide Web Virtual Library <http://www.dialogical .net/psychology/index.html>. A directory of selected links with brief descriptions. Areas covered include psychology of religion, transpersonal psychology, school psychology, mental health, and history of psychology. Maintained by Gene R. Thursby of the University of Florida.

Psych Web <http://www.psywww.com>. A selective directory linking to quality resources for teachers and students of psychology. Includes scholarly resources by subfield such as abnormal, behavioral, and forensic psychology, neuroscience, and sport psychology. Maintained by Russel A. Dewey.

Social Psychology Network <http://www.socialpsychology.org>. A deep directory of resources on topics such as gender and psychology, social cognition, and interpersonal psychology, as well as information on programs and organizations, research reports online, and social research groups. The site is maintained by Scott Plous at Wesleyan University.

Social Work and Social Services Web Sites <http://gwbweb.wustl .edu/websites.html>. A no-frills directory of links covering topics such as families, health care, poverty, crisis intervention, and welfare. The site is a service of the George Warren Brown School of Social Work, Washington University, St. Louis.

Reference books in psychology

Blackwell Dictionary of Cognitive Psychology. Ed. Andrew W. Ellis et al. Oxford: Blackwell, 1994. Contains surveys of major topics in cognition and provides selective bibliographies.

Companion Encyclopedia of Psychology. Ed. Andrew M. Colman. 2 vols. London: Routledge, 1994. Offers survey articles on major topics in psychology, including perception, learning, biological aspects of behavior, developmental psychology, abnormal psychology, and research methods. Each article is written at a fairly technical level and includes a selected bibliography and references.

Corsini Encyclopedia of Psychology and Behavioral Science. Ed. W. Edward Craighead and Charles B. Nemeroff. 3rd ed. 4 vols. New York: Wiley, 2001. Defines and discusses terms, theories, methodology, and issues in psychological practice and offers brief biographies of important psychologists.

Diagnostic and Statistical Manual of Mental Disorders (DSM-IV). 4th ed. rev. Washington: American Psychiatric Association, 2000. Classifies and describes mental disorders and includes diagrams to aid in the diagnosis of mental disorders as well as a glossary of technical terms.

Encyclopedia of Human Behavior. Ed. V. S. Ramachandran. 4 vols. San Diego: Academic Press, 1994. Offers articles on a wide range of topics, such as left- or right-handedness, blushing, interpersonal communications, and intelligence. Each article provides an overview of the current state of knowledge about a topic and provides references to research.

Encyclopedia of Human Intelligence. Ed. Robert J. Sternberg. 2 vols. New York: Macmillan, 1994. A collection of more than 250 articles on various aspects of intelligence, including reasoning, problem solving, aphasia, and measurement.

Encyclopedia of Mental Health. Ed. Howard S. Friedman et al. 3 vols. San Diego: Academic Press, 1998. Includes substantial articles on major disciplines in the field, research areas, and topics of public interest. Designed for both students and health professionals, this work provides current and thorough coverage of mental disorders, treatments, personality traits, and psychological aspects of such topics as television viewing, parenting, and homelessness.

Encyclopedia of Psychology. Ed. Alan E. Kazdin. 8 vols. Washington: American Psychological Association, 2000. The most thorough and scholarly treatment of psychology topics, including methodology, findings, advances in research, and applications.

Encyclopedia of Social Work. Ed. Richard L. Edwards et al. 19th ed. 3 vols. Washington: National Association of Social Workers Press, 1995. With supplements. Offers substantial articles, with bibliographies, on subjects such as foster care for children, adolescence, and public health services as well as short biographies of important figures in the field.

Mental Measurements Yearbook. Lincoln: Buros Institute of Mental Measurements, 1938–. An essential reference work for those interested in psychological tests. This work surveys and reviews tests of aptitude, education, achievement, and personality and includes bibliographies of related research. It is available in both print and electronic formats. The electronic version includes the full text of articles from 1983 through the present.

Sociology

Databases and indexes in sociology

Sociological Abstracts. San Diego: Sociological Abstracts, 1952–. The most detailed index for the field, covering approximately 2,000 journals from 55 countries as well as books and book chapters. All entries from 1974 on include abstracts. The index is available in print and online.

Web resources in sociology

SocioSite <http://www2.fmg.uva.nl/sociosite>. A host of links arranged in 18 categories and, within those categories, by country. Of particular note are the sections on sociologists, subjects in sociology, and data archives. The site is maintained by Albert Benschop of the University of Amsterdam.

Urban Institute <http://www.urban.org>. The Web site of a nonpartisan organization devoted to research on economic and social policy. Includes a wealth of reports by topic as well as analysis of issues.

WWW Virtual Library: Demography and Population Studies <http://demography.anu.edu.au/VirtualLibrary>. Lists more than 150 worldwide online population resources, including institutes, government resources, and organizations. The site is maintained by Diana Crow at the Australian National University.

Reference books in sociology

Encyclopedia of Sociology. Ed. Edgar G. Montgomery et al. 2nd ed. 5 vols. New York: Macmillan Library Reference, 2000. Provides scholarly discussions of such topics as class and race, ethnicity, economic sociology, and social structure. The articles are written by specialists and include excellent bibliographies.

Violence in America: An Encyclopedia. Ed. Ronald Gottsman and Richard Maxwell Brown. 3 vols. New York: Scribner, 1999. A wide-ranging exploration of political, social, and psychological aspects of violence, including violence in sports and popular culture as well as violence against the environment, economic aspects of violence, and violence against specific populations. Experts from many disciplines contributed over 600 essays; the third volume includes an index to the set.

Women's studies

Databases and indexes in women's studies

Contemporary Women's Issues. Farmington Hills: Gale Group, 1992–. A full-text database of journal articles, newsletters, alternative press publications, and reports produced by nongovernmental organizations on women's issues. International in scope, it includes material from 190 countries.

Feminae: Medieval Women and Gender Index <http://www.haverford .edu/library/reference/mschaus/mfi/mfi.html>. An index to journal articles, books, and dissertations on women in the Middle Ages. The index includes a sophisticated search engine and lists of broad topics and subjects. The site is hosted by Haverford College.

GenderWatch. Ann Arbor: ProQuest, 1998–. A database of full-text articles from 175 publications, some dating to the 1970s, on women's issues, including scholarly journals, magazines, and newsletters as well as conference proceedings and reports.

Women's Studies: Core Books <http://webcat.library.wisc.edu: 3200/ACRLWSS/ACRLWSSHome.html>. A searchable database of the most important books in print on issues ranging from girls and girlhood to aging, covering women's studies approaches to religion, sports, the arts, law, media, politics, and more. Books are chosen for inclusion by specialists in the Women's Studies Section of the Association of College and Research Libraries.

Women Studies Abstracts. Rush: Rush Publishing, 1972–. Offers abstracts of scholarly books, articles, and other publications focused on women's studies. Available in print and electronic formats.

Web resources in women's studies

Feminist Internet Gateway: Reviewed Links <http://www.feminist.org/gateway>. An extensive list of links on arts and media, education, health, LGBT information, politics, reproductive rights, and so on. The site, a project of the Feminist Majority Foundation, also provides a research center, court watch, a calendar, and more.

Institute for Women's Policy Research <http://www.iwpr.org>. Links to information on violence, employment and economic change, democracy and society, poverty and welfare, the family and work, and health care policy. The Institute for Women's Policy Research is a nonprofit organization that conducts scientific research for use by women's organizations.

Women's Studies/Women's Issues Resource Sites <http://research.umbc.edu/~korenman/wmst/links.html>. A substantial, selective directory of hundreds of sites on such topics as women and activism, cyberculture, health, higher education, sports and recreation, and women of color. All entries are annotated. The site also offers an international directory of women's studies programs and research centers. Maintained by Joan Korenman of the Center for Women and Information Technology, University of Maryland, Baltimore County.

WSSLinks: Women and Gender Studies <http://libr.org/wss/WSSLinks/index.html>. Selected, annotated links for women's studies covering art, education, film, health, history, sexuality, music, philosophy, politics, science and technology, and theology. Links are chosen by an editorial team from the Women's Studies Section of the Association of College and Research Libraries.

WWW Virtual Library: Women's History <http://www.iisg.nl/w3vlwomenshistory>. A directory of annotated links to women's history resources, arranged by chronological period, geographical location, and topic, with additional links to discussion lists, conferences, associations, and more. Maintained by Jenneke Quast for the International Institute of Social History.

Reference books in women's studies

The Dictionary of Feminist Theory. By Maggie Humm. 2nd ed. Columbus: Ohio State University Press, 1995. Covers theoretical issues in feminism and is particularly useful for putting them in historical context. The work is also helpful for pinpointing primary documents related to feminist theory.

Encyclopedia of Women and Gender: Sex Similarities and Differences and the Impact of Society on Gender. Ed. Judith Worell. 2 vols. San Diego: Academic Press, 2001. Provides lengthy, technical articles on the psychology of women and gender, covering such topics as gender and achievement, aging, child care, and body image concerns.

From Suffrage to the Senate: An Encyclopedia of American Women in Politics. By Suzanne O'Dea Schenken. 2 vols. Santa Barbara: ABC-CLIO, 1999. Coverage includes political leaders, issues and movements, organizations, and court cases.

Notable American Women, 1607–1950: A Biographical Dictionary. Ed. Edward T. James et al. 3 vols. Cambridge: Harvard University Press, 1974. With supplements and related series books. Provides lengthy and thorough biographies of women, followed by useful bibliographies. A supplement, *Notable American Women: The Modern Period,* published in 1983, profiles women who died between 1951 and 1975.

Routledge International Encyclopedia of Women: Global Women's Issues and Knowledge. Ed. Cheris Kramarae and Dale Spender. 4 vols. New York: Routledge, 2000. A record of women's knowledge and experience, offering essays on international approaches to the arts, economic development, education, health and reproduction, sexuality, households, families, politics, and peace and violence.

Women in the Third World: An Encyclopedia of Contemporary Issues. Ed. Edith H. Altbach and Nelly P. Stromquist. New York: Garland, 1998. Offers substantial overviews of topics related to women in the developing world, including theoretical issues, political and legal contexts, sex-role ideologies, demographics, economics, and the environment. It also provides regional surveys.

Women in World History: A Biographical Encyclopedia. Ed. Anne Commire and Deborah Klezmer. 17 vols. Waterford: Yorkin, 1999–2002. The largest compilation of biographical material on the world's women. This work contains biographies of historically significant women from all walks of life from all countries.

The Women's Chronology: A Year-by-Year Record, from Prehistory to the Present. By James Trager. New York: Holt, 1994. Provides brief descriptive entries on women through history. Entries are arranged chronologically and are marked with symbols indicating the topic area in which they fall.

Women's Studies Encyclopedia. Ed. Helen Tierney. 3 vols. rev. and expanded. New York: Greenwood, 1999. Provides overview articles on women's involvement in a wide variety of fields.

Researching in the Sciences

Research in the sciences generally involves recognizing a scientific problem to be solved, setting up an experiment designed to yield useful data, and interpreting the data in the context of other scientific knowledge. Researchers use library resources to

- keep up with current thinking in the field so they can recognize a question worth asking
- review what is known about a given phenomenon so they can place new knowledge in context
- locate specific information they need to successfully carry out an experiment or project

The large volume of scientific literature being produced can be daunting at first. However, a number of resources are available to help you find what is relevant to your research, and most of the resources are searchable online. Students planning to search for scientific materials should be prepared to

- choose search terms carefully so that they match those used by the sources
- work from the most recent publications to earlier ones, sorting out schools of thought and lines of inquiry
- know when to stop, when they have uncovered a selection of the most important and relevant research for their topic

The resources listed here will give you an idea of where to start. Consult a librarian to determine which resources are best for your research and whether they are available in electronic format.

General resources in the sciences

Databases and indexes in the sciences

General Science Index. New York: Wilson, 1978–. An index designed for the nonspecialist, covering about 190 major research publications and popular science magazines. Available in print and electronic formats. Some libraries may subscribe to an electronic version that includes abstracts and full text of selected articles.

Science Citation Index. Philadelphia: Institute for Scientific Information, 1961–. An interdisciplinary index to nearly 6,000 science journals. The index, updated weekly, provides citations and abstracts. It can be searched by author or keyword and allows searches by cited source, an efficient way to trace the influence of a piece of research. The electronic version, part of the *Web of Science,* has a powerful "related records" search, which identifies articles that cite one or more of the same sources.

Web resources in the sciences

EurekAlert <http://www.eurekalert.org>. A regularly updated source for information about research advances in science, medicine, health, and technology. The site includes links to other science sites, access to databases, and a searchable archive of news releases. Content for the site is screened by an advisory committee of journalists and public information specialists. The site was founded by the American Association for the Advancement of Science.

National Science Digital Library <http://nsdl.org>. Sponsored by the National Science Foundation, this site offers hundreds of collections of digitized material about math and science, intended to enhance science education at all levels. Users can search or browse collections or submit a question to a panel of experts.

Science.gov <http://www.science.gov>. A portal for science information from the U.S. government. The site includes cross-searching of 30 databases as well as links to science pages contributed by 12 federal agencies. It offers an advanced search as well as a browsable directory of resources by topic.

Scirus <http://www.scirus.com>. A search engine that focuses on science materials only. It searches both free Web content and several databases that include abstracts to published research, including *Medline, Science Direct,* and *NASA Technical Reports.* The site is sponsored by Elsevier, a major science publisher.

Reference books in the sciences

Dictionary of Scientific Biography. Ed. Charles Coulston Gillispie, 14 vols. New York: Macmillan Library Reference, 1970–2000. With supplements. Profiles scientists from early to modern times, considering both their lives and technical aspects of their work. Each biography is followed by a bibliography of primary and secondary sources. For basic biographical information on living scientists, consult *American Men and Women of Science,* published by Thomson Gale.

McGraw-Hill Dictionary of Scientific and Technical Terms. 6th ed. New York: McGraw-Hill, 2003. Offers concise, up-to-date definitions of technical terms beyond those found in a standard dictionary.

McGraw-Hill Encyclopedia of Science and Technology. 9th ed. 20 vols. New York: McGraw-Hill, 2002. A specialized encyclopedia covering scientific topics in detail. Technical discussions are fully illustrated with charts, diagrams, and photographs.

Biology

Databases and indexes in biology

Agricola. Beltsville: National Agricultural Library, 1970–. A database of books, articles, and documents on agriculture, including veterinary science, entomology, plant sciences, forestry, aquaculture and fisheries, farming and farming systems, agricultural economics, and nutrition. Searches can be limited to books in the National Agricultural Library, to articles, or both. The database is available free at <http://agricola.nal.usda.gov>.

Biological Abstracts. Philadelphia: Biosis, 1926–. The most thorough index to biological literature, with more than 5 million records of biology research. The electronic version of this work is called *BIOSIS.*

Biological and Agricultural Index. New York: Wilson, 1964–. An index to about 300 basic journals in biology and agriculture. This work is available in both print and electronic formats. In some libraries, abstracts and full text of selected articles are included.

CSA Biological Sciences. Bethesda: Cambridge Scientific Abstracts, 1994–. Provides citations and abstracts to the contents of over 6,000 biology journals as well as selected conference proceedings and books, covering publications from 1982 to the present.

Web resources in biology

Animal Diversity Web <http://animaldiversity.ummz.umich.edu/site/index.html>. Provides information on animals: mammals, birds, amphibians, reptiles, sharks, bony fish, mollusks, arthropods, and echinoderms. Each animal is classified by phylum, order, class, and family; pictures, sounds, and background information are provided for many of them. The site is a service of the University of Michigan Museum of Zoology.

National Center for Biotechnology Information <http://www.ncbi.nlm.nih.gov>. Provides highly technical molecular biology information and tools. The site includes molecular databases, nucleotide and protein sequences, and genome databases as well as links to the *PubMed* database of medical research and *PubMed Central,* an archive of full-text life sciences journals. The center is part of the U.S. National Library of Medicine.

Tree of Life Web Project <http://tolweb.org/tree/phylogeny.html>. A collaborative project compiled by biologists around the world. The site offers more than 1,300 schematic trees that map biological relationships and provide information about organisms. Detailed bibliographies are inlcuded.

WWW Virtual Library: Bio Sciences <http://www.vlib.org/Biosciences.html>. An index to several *Virtual Library* pages related to biology, with links to biodiversity and ecology, biotechnology, botany, cell biology, medicine, zoology, and more.

Reference books in biology

Encyclopedia of Human Biology. Ed. Renato Dulbecco. 2nd ed. 9 vols. San Diego: Academic Press, 1997. Offers substantial articles on topics in human biology, including behavior, biochemistry, genetics, psychology, and medical research. The final volume includes an index to the set.

Encyclopedia of Microbiology. Ed. Joshua Lederberg. 2nd ed. 4 vols. San Diego: Academic Press, 2000. Covers topics in microbiology, reviewing research in such areas as bacteriophages, anaerobic respiration, and AIDS. The articles, written for the informed nonspecialist, are substantial and include bibliographies.

Fieldbook of Natural History. Ed. E. L. Palmer and G. A. Parker. 2nd ed. New York: McGraw-Hill, 1975. A handy compilation of information on the natural world, devoted chiefly to the description of plants and animals with some information on their environment and behavior. The work is arranged by topic with an alphabetical index.

Grzimek's Animal Life Encyclopedia. Ed. Bernhard Grzimek. 2nd ed. 17 vols. Detroit: Gale Group, 2003–04. A survey of animals, organized by taxonomic class. Entries discuss species' distribution, behavior, and appearance; the work includes numerous color plates.

Oxford Companion to Animal Behavior. New York: Oxford University Press, 1982. Offers short articles, arranged alphabetically, covering topics in ethnology, defining terms, and discussing theories and discoveries in the field.

Walker's Mammals of the World. By Ronald M. Nowak. 6th ed. 2 vols. Baltimore: Johns Hopkins University Press, 1999. Describes the appearance, habitat, behavior, and biology of every genus of living mammal. The work is arranged taxonomically.

Chemistry

Databases and indexes in chemistry

Beilstein. Frankfurt: Beilstein Information, 1997–. A database of references to publications about organic compounds, based on *Beilstein's Handbook for Organic Chemistry.* The work covers organic chemistry research back to the eighteenth century, updated with the contents of current journals. Electronic versions are called variously *CrossFire, MDL Commander,* and *Beilstein Online;* one is also available through *ChemWeb,* below. Inorganic compounds are covered in *Gmelin's Handbuch der Anorganischen Chemie,* which is also available online as *Gmelin Database.*

Chemical Abstracts. Columbus: American Chemical Society, 1907–. A comprehensive index to chemistry publications. Searches can be conducted by author, subject, chemical structure, formula, and more. Online access is provided through the services *STN* and *SciFinder Scholar.*

Web resources in chemistry

ChemFinder <http://chemfinder.cambridgesoft.com>. Databases for common types of chemicals, including physical property data and two-dimensional chemical structures. Though chemical structures, manufacturer's information, and organic syntheses published in a respected annual series can be searched at no cost, some of the databases at this site are available only by subscription.

ChemWeb <http://www.chemweb.com>. Offers a wide variety of information, including breaking news and a preprint archive. Registration is required. Most of the material is free, but some journals and databases are available only by subscription.

Molecule of the Month <http://www.chm.bris.ac.uk/motm/motm .htm>. Provides detailed graphic and textual information on molecules, from mustard gas to aspirin. Pages are contributed by chemists in universities and research labs around the world. Emphasis is on molecules of popular interest. The site is maintained by Paul May at the School of Chemistry, University of Bristol.

NIST Chemistry WebBook <http://webbook.nist.gov/chemistry>. Provides chemical structure and thermochemical data for over 6,500 organic and small inorganic compounds and over 9,800 reactions as well as a variety of spectra data. A service of the National Institute of Standards and Technology, the site is searchable by physical property, name, formula, and more.

WebElements Periodic Table <http://www.webelements.com>. Offers information about elements based on the periodic table. The "professional edition" portion of the site provides data about physical, electronic, and nuclear properties as well as information about abundance, use, and more. The "scholar edition" presents similar information in a more accessible style. The site is maintained by Mark Winter at the University of Sheffield.

Reference books in chemistry

Encyclopedia of Reagents for Organic Synthesis. Ed. Leo A. Paquette. 8 vols. Chichester: Wiley, 1995. Comprehensively covers over 3,000 reagents in alphabetical order. The work is indexed by formula, reagent structural class, and reagent function. Each article includes ring diagrams and a bibliography of research sources. The online version is called *e-EROS.*

Kirk-Othmer Encyclopedia of Chemical Technology. 4th ed. 25 vols. New York: Wiley, 1991–. Provides in-depth articles on chemical properties, manufacturing, and technology. A fifth edition began publication in 2004. A single-volume concise edition is also available.

Macmillan Encyclopedia of Chemistry. Ed. Joseph J. Lagowski. 4 vols. New York: Macmillan Library Reference, 1997. A wide range of brief, accessible articles on research and practical concepts in chemistry, including key ideas in the field, individual chemists and their contributions, and common chemical substances.

Merck Index: An Encyclopedia of Chemicals, Drugs, and Biologicals. Ed. Maryadele J. O'Neil. 13th ed. Whitehouse Station: Merck, 2001. Contains about 10,000 entries on chemicals, including many pharmaceuticals, as well as chemical formulas, properties, uses, and references to literature.

World of Chemistry. Ed. Robin V. Young. Detroit: Gale Group, 2000. A collection of articles on theories, discoveries, concepts, and key scientists in chemistry.

Computer science

Databases and indexes in computer science

ACM Digital Library. New York: Association for Computing Machinery, 1947–. Contains full-text articles from journals, newsletters, and conference proceedings published by the Association for Computing Machinery.

Web resources in computer science

ACM Portal: The Guide to Computing Literature <http://portal .acm.org/guide.cfm>. A database of references, many with abstracts, to over 700,000 publications in the field, including books, journals, conference proceedings, dissertations, and technical reports. The advanced search option is available only to ACM members, but the basic search and browse features are useful and free. Though many of the items include links, most require subscriptions to materials that may be in your library. Sponsored by the association for Computing Machinery.

FOLDOC: Free Online Dictionary of Computing <http://wombat.doc .ic.ac.uk/foldoc/index.html>. A searchable dictionary of computer terms, including acronyms, jargon, computer languages, operating systems, companies, and theory. The site is maintained by the Department of Computing at the Imperial College, London.

Virtual Computer Library <http://www.utexas.edu/computer/ vcl>. Provides a collection of documentation, news sources, journals, online books, and other information of particular interest to users of college computer resources. Sponsored by the University of Texas at Austin.

WWW Virtual Library: Computing and Computer Science <http:// vlib.org/Computing>. An index page for a wide variety of computer-related Web directories in the *WWW Virtual Library,* including cryptography, logic programming, and software engineering.

Reference books in computer science

Encyclopedia of Computers and Computer History. Ed. Raúl Rojas. 2 vols. Chicago: Fitzroy Dearborn, 2001. An accessible work that provides entries on people, organizations, and developments in the history of computing, "from the abacus to eBay."

Encyclopedia of Computer Science. Ed. Anthony Ralston, Edwin D. Reilly, and David Hemmendinger. 4th ed. London: Nature, 2000. A technical compendium that covers hardware, computer systems, information and data, software, the mathematics of computing, theory of computation, methodologies, applications, and computing in general. This is an authoritative reference work for the field.

Engineering

Databases and indexes in engineering

Applied Science and Technology Index. New York: Wilson, 1983–. Covers over 400 core scientific and technical journals and important trade and industrial publications in engineering, mathematics, computer technology, the environment, and natural science. Available in print and electronic formats. Some libraries also have access to abstracts and selected full-text articles.

CE Database <http://www.pubs.asce.org/cedbsrch.html>. A database of journal articles, conference proceedings, books, manuals, and other publications produced by the American Society of Civil Engineers from 1970 to the present concerning all aspects of civil engineering.

EI Engineering Village 2. Hoboken: Elsevier Engineering Information, 2000–. The most comprehensive resource covering all engineering disciplines with over 5 million abstracts of journal articles, technical reports, selected Web sites, conference papers, and proceedings. Includes the contents of several long-running databases, among them *Compendex* and *Inspec,* and other industry-related resources.

TRIS Online <http://trisonline.bts.gov/sundev/search.cfm>. A comprehensive database of publications on transportation issues. In some cases, links to full text are provided. This work is a joint project of the National Transportation Library, the Transportation Research Board, and the Bureau of Transportation Statistics.

Web resources in engineering

EEVL: The Internet Guide to Engineering, Mathematics, and Computing <http://www.eevl.ac.uk>. Provides reviews of and access to reputable sites on engineering topics such as bioengineering and manufacturing and to online scholarly and trade journals. Particularly useful sites are designated as "key sites."

Searches can be limited to key sites, to cataloged descriptions, or to the entire contents of included Web sites.

MatWeb: The Online Materials Information Resource <http://www .matweb.com>. Links to over 40,000 material datasheets from manufacturers and professional societies covering plastics, metals, ceramics, and composites. May be searched by physical properties or by material type, manufacturer, or trade name. Though access to the datasheets is free, some search features are available only by subscription.

WWW Virtual Library: Electrical and Electronics Engineering <http://www.cem.itesm.mx/vlee>. A directory to Web sources on institutions, standards, technical publications, products, and information on topics such as electronic circuit analysis and electronics tutorials. Maintained by Alejandro C. Alemán of the Monterrey Tech (Mexico) Department of Electrical and Electronics Engineering.

Reference books in engineering

The Electronics Handbook. Ed. Jerry Whitaker. Boca Raton: CRC, 1996. Covers theory and principles governing electronic devices and systems.

McGraw-Hill Dictionary of Engineering. 2nd ed. New York: McGraw-Hill, 2003. Covers all fields of engineering, including building construction. This work is based on the *McGraw-Hill Dictionary of Scientific and Technical Terms.*

Mechanical Engineers' Handbook. Ed. Myer Kutz. 2nd ed. New York: Wiley, 1998. Covers fundamental topics and emerging issues in mechanical engineering.

Perry's Chemical Engineers' Handbook. 7th ed. New York: McGraw-Hill, 1998. Covers all aspects of chemical engineering, including chemical and physical property data and fundamentals of chemical engineering.

Standard Handbook of Engineering Calculations. Ed. Tyler G. Hicks et al. 3rd ed. New York: McGraw-Hill, 1995. A classic compendium of step-by-step calculations for solving the most frequently encountered engineering problems in many engineering disciplines.

Structural Engineering Handbook. Ed. Wai-Fah Chen and Eric M. Lui. 2nd ed. Boca Raton: CRC, 2004. Covers a variety of engineering structures, theories, and topics such as seismic loading and fatigue and fracture.

Environmental sciences

Databases and indexes in environmental sciences

Environmental Sciences and Pollution Management. Bethesda: Cambridge Scientific Abstracts, 1994–. Provides abstracts of research from nearly 6,000 journals as well as reports, conference proceedings, and books published since 1967 on ecology, energy, pollution, waste management, toxicology, risk assessment, environmental biotechnology, and water resources.

Web resources in environmental sciences

Environmental Media Services <http://www.ems.org>. A nonprofit clearinghouse for environmental and public health issues. Includes breaking news, "backgrounders" on topics in environmental health, transportation, climate and air quality, land use, and oceans and water. For each topic, there are fast facts, background, links to sources, and often contacts. Aimed at working journalists, this site is a good source of news and information.

National Library for the Environment <http://www.ncseonline .org/NLE>. A digital archive of material, including reports on "hot topics," Congressional Research Service reports, and abstracts and links to over 14,000 reports on population and the environment. This site is a project of the National Council for Science and the Environment.

U.S. Environmental Protection Agency <http://www.epa.gov>. Offers information on topics such as acid rain, lead, ozone, and wetlands, as well as technical publications, legal and regulatory information, and a database of enforcement and compliance actions taken by the EPA. The *Envirofacts* portal at <http://www.epa.gov/ enviro/index_java.html> provides detailed environmental data on local water quality, toxic emissions, and other information, searchable by zip code.

World Resources Institute <http://www.wri.org>. Offers many digital publications on environmental issues, including country profiles and *EarthTrends* (<http://earthtrends.wri.org>), a portal for a wealth of data on environmental topics including population, energy, water resources, biodiversity, and economic issues affecting the environment.

Reference books in environmental sciences

Encyclopedia of Biodiversity. Ed. Simon Asher Levin. 5 vols. San Diego: Academic Press, 2001. Provides in-depth, scholarly articles on topics ranging from agriculture, conservation, economic aspects of biodiversity, microbial biodiversity, public policy, and systematics.

Encyclopedia of Endangered Species. 2 vols. Detroit: Gale Group, 1994. Describes over 700 animals and plants currently threatened with extinction. Arranged taxonomically; an index provides access by common and scientific names. For each species the status, description and biology, habitat and current distribution, and history and conservation measures are described. Includes indexes by geographic location and a list of wildlife and conservation organizations.

Encyclopedia of Energy, Technology, and the Environment. Ed. Attilio Bisio and Sharon Boots. 4 vols. New York: Wiley, 1995. Provides lengthy articles on the technologies used to produce energy and their effects on the environment. There are many tables, graphs, and diagrams, and most articles, written by experts in the field, are followed by extensive bibliographies. *Wiley Encyclopedia of Energy and the Environment* (1997) is a condensed edition in two volumes.

Encyclopedia of the Biosphere. Ed. Ramon Folch. 11 vols. Detroit: Gale Group, 2000. Covers world habitats such as tropical rain forests, savannahs, prairies, and lakes, in lavishly illustrated volumes. The work is based on a 1998 Catalan publication compiled under the sponsorship of UNESCO.

Encyclopedia of World Environmental History. Ed. Shepard Krech, J. R. McNeill, and Carolyn Merchant. 3 vols. New York: Routledge, 2004. Covers topics, events, people, natural resources, and aspects of human interaction with the environment worldwide. This work provides historical surveys of environmental issues such as deforestation and extinction; it also offers regional and national overviews as well as essays on subfields such as environmental philosophy.

Vital Signs: The Environmental Trends That Are Shaping Our Future. Ed. Lester R. Brown. New York: Norton, 1992–. A compilation of statistics and analysis of major trends in food production, energy, atmosphere, the economy, and social factors such as population growth, epidemics, and refugees. This work was produced under the auspices of the Worldwatch Institute.

Geology

Databases and indexes in geology

Bibliography and Index of Geology. Alexandria: American Geological Institute, 1966–. A comprehensive index of more than 2.3 million bibliographic citations to articles, books, maps, papers, reports, and theses covering the geosciences internationally. This index is maintained and updated monthly by the AGI; the electronic version is called *GeoRef.* An earlier index of North American Geology covers publications back to 1907.

Web resources in geology

Links for Mineralogists <http://www.uni-wuerzburg.de/mineralogie/links.html>. A large directory of links to information on petrology, geochemistry, crystallography, materials science, and ore and mineral deposits. The site is maintained by Klaus-Peter Kelber at the Institute of Mineralogy, University of Würzburg.

Minerals Information <http://minerals.usgs.gov/minerals>. Includes an online version of *The Minerals Yearbook* with profiles of over 90 minerals as well as international industry surveys and statistics, current and historical. From the U.S. Geological Survey.

National Map: The Nation's Topographic Map for the 21st Century <http://nationalmap.usgs.gov>. An amazing tool from the U.S. Geological Survey. The viewer allows users to zoom in on any part of the United States and choose map layers such as elevation, roads, water, land use, and even detailed aerial satellite images. Whether you're examining a region, a state, or a few city blocks, this tool offers access to a wealth of topographic information.

Petroleum Engineering Reading Room <http://www.pge.utexas .edu/reading/info.cfm>. Offers digital collections of publications on petroleum worldwide as well as information about government and commercial sites and research centers. Part of the *WWW Virtual Library* and compiled by the Department of Petroleum and Geosystems Engineering at the University of Texas at Austin.

Tour of Geologic Time <http://www.ucmp.berkeley.edu/exhibits/ geologictime.php>. A "journey through the history of the Earth," covering the geologic time scale and details about each geologic era. Sponsored by the University of California Museum of Paleontology.

U.S. Geological Survey <http://www.usgs.gov>. Since 1879, this federal project has provided the nation with geologic information and mapping services. Its Web site provides information about earthquakes, environmental and biological material, geospatial data and mapping projects, and other geologic resources.

Reference books in geology

Encyclopedia of Earth Sciences Series. Ed. Rhodes W. Fairbridge et al. 20 vols. Boston: Kluwer Academic Publishers, 1966–99. Offers scholarly articles on oceanography, atmospheric sciences and astrogeology, geochemistry, regional geography, climatology, and structural geology. Each volume covers a different aspect of earth sciences.

Encyclopedia of Paleontology. Ed. Ronald Singer. 2 vols. Chicago: Fitzroy Dearborn, 1999. Includes information on principles and methods of the field as well as on paleontologists and their findings throughout the world. Entries cover dinosaurs and other animals and plants found in the fossil record.

Lexicon of Geologic Names of the United States (including Alaska). 2 vols. Washington: Government Printing Office, 1936. With supplements. Provides information from records kept since the 1880s by the Geological Names Committee of the U.S. Geological Survey. This work identifies the names of geological features by time period and location and provides reviews of the literature referring to the names. Supplements provide information on more recently named features. Most of the names from the print volumes are also provided online in the *Geolex* database: <http://ngmdb.usgs.gov/ Geolex/geolex_home.html>.

Macmillan Encyclopedia of Earth Sciences. Ed. Julius E. Dasch. 2 vols. New York: Macmillan, 1996. Offers nearly 400 accessible articles on all aspects of earth science, including solid earth, oceanographic, and atmospheric sciences, as well as some coverage of the place of the earth in the solar system.

Mathematics

Databases and indexes in mathematics

Mathematical Reviews. Lancaster: American Mathematical Society, 1940–. The most comprehensive database for mathematics research, covering all types of publications with annotations written by reviewers. The online version of this database is called *MathSciNet.*

Web resources in mathematics

Biographies of Women Mathematicians <http://www.agnesscott .edu/lriddle/women/women.htm>. An extensive collection of biographical information about the contributions of women to mathematics. The site can be searched or browsed alphabetically or chronologically. Profiles are compiled by students and faculty at Agnes Scott College.

MacTutor History of Mathematics Archive <http://www-history.mcs .st-andrews.ac.uk/history/index.html>. Provides biographies, historical overviews of topics, the history of mathematics in different cultures, and a "famous curves" page with illustrations, formulas, and other information. Maintained by staff at the St. Andrews University (Scotland) School of Mathematics and Statistics.

Math on the Web <http://www.ams.org/mathweb>. A directory of mathematics resources from the American Mathematical Society. The selection of sites by topic is particularly useful.

Reference books in mathematics

Companion Encyclopedia of the History and Philosophy of Mathematical Sciences. Ed. I. Grattan-Guinness. 2 vols. London:

Routledge, 1994. Offers lengthy, well-documented articles on the historical basis of mathematics and the cultural production of mathematical understanding.

CRC Concise Encyclopedia of Mathematics. Ed. Eric W. Weisstein. Boca Raton: CRC, 1999. Offers nearly 2,000 pages of accessible information about mathematics and its applications in physics, biochemistry, chemistry, biophysics, and engineering.

Encyclopedia of Statistical Sciences. Ed. Samuel Kotz and Norman L. Johnson. 8 vols. New York: Wiley, 1982. With supplements. An in-depth exploration of all fields of inquiry in which statistical methods are used. The work includes articles on statistical terminology.

The World of Mathematics: A Small Library of the Literature of Mathematics from A'h-mose the Scribe to Albert Einstein. 4 vols. New York: Simon and Schuster, 1956. This gem can sometimes provide answers to the most arcane questions, while conducting a tour through the history and traditions of mathematics. It is dated, so it does not cover recent developments, but it has excellent background material easily accessed using the thorough index.

Nursing and health sciences

Databases and indexes in nursing and health sciences

Cumulative Index to Nursing and Allied Health Literature. Glendale: Cinahl Information Systems, 1977–. Covers publications related to nursing research and practice, providing references to articles, books and book chapters, pamphlets and other documents, and standards of professional practice and research. The online version is called *CINAHL* and in some libraries includes selected full-text articles.

Web resources in nursing and health sciences

Centers for Disease Control and Prevention <http://www.cdc.gov>. The CDC is the federal government's lead agency for preventing disease and promoting health. The agency's Web site provides information on health and safety topics, an A-to-Z index of health information, technical publications such as *The Mortality and Morbidity Weekly Report,* and current news about health risks.

HealthWeb <http://healthweb.org/index.cfm>. A clearly organized and thoroughly annotated list of high-quality medical sites chosen by medical librarians in an ongoing collaborative project.

National Center for Health Statistics <http://www.cdc.gov/nchs>. Provides a wealth of statistical data on health in the United States, including analysis of trends, health reports on specific populations, and leading causes of death. The center is part of the Centers for Disease Control.

National Institute of Nursing Research <http://ninr.nih.gov/ninr>. A U.S. government program devoted to clinical and basic research efforts in patient care. Included on the site are many publications and an online course for nurses who wish to conduct research.

National Institutes of Health <http://www.nih.gov>. Offers information on current medical research funded by the U.S. government in the areas of cancer, mental health, human genomes, drug and alcohol abuse, and a wide variety of other illnesses and medical specialties. Though much of the information available from the NIH is technical, every subject area contains information written for a nonspecialist audience. The NIH is part of the U.S. Department of Health and Human Services.

PubMed <http://www.ncbi.nlm.nih.gov/entrez/query.fcgi>. The most comprehensive database of medical research. Sometimes referred to as *Medline,* this tool provides over 15 million abstracts of publications in medicine, nursing, dentistry, veterinary medicine, the health care system, and the preclinical sciences published from the 1950s to the present. *PubMed* is a service of the National Library of Medicine and was developed by the National Center for Biotechnology Information.

Virtual Hospital: A Digital Library of Health Information <http://www.vh.org>. Offers a tremendous amount of information for health care providers and their patients. A service of the University of Iowa Health Care Program, the site includes the full text of scores of medical textbooks as well as easily accessible patient and provider information arranged by topic.

Reference books in nursing and health sciences

Cambridge World History of Human Disease. Ed. Kenneth F. Kiple. Cambridge: Cambridge University Press, 1993. A scholarly guide to the history of specific diseases across time and in all parts of the world.

Cecil Textbook of Medicine. Ed. Lee Goldman and Dennis Ausiello. 22nd ed. Philadelphia: Saunders, 2004. A classic general textbook of medicine.

Conn's Current Therapy: Latest Approved Methods of Treatment for the Practicing Physician. Ed. Robert E. Rackel and Edward T. Bope. Philadelphia: Saunders, annual. A basic guide to current diagnosis and treatment of diseases and injuries.

Encyclopedia of Public Health. Ed. Lester Breslow. 4 vols. New York: Macmillan Reference, 2002. Contains entries relevant to public health, promotion of health and prevention of disease, injuries, and premature death. Topics covered include common ailments, environmental factors affecting health, organizations, and so on.

Gale Encyclopedia of Medicine. Ed. Jacqueline Longe. 2nd ed. 5 vols. Detroit: Gale Group, 2002. Covers basic consumer information on hundreds of medical disorders, tests, and treatments, written in accessible, nontechnical language.

Handbook of Clinical Nursing Research. Ed. Ada Sue Hinshaw et al. Newbury Park: Sage, 1999. Provides a comprehensive review and critique of nursing research.

Stedman's Medical Dictionary for Nursing and Health Professionals. 5th ed. Philadelphia: Lippincott Williams and Wilkins, 2005. Contains brief, illustrated definitions of medical terms. This work is an adaptation of a longer, classic work, *Stedman's Medical Dictionary,* for practitioners.

Physics and astronomy

Databases and indexes in physics and astronomy

Physical Review Online Archive (*PROLA*). College Park: American Physical Society, 1997–. Indexes and provides full-text access to articles published in the most prominent series of physics research journals from 1893 to the most recent five years. The database includes abstracts of current articles, but only those to which a library subscribes are available in full text.

Physics Abstracts. London: Institute of Electrical Engineers, 1903–. Provides abstracts of publications in physics, electrical engineering, electronics, communications, control engineering, computers and computing, and information technology. The online version of this database is called *INSPEC.*

Web resources in physics and astronomy

AstroWeb: Astronomy/Astrophysics on the Web <http:// www.vilspa .esa.es/astroweb/astronomy.html>. Offers links to research material from observatories, to people, publications, and organizations in the field, and to information on topics such as radio, planetary, and solar astronomy.

Energy Citations Database <http://www.osti.gov/energycitations>. Provides abstracts and, in some cases, links to full text of research publications in fields such as chemistry, physics, materials science, environmental science, geology, engineering, mathematics, and related disciplines. This database covers publications from 1948 to the present and is made available by the Office of Scientific and Technical Information at the U.S. Department of Energy.

Information Bridge <http://www.osti.gov/bridge>. A searchable database of full-text reports of research projects sponsored by the Department of Energy in physics, chemistry, materials science, biology, environmental science, energy technologies, engineering, renewable energy, and other topics from 1995 to present. The database is made available by the Office of Scientific and Technical Information at the U.S. Department of Energy.

NASA Astrophysics Data System <http://adswww.harvard.edu>. A database of nearly 4 million abstracts of publications from journals, colloquia, symposia, proceedings, and internal NASA reports from 1993 to the present. The database covers astronomy and astrophysics, instrumentation, physics, and geophysics and includes preprints in astronomy. It is made available by the Harvard-Smithsonian Center for Astrophysics.

National Aeronautics and Space Administration (*NASA*) <http://www.nasa.gov>. Offers information for scientists and the public, including many visual resources and information about space missions.

Physics Reference Data <http://physics.nist.gov/PhysRefData/contents.html>. Includes physical constants, atomic and molecular spectroscopy data, X-ray and gamma-ray data, and nuclear physics data. From the National Institute of Standards and Technology.

PhysicsWeb <http://physicsweb.org>. News from the world of physics. Sponsored by the Institute of Physics, this site includes a "Best of *PhysicsWeb*" section with a selection of articles organized by subfield as well as a collection of resources for physicists and physics students.

PhysLink <http://www.physlink.com>. A commercial site rich in news and general information. It contains links to reference sites and materials for physics teachers and students.

Reference books in physics and astronomy

AIP Physics Desk Reference. Ed. E. Richard Cohen, David R. Lide, and George L. Trigg. 3rd ed. New York: American Institute of Physics, 1995. A concise source of tables, formulas, and bibliographies in 22 subdisciplines related to physics, including acoustics, astronomy, biological physics, quantum physics, optics, fluid mechanics, and molecular spectroscopy. This work includes sections on "mathematical basics" and practical laboratory data.

Dictionary of Physics. 4 vols. London: Macmillan, 2004. An updated translation of *Lexikon der Physik,* this work provides brief, technical articles on a wide variety of topics in the field.

Dictionary of Pure and Applied Physics. Ed. Dipak Basu. Boca Raton: CRC, 2001. Defines over 3,000 terms in the fields of acoustics, biophysics, medical physics, communication, electricity, electronics, geometrical optics, low-temperature physics, magnetism, and physical optics.

Encyclopedia of Astronomy and Astrophysics. Ed. Paul Murdin. 4 vols. Bristol: Institute of Physics, 2001. Includes 700 long articles on topics and themes in the field as well as hundreds of shorter articles that define terms and provide profiles of people and institutions.

Macmillan Encyclopedia of Physics. Ed. John S. Rigden. 4 vols. New York: Macmillan Library Reference, 1996. Covers laws, concepts, fundamental theories, and the lives and work of important physicists throughout history in accessible form.

The World of Physics: A Small Library of the Literature of Physics from Antiquity to the Present. 3 vols. New York: Simon and Schuster, 1987. An anthology of key historical texts in physics, presented with informative introductory essays. This work is a useful collection of primary sources in the history of physics.

PART IV. DOCUMENTATION STYLES

In academic research papers and in any other writing that borrows information from sources, the borrowed information — quotations, summaries, paraphrases, and any facts or ideas that are not common knowledge — must be clearly documented.

Each academic discipline uses a particular editorial style for citing sources and for listing the works that have been cited in a paper. The following sections give details for four documentation styles: MLA (Modern Language Association), used in English and other humanities; APA (American Psychological Association), used in psychology and the social sciences; *Chicago,* used in history and some humanities; and CSE (Council of Science Editors), used in biology and other sciences.

MLA Style: English and Other Humanities

In English and in some humanities classes, you will be asked to use the MLA system for documenting sources, which is set forth in the *MLA Handbook for Writers of Research Papers,* 6th ed. (New York: MLA, 2003). MLA recommends in-text citations that refer readers to a list of works cited.

An in-text citation names the author of the source, often in a signal phrase, and gives the page number in parentheses. At the end of the paper, a list of works cited provides publication information about the source; the list is alphabetized by authors' last names (or by titles for works without authors).

IN-TEXT CITATION

Matt Sundeen notes that drivers with cell phones place an estimated 98,000 emergency calls each day and that the phones "often reduce emergency response times and actually save lives" (1).

ENTRY IN THE LIST OF WORKS CITED

Sundeen, Matt. "Cell Phones and Highway Safety: 2000 State
Legislative Update." <u>National Conference of State
Legislatures</u>. Dec. 2000. 9 pp. 27 Feb. 2001
<http://ncsl.org/programs/esnr/cellphone.pdf>.

For a list of works cited with this entry, see pages 184–85.

NOTE: If your instructor allows italics for the titles of long
works such as books and for the names of publications,
simply substitute italics for underlining in all the models in
this section.

MLA in-text citations

MLA in-text citations are made with a combination of signal
phrases and parenthetical references. A signal phrase indicates that something taken from a source (a quotation,
summary, paraphrase, or fact) is about to be used; usually
the signal phrase includes the author's name. The parenthetical reference, which comes after the cited material,
normally includes at least a page number.

IN-TEXT CITATION

One driver, Peter Cohen, says that after he was rear-ended, the
guilty party emerged from his vehicle still talking on the phone
(127).

Readers can look up the author's last name in the alphabetized list of works cited, where they will learn the work's
title and other publication information. When readers
decide to consult the source, the page number will take
them straight to the passage that has been cited.

Basic rules for print and electronic sources

The MLA system of in-text citations, which depends heavily on authors' names and page numbers, was created in the early 1980s with print sources in mind. Because some of today's electronic sources have unclear authorship and lack page numbers, they present a special challenge. Nevertheless, the basic rules are the same for both print and electronic sources.

The models in this section (items 1–5) show how the MLA system usually works and explain what to do if your source has no author or page numbers.

■ **1. AUTHOR NAMED IN A SIGNAL PHRASE** Ordinarily, introduce the material being cited with a signal phrase that includes the author's name. In addition to preparing readers for the source, the signal phrase allows you to keep the parenthetical citation brief.

> Christine Haughney reports that shortly after Japan made it illegal to use a handheld phone while driving, "accidents caused by using the phones dropped by 75 percent" (A8).

The signal phrase — *Christine Haughney reports that* — names the author; the parenthetical citation gives the page number where the quoted words may be found.

Notice that the period follows the parenthetical citation. When a quotation ends with a question mark or an exclamation point, leave the end punctuation inside the quotation mark and add a period after the parentheses: ". . . ?" (8).

■ **2. AUTHOR NAMED IN PARENTHESES** If a signal phrase does not name the author, put the author's last name in parentheses along with the page number.

> Most states do not keep adequate records on the number of times
> cell phones are a factor in accidents; as of December 2000, only
> ten states were trying to keep such records (Sundeen 2).

Use no punctuation between the name and the page number.

■ **3. AUTHOR UNKNOWN** Either use the complete title in a
signal phrase or use a short form of the title in parentheses.
Titles of books are underlined; titles of articles are put in
quotation marks.

> As of 2001, at least three hundred towns and municipalities had
> considered legislation regulating use of cell phones while driving
> ("Lawmakers" 2).

TIP: Before assuming that a Web source has no author, do
some detective work. Often the author's name is available
but is not easy to find. For example, it may appear at the
end of the source, in tiny print. Or it may appear on another
page of the site, such as the home page.

NOTE: If a source has no author and is sponsored by a corporate entity, such as an organization or a government
agency, name the corporate entity as the author (see item 9
on p. 136).

■ **4. PAGE NUMBER UNKNOWN** You may omit the page number if a work lacks page numbers, as is the case with many
Web sources. Although printouts from Web sites usually
show page numbers, printers don't always provide the same
page breaks; for this reason, MLA recommends treating
such sources as unpaginated.

> The California Highway Patrol opposes restrictions on the use of
> phones while driving, claiming that distracted drivers can already
> be prosecuted (Jacobs).

According to Jacobs, the California Highway Patrol opposes restrictions on the use of phones while driving, claiming that distracted drivers can already be prosecuted.

When the pages of a Web source are stable (as in PDF files), however, supply a page number in your in-text citation.

NOTE: If a Web source numbers its paragraphs or screens, give the abbreviation "par." or "pars." or the word "screen" or "screens" in the parentheses: (Smith, par. 4).

■ **5. ONE-PAGE SOURCE** If the source is one page long, MLA allows (but does not require) you to omit the page number. Many instructors will want you to supply the page number because without it readers may not know where your citation ends or, worse, may not realize that you have provided a citation at all.

No page number given

Milo Ippolito reports that the driver who struck and killed a two-year-old while using her cell phone got off with a light sentence even though she left the scene of the accident and failed to call 911 for help. In this and in similar cases, traffic offenders distracted by cell phones have not been sufficiently punished under laws on reckless driving.

Page number given

Milo Ippolito reports that the driver who struck and killed a two-year-old while using her cell phone got off with a light sentence even though she left the scene of the accident and failed to call 911 for help (J1). In this and in similar cases, traffic offenders distracted by cell phones have not been sufficiently punished under laws on reckless driving.

Variations on the basic rules

This section describes the MLA guidelines for handling a variety of situations not covered by the basic rules just given. Again, these rules on in-text citations are the same for both traditional print sources and electronic sources.

■   **6. TWO OR MORE TITLES BY THE SAME AUTHOR**   If your list of works cited includes two or more titles by the same author, mention the title of the work in the signal phrase or include a short version of the title in the parentheses.

> On December 6, 2000, reporter Jamie Stockwell wrote that distracted driver Jason Jones had been charged with "two counts of vehicular manslaughter . . . in the deaths of John and Carole Hall" ("Phone" B1). The next day Stockwell reported the judge's ruling: Jones "was convicted of negligent driving and fined $500, the maximum penalty allowed" ("Man" B4).

Titles of articles and other short works are placed in quotation marks, as in the example just given. Titles of books are underlined.

In the rare case when both the author's name and a short title must be given in parentheses, separate them with a comma.

> According to police reports, there were no skid marks indicating that the distracted driver who killed John and Carole Hall had even tried to stop (Stockwell, "Man" B4).

■   **7. TWO OR THREE AUTHORS**   Name the authors in a signal phrase, as in the following example, or include their last names in the parenthetical reference: (Redelmeier and Tibshirani 453).

Redelmeier and Tibshirani found that "the risk of a collision when using a cellular telephone was four times higher than the risk when a cellular telephone was not being used" (453).

When three authors are named in the parentheses, separate the names with commas: (Alton, Davies, and Rice 56).

■ **8. FOUR OR MORE AUTHORS** Name all of the authors or include only the first author's name followed by "et al." (Latin for "and others"). Make sure that your citation matches the entry in the list of works cited (see item 2 on pp. 144–45).

The study was extended for two years, and only after results were reviewed by an independent panel did the researchers publish their findings (Blaine et al. 35).

■ **9. CORPORATE AUTHOR** When the author is a corporation, an organization, or a government agency, name the corporate author either in the signal phrase or in the parentheses.

Researchers at the Harvard Center for Risk Analysis claim that the risks of driving while phoning are small compared with other driving risks (3-4).

In the list of works cited, the Harvard Center for Risk Analysis is treated as the author and alphabetized under *H*.

When a government agency is treated as the author, it will be alphabetized in the list of works cited under the name of the government, such as "United States" (see item 3 on p. 145). For this reason, you must name the government in your in-text citation.

The United States Department of Transportation provides nationwide statistics on traffic fatalities.

■   **10. AUTHORS WITH THE SAME LAST NAME** If your list of works cited includes works by two or more authors with the same last name, include the author's first name in the signal phrase or first initial in the parentheses.

> Estimates of the number of accidents caused by distracted
> drivers vary because little evidence is being collected
> (D. Smith 7).

■   **11. INDIRECT SOURCE (SOURCE QUOTED IN ANOTHER SOURCE)** When a writer's or a speaker's quoted words appear in a source written by someone else, begin the parenthetical citation with the abbreviation "qtd. in."

> According to Richard Retting, "As the comforts of home and
> the efficiency of the office creep into the automobile, it is
> becoming increasingly attractive as a work space" (qtd. in
> Kilgannon A23).

■   **12. ENCYCLOPEDIA OR DICTIONARY** Unless an encyclopedia or a dictionary has an author, it will be alphabetized in the list of works cited under the word or entry that you consulted — not under the title of the reference work itself (see item 13 on p. 149). Either in your text or in your parenthetical reference, mention the word or the entry. No page number is required, since readers can easily look up the word or entry.

> The word <u>crocodile</u> has a surprisingly complex etymology
> ("Crocodile").

■   **13. MULTIVOLUME WORK** If your paper cites more than one volume of a multivolume work, indicate in the parentheses the volume you are referring to, followed by a colon and the page number.

> In his studies of gifted children, Terman describes a pattern of
> accelerated language acquisition (2: 279).

If your paper cites only one volume of a multivolume work,
you will include the volume number in the list of works
cited and will not need to include it in the parentheses.

■   **14. TWO OR MORE WORKS**   To cite more than one source
in the parentheses, give the citations in alphabetical order
and separate them with a semicolon.

> The effects of sleep deprivation have been well documented
> (Cahill 42; Leduc 114; Vasquez 73).

Multiple citations can be distracting, however, so you
should not overuse the technique. If you want to alert readers to several sources that discuss a particular topic, consider using an information note instead (see p. 173).

■   **15. AN ENTIRE WORK**   Use the author's name in a signal
phrase or a parenthetical reference. There is of course no
need to use a page number.

> Robinson succinctly describes the status of the mountain lion
> controversy in California.

■   **16. WORK IN AN ANTHOLOGY**   Put the name of the author
of the work (not the editor of the anthology) in the signal
phrase or the parentheses.

> In "A Jury of Her Peers," Mrs. Hale describes both a style of
> quilting and a murder weapon when she utters the last words of
> the story: "We call it--knot it, Mr. Henderson" (Glaspell 210).

In the list of works cited, the work is alphabetized under Glaspell, not under the name of the editor of the anthology.

Glaspell, Susan. "A Jury of Her Peers." Literature and Its Writers: A
    Compact Introduction to Fiction, Poetry, and Drama. Ed. Ann
    Charters and Samuel Charters. 3rd ed. Boston: Bedford, 2004.
    194-210.

■ **17. LEGAL SOURCE** For well-known historical documents, such as articles of the United States Constitution,
and for laws in the United States Code, provide a parenthetical citation in the text: (US Const., art. 1, sec. 2) or (12
USC 3412, 2000). There is no need to provide a works cited
entry.

Legislative acts and court cases are included in the
works cited list (see item 50 on p. 171). Your in-text citation
should name the act or case either in a signal phrase or in
parentheses. In the text of a paper, names of acts are not
underlined, but names of cases are.

The Jones Act of 1917 granted US citizenship to Puerto Ricans.

In 1857, Chief Justice Roger B. Taney declared in the case of
Dred Scott v. Sandford that blacks, whether enslaved or free,
could not be citizens of the United States.

Literary works and sacred texts

Literary works and sacred texts are usually available in a
variety of editions. Your list of works cited will specify which
edition you are using, and your in-text citation will usually
consist of a page number from the edition you consulted
(see item 18).

However, MLA suggests that when possible you should give enough information — such as book parts, play divisions, or line numbers — so that readers can locate the cited passage in any edition of the work (see items 19–21).

■ **18. LITERARY WORKS WITHOUT PARTS OR LINE NUMBERS** Many literary works, such as most short stories and many novels and plays, do not have parts or line numbers that you can refer to. In such cases, simply cite the page number.

> At the end of Kate Chopin's "The Story of an Hour," Mrs. Mallard drops dead upon learning that her husband is alive. In the final irony of the story, doctors report that she has died of a "joy that kills" (25).

■ **19. VERSE PLAYS AND POEMS** For verse plays, MLA recommends giving act, scene, and line numbers that can be located in any edition of the work. Use arabic numerals, and separate the numbers with periods.

> In Shakespeare's <u>King Lear</u>, Gloucester, blinded for suspected treason, learns a profound lesson from his tragic experience: "A man may see how this world goes / with no eyes" (4.2.148-49).

For a poem, cite the part (if there are a number of parts) and the line numbers, separated by a period.

> When Homer's Odysseus comes to the hall of Circe, he finds his men "mild / in her soft spell, fed on her drug of evil" (10.209-10).

For poems that are not divided into parts, use line numbers. For a first reference, use the word "lines": (lines 5-8). Thereafter use just the numbers: (12-13).

■   **20. NOVELS WITH NUMBERED DIVISIONS**   When a novel has numbered divisions, put the page number first, followed by a semicolon, and then indicate the book, part, or chapter in which the passage may be found. Use abbreviations such as "bk." and "ch."

> One of Kingsolver's narrators, teenager Rachel, pushes her vocabulary beyond its limits. For example, Rachel complains that being forced to live in the Congo with her missionary family is "a sheer tapestry of justice" because her chances of finding a boyfriend are "dull and void" (117; bk. 2, ch. 10).

■   **21. SACRED TEXTS**   When citing a sacred text such as the Bible or the Qur'an, name the edition you are using in your works cited entry (see item 14 on p. 150). In your parenthetical citation, give the book, chapter, and verse (or their equivalent), separated by periods. Common abbreviations for books of the Bible are acceptable.

> Consider the words of Solomon: "If your enemies are hungry, give them food to eat. If they are thirsty, give them water to drink" (Holy Bible, Prov. 25.21).

MLA list of works cited

An alphabetized list of works cited, which appears at the end of your research paper, gives publication information for each of the sources you have cited in the paper. (For information about preparing the list, see pp. 176–77; for a sample list of works cited, see pp. 184–85.)

NOTE: Unless your instructor asks for them, omit sources not actually cited in the paper, even if you read them.

Directory to MLA works cited entries

General guidelines for listing authors

Alphabetize entries in the list of works cited by authors' last names (if a work has no author, alphabetize it by its title). The author's name is important because citations in the text of the paper refer to it and readers will be looking for it at the beginning of an entry in the alphabetized list.

NAME CITED IN TEXT

According to Matt Sundeen, . . .

BEGINNING OF WORKS CITED ENTRY

Sundeen, Matt.

Items 1–5 show how to begin an entry for a work with a single author, multiple authors, a corporate author, an unknown author, and multiple works by the same author. What comes after this first element of your citation will depend on the kind of source you are citing. (See items 6–56.)

NOTE: For a book, an entry in the works cited list will sometimes begin with an editor (see item 9 on p. 147).

■ **1. SINGLE AUTHOR** For a work with one author, begin with the author's last name, followed by a comma; then give the author's first name, followed by a period.

Tannen, Deborah.

■ **2. MULTIPLE AUTHORS** For works with two or three authors, name the authors in the order in which they are listed in the source. Reverse the name of only the first author.

Walker, Janice R., and Todd Taylor.

Wilmut, Ian, Keith Campbell, and Colin Tudge.

For a work with four or more authors, either name all of the authors or name the first author, followed by "et al." (Latin for "and others").

Sloan, Frank A., Emily M. Stout, Kathryn Whetten-Goldstein, and Lan
    Liang.

Sloan, Frank A., et al.

■ **3. CORPORATE AUTHOR** When the author of a print document or Web site is a corporation, a government agency, or some other organization, begin your entry with the name of the group.

First Union.

United States. Bureau of the Census.

American Automobile Association.

NOTE: Make sure that your in-text citation also treats the organization as the author (see item 9 on p. 136).

■ **4. UNKNOWN AUTHOR** When the author of a work is unknown, begin with the work's title. Titles of articles and other short works, such as brief documents from Web sites, are put in quotation marks. Titles of books and other long works, such as entire Web sites, are underlined.

Article or other short work
"Media Giants."

Book or other long work
<u>Atlas of the World</u>.

Before concluding that the author of a Web source is unknown, check carefully (see the tip on p. 133). Also remember that an organization may be the author (see item 3 above).

■ **5. TWO OR MORE WORKS BY THE SAME AUTHOR**   If your list of works cited includes two or more works by the same author, use the author's name only for the first entry. For other entries, use three hyphens followed by a period. The three hyphens must stand for exactly the same name or names as in the first entry. List the titles in alphabetical order (ignoring the article *A*, *An*, or *The* at the beginning of a title).

García, Cristina. <u>The Agüero Sisters</u>. New York: Ballantine, 1998.

---. <u>Monkey Hunting</u>. New York: Ballantine, 2003.

Books

Items 6–19 apply to print books. For online books, see item 29 on page 160.

■ **6. BASIC FORMAT FOR A BOOK**   For most books, arrange the information into three units, each followed by a period and one space: the author's name; the title and subtitle, underlined; and the place of publication, the publisher, and the date.

Tan, Amy. <u>The Bonesetter's Daughter</u>. New York: Putnam, 2001.

Take the information about the book from its title page and copyright page. Use a short form of the publisher's name; omit terms such as *Press, Inc.,* and *Co.* except when naming university presses (Harvard UP, for example). If the copyright page lists more than one date, use the most recent one.

■ **7. AUTHOR WITH AN EDITOR**   Begin with the author and title, followed by the name of the editor. In this case the abbreviation "Ed." means "Edited by," so it is the same for one or multiple editors.

Plath, Sylvia. <u>The Unabridged Journals of Sylvia Plath</u>. Ed. Karen V.
Kukil. New York: Anchor-Doubleday, 2000.

■ **8. AUTHOR WITH A TRANSLATOR** Begin with the name of the author. After the title, write "Trans." (for "Translated by") and the name of the translator.

Allende, Isabel. <u>Daughter of Fortune</u>. Trans. Margaret Sayers Peden.
New York: Harper, 2000.

■ **9. EDITOR** An entry for a work with an editor is similar to that for a work with an author except that the name is followed by a comma and the abbreviation "ed." for "editor" (or "eds." for "editors").

Craig, Patricia, ed. <u>The Oxford Book of Travel Stories</u>. Oxford: Oxford
UP, 1996.

■ **10. WORK IN AN ANTHOLOGY** Begin with (1) the name of the author of the selection, not with the name of the editor of the anthology. Then give (2) the title of the selection; (3) the title of the anthology; (4) the name of the editor (preceded by "Ed." for "Edited by"); (5) publication information; and (6) the pages on which the selection appears.

```
  ┌── 1 ──┐ ┌──── 2 ────┐┌──────── 3 ────────┐
Desai, Anita. "Scholar and Gypsy." The Oxford Book of Travel Stories.

    ┌──── 4 ────┐ ┌──── 5 ────┐ ┌─ 6 ─┐
  Ed. Patricia Craig. Oxford: Oxford UP, 1996. 251-73.
```

If you wish, you may cross-reference two or more works from the same anthology. Provide an entry for the anthology (see item 9 above). Then in separate entries list the author and title of each selection, followed by the last name

Citation at a glance: Book (MLA)

To cite a book in MLA style, include the following elements:

1 Author
2 Title and subtitle
3 City of publication

4 Publisher
5 Date of publication

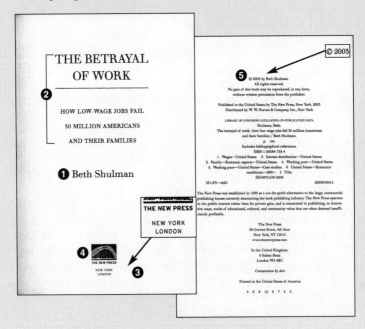

WORKS CITED ENTRY FOR A BOOK

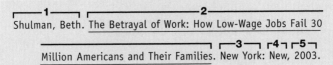

```
┌──1──┐ ┌────────────2────────────────────────
Shulman, Beth. The Betrayal of Work: How Low-Wage Jobs Fail 30

                                    ┌──3──┐ ┌4┐ ┌5┐
Million Americans and Their Families. New York: New, 2003.
```

of the editor of the anthology and the page numbers on which the selection appears.

Desai, Anita. "Scholar and Gypsy." Craig 251-73.

Malouf, David. "The Kyogle Line." Craig 390-96.

Alphabetize the entry for the anthology under the name of its editor (Craig); alphabetize the entries for the selections under the names of the authors (Desai, Malouf).

■ **11. EDITION OTHER THAN THE FIRST** If you are citing an edition other than the first, include the number of the edition after the title (or after the names of any translators or editors that appear after the title): 2nd ed., 3rd ed., and so on.

Auletta, Ken. The Underclass. 2nd ed. Woodstock: Overlook, 2000.

■ **12. MULTIVOLUME WORK** Include the total number of volumes before the city and publisher, using the abbreviation "vols."

Conway, Jill Ker, ed. Written by Herself. 2 vols. New York: Random, 1996.

If your paper cites only one of the volumes, give the volume number before the city and publisher and give the total number of volumes after the date.

Conway, Jill Ker, ed. Written by Herself. Vol. 2. New York: Random, 1996. 2 vols.

■ **13. ENCYCLOPEDIA OR DICTIONARY ENTRY** When an encyclopedia or a dictionary is well known, simply list the author of the entry (if there is one), the title of the entry, the title of the reference work, the edition number (if any), and the date of the edition.

Posner, Rebecca. "Romance Languages." <u>The New Encyclopaedia
    Britannica: Macropaedia</u>. 15th ed. 1987.

"Sonata." <u>The American Heritage Dictionary of the English Language</u>.
    4th ed. 2000.

Volume and page numbers are not necessary because the entries in the source are arranged alphabetically and therefore are easy to locate.

If a reference work is not well known, provide full publication information as well.

■   **14. SACRED TEXT**   Give the title of the edition of the sacred text (taken from the title page), underlined; the editor's or translator's name (if any); and publication information.

<u>Holy Bible</u>. Wheaton: Tyndale, 2005.

<u>The Qur'an: Translation</u>. Trans. Abdullah Yusuf Ali. Elmhurst: Tahrike,
    2000.

■   **15. FOREWORD, INTRODUCTION, PREFACE, OR AFTERWORD**
Begin with the author of the foreword or other book part, followed by the name of that part. Then give the title of the book; the author of the book, preceded by the word "By"; and the editor of the book (if any). After the publication information, give the page numbers for the part of the book being cited.

Morris, Jan. Introduction. <u>Letters from the Field, 1925-1975</u>.
    By Margaret Mead. New York: Perennial-Harper, 2001. xix-xxiii.

If the book part being cited has a title, include it in quotation marks immediately after the author's name.

Ozick, Cynthia. "Portrait of the Essay as a Warm Body." Introduction.
　　The Best American Essays 1998. Ed. Ozick. Boston: Houghton,
　　1998. xv-xxi.

■ **16. BOOK WITH A TITLE IN ITS TITLE** If the book contains a title normally underlined, neither underline the internal title nor place it in quotation marks.

King, John N. Milton and Religious Controversy: Satire and Polemic in
　　Paradise Lost. Cambridge: Cambridge UP, 2000.

If the title within the title is normally put in quotation marks, retain the quotation marks and underline the entire title.

Knight, Denise D., and Cynthia J. Davis. Approaches to Teaching
　　Gilman's "The Yellow Wall-Paper" and Herland. New York: Mod.
　　Lang. Assn., 2003.

■ **17. BOOK IN A SERIES** Before the publication information, cite the series name as it appears on the title page, followed by the series number, if any.

Malena, Anne. The Dynamics of Identity in Francophone Caribbean
　　Narrative. Francophone Cultures and Lits. Ser. 24. New York: Lang,
　　1998.

■ **18. REPUBLISHED BOOK** After the title of the book, cite the original publication date, followed by the current publication information. If the republished book contains new material, such as an introduction or afterword, include information about the new material after the original date.

Hughes, Langston. Black Misery. 1969. Afterword Robert O'Meally. New
York: Oxford UP, 2000.

■ **19. PUBLISHER'S IMPRINT** If a book was published by an
imprint (a division) of a publishing company, link the name
of the imprint and the name of the publisher with a hyphen,
putting the imprint first.

Truan, Barry. Acoustic Communication. Westport: Ablex-Greenwood,
2000.

Articles in periodicals

This section shows how to prepare works cited entries for
articles in magazines, scholarly journals, and newspapers.
In addition to consulting the models in this section, you will
at times need to turn to other models as well:

- More than one author: see item 2
- Corporate author: see item 3
- Unknown author: see item 4
- Online article: see item 32
- Article from a subscription service: see item 31

NOTE: For articles appearing on consecutive pages, provide
the range of pages (see items 21 and 22). When an article
does not appear on consecutive pages, give the number of
the first page followed by a plus sign: 32+.

■ **20. ARTICLE IN A MAGAZINE** List, in order, separated by
periods, the author's name; the title of the article, in quotation marks; and the title of the magazine, underlined. Then
give the date and the page numbers, separated by a colon.
If the magazine is issued monthly, give just the month and

year. Abbreviate the names of the months except May, June, and July.

Fay, J. Michael. "Land of the Surfing Hippos." <u>National Geographic</u>
Aug. 2004: 100+.

If the magazine is issued weekly, give the exact date.

Lord, Lewis. "There's Something about Mary Todd." <u>US News and World</u>
<u>Report</u> 19 Feb. 2001: 53.

■ **21. ARTICLE IN A JOURNAL PAGINATED BY VOLUME**   Many scholarly journals continue page numbers throughout the year instead of beginning each issue with page 1; at the end of the year, the issues are collected in a volume. To find an article, readers need only the volume number, the year, and the page numbers.

Ryan, Katy. "Revolutionary Suicide in Toni Morrison's Fiction." <u>African</u>
<u>American Review</u> 34 (2000): 389-412.

■ **22. ARTICLE IN A JOURNAL PAGINATED BY ISSUE**   If each issue of the journal begins with page 1, you need to indicate the number of the issue. After the volume number, put a period and the issue number.

Wood, Michael. "Broken Dates: Fiction and the Century." <u>Kenyon</u>
<u>Review</u> 22.3 (2000): 50-64.

■ **23. ARTICLE IN A DAILY NEWSPAPER**   Begin with the name of the author, if known, followed by the title of the article. Next give the name of the newspaper, the date, and the page numbers (including the section letter). Use a plus sign (+) after the page number if the article does not appear on consecutive pages.

Citation at a glance: Article in a periodical (MLA)

To cite an article in a periodical in MLA style, include the following elements:

1 Author

2 Title of article

3 Name of periodical

4 Date of publication

5 Page numbers

WORKS CITED ENTRY FOR AN ARTICLE IN A PERIODICAL

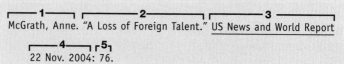

McGrath, Anne. "A Loss of Foreign Talent." US News and World Report 22 Nov. 2004: 76.

Brummitt, Chris. "Indonesia's Food Needs Expected to Soar." <u>Boston</u>
<u>Globe</u> 1 Feb. 2005: A7.

If the section is marked with a number rather than a letter, handle the entry as follows:

Wilford, John Noble. "In a Golden Age of Discovery, Faraway Worlds
Beckon." <u>New York Times</u> 9 Feb. 1997, late ed., sec. 1: 1+.

When an edition of the newspaper is specified on the masthead, name the edition after the date and before the page reference (eastern ed., late ed., natl. ed., and so on), as in the example just given.

If the city of publication is not obvious, include it in brackets after the name of the newspaper: *City Paper* [Washington, DC].

■   **24. EDITORIAL IN A NEWSPAPER**   Cite an editorial as you would an article with an unknown author, adding the word "Editorial" after the title.

"All Wet." Editorial. <u>Boston Globe</u> 12 Feb. 2001: A14.

■   **25. LETTER TO THE EDITOR**   Name the writer, followed by the word "Letter" and the publication information for the periodical in which the letter appears.

Shrewsbury, Toni. Letter. <u>Atlanta Journal-Constitution</u> 17 Feb. 2001:
A13.

■   **26. BOOK OR FILM REVIEW**   Name the reviewer and the title of the review, if any, followed by the words "Rev. of" and the title and author or director of the work reviewed. Add the publication information for the periodical in which the review appears.

Gleick, Elizabeth. "The Burdens of Genius." Rev. of <u>The Last Samurai</u>,
     by Helen DeWitt. <u>Time</u> 4 Dec. 2000: 171.

Denby, David. "On the Battlefield." Rev. of <u>The Hurricane</u>, dir. Norman
     Jewison. <u>New Yorker</u> 10 Jan. 2000: 90-92.

Electronic sources

This section shows how to prepare works cited entries for a
variety of electronic sources, including Web sites, online
books, articles in online periodicals and databases, and
e-mail.

NOTE: When a Web address in a works cited entry must be
divided at the end of a line, MLA recommends that you
break it after a slash. Do not insert a hyphen.

■ **27. AN ENTIRE WEB SITE** Begin with the name of the
author or corporate author (if known) and the title of the site,
underlined. Then give the names of any editors, the date of
publication or last update, the name of any sponsoring organization, the date you accessed the source, and the URL in
angle brackets. Provide as much of this information as is
available.

With author
Peterson, Susan Lynn. <u>The Life of Martin Luther</u>. 2002. 24 Jan. 2005
     <http://www.susanlynnpeterson.com/luther/home.html>.

With corporate (group) author
United States. Environmental Protection Agency. <u>Drinking Water</u>
     <u>Standards</u>. 8 July 2004. 24 Jan. 2005 <http://www.epa.gov/
     safewater/standards.html>.

Author unknown

Margaret Sanger Papers Project. 18 Oct. 2000. History Dept., New York
 U. 6 Dec. 2004 <http://www.nyu.edu/projects/sanger>.

With editor

Exploring Ancient World Cultures. Ed. Anthony F. Beavers. 1997. U of
 Evansville. 24 Jan. 2005 <http://eawc.evansville.edu/index.htm>.

NOTE: If the site has no title, substitute a description, such
as "Home page," for the title. Do not underline the words or
put them in quotation marks.

Yoon, Mina. Home page. 29 Sept. 2004. 12 Jan. 2005 <http://
 www.pa.msu.edu/~mnyoon>.

■ **28. SHORT WORK FROM A WEB SITE** Short works are those
that appear in quotation marks in MLA style: articles,
poems, and other documents that are not book length. For
a short work from a Web site, include as many of the following elements as apply and as are available: author's
name; title of the short work, in quotation marks; title of the
site, underlined; date of publication or last update; sponsor
of the site (if not named as the author or given as the title
of the site); date you accessed the source; and the URL in
angle brackets.

Usually at least some of these elements will not apply
or will be unavailable. In the following example, no sponsor
or date of publication was available. (The date given is the
date on which the researcher accessed the source.) For an
annotated example, see pages 158–59.

With author

Shiva, Vandana. "Bioethics: A Third World Issue." NativeWeb. 15 Sept.
 2004 <http://www.nativeweb.org/pages/legal/shiva.html>.

Citation at a glance: Short work from a Web site (MLA)

To cite a short work from a Web site in MLA style, include the following elements:

1 Author
2 Title of short work
3 Title of Web site
4 Date of publication or latest update
5 Sponsor of site
6 Date of access
7 URL

ON-SCREEN VIEW OF SHORT WORK

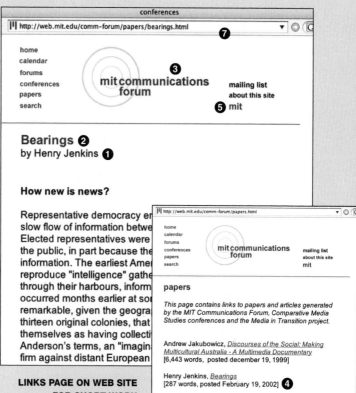

LINKS PAGE ON WEB SITE FOR SHORT WORK

BROWSER PRINTOUT OF SHORT WORK

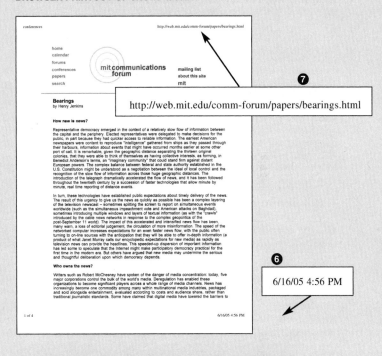

http://web.mit.edu/comm-forum/papers/bearings.html

⑦

⑥

6/16/05 4:56 PM

WORKS CITED ENTRY FOR A SHORT WORK FROM A WEB SITE

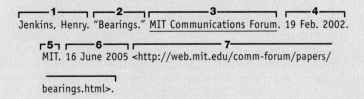

┌───1───┐ ┌───2───┐ ┌──────3──────┐ ┌───4───┐
Jenkins, Henry. "Bearings." <u>MIT Communications Forum</u>. 19 Feb. 2002.

┌─5─┐ ┌───6───┐ ┌──────────7──────────┐
MIT. 16 June 2005 <http://web.mit.edu/comm-forum/papers/

bearings.html>.

Author unknown

"Media Giants." Frontline: The Merchants of Cool. 2001. PBS Online.
    7 Feb. 2005 <http://www.pbs.org/wgbh/pages/frontline/shows/
    cool/giants>.

NOTE: When the URL for a short work from a Web site is very
long, you may give the URL for the home page and indicate
the path by which readers can access the source.

"Obesity Trends among US Adults between 1985 and 2001." Centers
    for Disease Control and Prevention. 3 Jan. 2003. 17 Feb. 2003
    <http://www.cdc.gov>. Path: Health Topics A-Z; Obesity Trends;
    US Obesity Trends 1985 to 2001.

■   **29. ONLINE BOOK**   When a book or a book-length work
such as a play or a long poem is posted on the Web as its
own site, give as much publication information as is available, followed by your date of access and the URL. (See also
the models for print books: items 6–19.)

Rawlins, Gregory J. E. Moths to the Flame. Cambridge: MIT P, 1996.
    11 Nov. 2004 <http://mitpress.mit.edu/e-books/Moths/
    contents.html>.

If the book-length work is posted on a scholarly Web
site, provide information about that site.

Jacobs, Harriet Ann. Incidents in the Life of a Slave Girl. Boston,
    1861. Documenting the American South: The Southern Experience
    in Nineteenth-Century America. Ed. Ji-Hae Yoon and Natalia
    Smith. 1998. Academic Affairs Lib., U of North Carolina, Chapel
    Hill. 3 Mar. 2005 <http://docsouth.unc.edu/jacobs/
    jacobs.html>.

■ **30. PART OF AN ONLINE BOOK**   Place the part title before the book's title. If the part is a short work such as a poem or an essay, put its title in quotation marks. If the part is an introduction or other division of the book, do not use quotation marks.

Adams, Henry. "Diplomacy." The Education of Henry Adams. Boston:

   Houghton, 1918. Bartleby.com: Great Books Online. 1999. 8 Jan.

   2005 <http://bartleby.com/159/8.html>.

■ **31. WORK FROM A SERVICE SUCH AS *INFOTRAC***   For sources retrieved from a library's subscription database service, give as much of the following information as is available: publication information for the source (see items 20–26); the name of the database, underlined; the name of the service; the name and location of the library where you retrieved the source; your date of access; and the URL of the service.

The following models are for articles retrieved through three popular library subscription services. The *InfoTrac* source is a scholarly article in a journal paginated by volume (see item 21); the *EBSCOhost* source is an article in a bimonthly magazine (see item 20); and the *ProQuest* source is an article in a daily newspaper (see item 23).

InfoTrac

Johnson, Kirk. "The Mountain Lions of Michigan." Endangered Species

   Update 19.2 (2002): 27+. Expanded Academic Index. InfoTrac.

   U of Michigan Lib., Ann Arbor. 26 Nov. 2002 <http://

   infotrac.galegroup.com>.

EBSCOhost

Barrera, Rebeca María. "A Case for Bilingual Education." Scholastic

   Parent and Child Nov.–Dec. 2004: 72-73. Academic Search

   Premier. EBSCOhost. St. Johns River Community Coll. Lib.,

   Palatka, FL. 1 Feb. 2005 <http://search.epnet.com>.

ProQuest

Kolata, Gina. "Scientists Debating Future of Hormone Replacement."
New York Times 23 Oct. 2002: A20. ProQuest. Drew U Lib.,
Madison, NJ. 26 Nov. 2002 <http://www.proquest.com>.

NOTE: When you access a work through a personal subscription service such as *America Online,* give the information about the source, the name of the service, the date of access, and the keyword used to retrieve the source.

Conniff, Richard. "The House That John Built." Smithsonian Feb. 2001.
America Online. 11 Mar. 2001. Keyword: Smithsonian Magazine.

■ **32. ARTICLE IN AN ONLINE PERIODICAL** When citing online articles, follow the guidelines for printed articles (see items 20–26), giving whatever information is available in the online source. End the citation with your date of access and the URL.

NOTE: In some online articles, paragraphs are numbered. For such articles, include the total number of paragraphs in your citation, as in the next example.

From an online scholarly journal

Belau, Linda. "Trauma and the Material Signifier." Postmodern
Culture 11.2 (2001): 37 pars. 30 Mar. 2001 <http://
jefferson.village.virginia.edu/pmc/current.issue/
11.2belau.html>.

From an online magazine

Morgan, Fiona. "Banning the Bullies." Salon.com 15 Mar. 2001.
21 Sept. 2004 <http://www.salon.com/news/feature/2001/03/15/
bullying/index.html>.

From an online newspaper

Rubin, Joel. "Report Faults Charter School." Los Angeles Times 22 Jan.

   2005. 24 Jan. 2005 <http://pqasb.pqarchiver.com/latimes/

   search.html>.

■ **33. CD-ROM**   Treat a CD-ROM as you would any other source, but name the medium before the publication information.

"Pimpernel." The American Heritage Dictionary of the English Language.

   4th ed. CD-ROM. Boston: Houghton, 2000.

Wattenberg, Ruth. "Helping Students in the Middle." American Educator

   19.4 (1996): 2-18. ERIC. CD-ROM. SilverPlatter. Sept. 1996.

■ **34. E-MAIL**   To cite an e-mail, begin with the writer's name and the subject line. Then write "E-mail to" followed by the name of the recipient. End with the date of the message.

Wilde, Lisa. "Review questions." E-mail to the author. 15 Mar. 2005.

■ **35. POSTING TO AN ONLINE LIST, FORUM, OR GROUP**
Communications through e-mail discussion lists (often called LISTSERVs), Web forums, and Usenet newsgroups do not take place in real time. (For real-time online communications, see item 36.) When possible, cite archived versions of postings, which are more permanent and easier to retrieve. If you cannot locate an archived version, keep a copy of the posting for your records.

   Begin the entry with the author's name, followed by the title or subject line; the words "Online posting"; the date of the posting; the name of the list, forum, or newsgroup; and your date of access. Then, for a discussion list, give the URL of the list if it is available; otherwise give the e-mail address of the list moderator. For a Web forum, give the network

Citation at a glance: Article from a database (MLA)

To cite an article from a database in MLA style, include the following elements:

1 Author
2 Title of article
3 Name of periodical, volume and issue numbers
4 Date of publication
5 Inclusive pages

6 Name of database
7 Name of subscription service
8 Library at which you retrieved the source
9 Date of access
10 URL of service

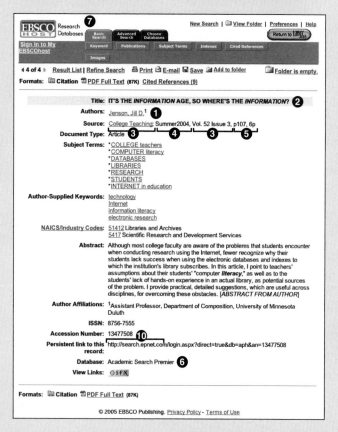

WORKS CITED ENTRY FOR AN ARTICLE FROM A DATABASE

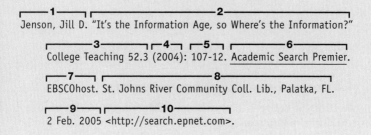

Jenson, Jill D. "It's the Information Age, so Where's the Information?"

College Teaching 52.3 (2004): 107-12. Academic Search Premier.

EBSCOhost. St. Johns River Community Coll. Lib., Palatka, FL.

2 Feb. 2005 <http://search.epnet.com>.

address. For a Usenet group, use the prefix "news:" followed by the name of the newsgroup.

Discussion list posting

Edwards, David. "Media Lens." Online posting. 20 Dec. 2001. Media
     Lens Archives. 10 Apr. 2002 <http://groups.yahoo.com/group/
     medialens/message/25>.

Web forum posting

Brown, Oliver. "Welcome." Online posting. 8 Oct. 2002. Chester Coll.
     Students Web Forum. 20 Feb. 2003 <http://www.voy.com/
     113243>.

Newsgroup posting

Reedy, Tom. "Re: Macbeth an Existential Nightmare?" Online posting.
     9 Mar. 2002. 8 Apr. 2002 <news:humanities.lit.authors.shakespe>.

■ **36. POSTING TO A MUD OR A MOO** MUDs and MOOs are forums that allow communication in real time. Include the writer's name (if relevant), a description and date of the event, the title of the forum, the date of access, and the electronic address, beginning with the prefix "telnet://."

Carbone, Nick. Planning for the future. 1 Mar. 2001. TechRhet's
    Thursday night MOO. 1 Mar. 2001 <telnet://
    connections.moo.mud.org:3333>.

If possible, cite an archived version of the posting.

Multimedia sources (including online versions)

Multimedia sources include visuals (such as works of art),
audio works (such as sound recordings), audiovisuals (such
as films), and live events (such as the performance of a
play).

When citing multimedia sources that you retrieved
online, consult the appropriate model in this section and
give whatever information is available for the online source;
then end the citation with your date of access and the URL.
(See items 37, 40, and 44 for examples.)

■ **37. WORK OF ART** Cite the artist's name, followed by the
title of the artwork, usually underlined, and the institution
and city in which the artwork can be found. If you want to
indicate the work's date, include it after the title. For a work
of art you viewed online, end your citation with your date of
access and the URL.

Constable, John. Dedham Vale. Victoria and Albert Museum, London.

van Gogh, Vincent. The Starry Night. 1889. Museum of Mod. Art,
    New York. 3 Feb. 2003 <http://moma.org/collection/depts/
    paint_sculpt/blowups/paint_sculpt_003.html>.

■ **38. CARTOON** Begin with the cartoonist's name, the title
of the cartoon (if it has one) in quotation marks, the word
"Cartoon," and the publication information for the publication in which the cartoon appears.

Sutton, Ward. "Why Wait 'til November?" Cartoon. Village Voice 7-13
    July 2004: 6.

■ **39. ADVERTISEMENT** Name the product or company being advertised, followed by the word "Advertisement." Give
publication information for the source in which the advertisement appears.

Truth by Calvin Klein. Advertisement. Vogue Dec. 2000: 95-98.

■ **40. MAP OR CHART** Cite a map or a chart as you would a
book or a short work within a longer work. Add the word
"Map" or "Chart" following the title.

Serbia. Map. 2 Feb. 2001. 17 Mar. 2003 <http://www.biega.com/
    serbia.html>.

Joseph, Lori, and Bob Laird. "Driving While Phoning Is Dangerous."
    Chart. USA Today 16 Feb. 2001: 1A.

■ **41. MUSICAL COMPOSITION** Cite the composer's name,
followed by the title of the work. Underline the title of an
opera, a ballet, or a composition identified by name, but do
not underline or use quotation marks around a composition
identified by number or form.

Ellington, Duke. Conga Brava.

Haydn, Franz Joseph. Symphony no. 88 in G.

■ **42. SOUND RECORDING** Begin with the name of the person you want to emphasize: the composer, conductor, or
performer. For a long work, give the title, underlined, followed by names of pertinent artists (such as performers,

readers, or musicians) and the orchestra and conductor (if relevant). End with the manufacturer and the date.

Bizet, Georges. <u>Carmen</u>. Perf. Jennifer Laramore, Thomas Moser, Angela
    Gheorghiu, and Samuel Ramey. Bavarian State Orch. and Chorus.
    Cond. Giuseppe Sinopoli. Warner, 1996.

For a song, put the title in quotation marks. If you include the name of the album, underline it.

Counting Crows. "Holiday in Spain." <u>Hard Candy</u>. Geffen, 2002.

■ **43. FILM OR VIDEO**   Begin with the title, underlined. For a film, cite the director and the lead actors or narrator ("Perf." or "Narr."), followed by the name of the distributor and the year of the film's release. For a videotape or DVD, add "Videocassette" or "DVD" before the name of the distributor.

<u>Finding Neverland</u>. Dir. Marc Forster. Perf. Johnny Depp, Kate Winslet,
    Julie Christie, Radha Mitchell, and Dustin Hoffman. Miramax,
    2004.

<u>High Fidelity</u>. Dir. Stephen Frears. Perf. John Cusack, Iben Hjejle,
    Jack Black, and Todd Louiso. 2000. Videocassette. Walt Disney
    Video, 2001.

■ **44. RADIO OR TELEVISION PROGRAM**   Begin with the title of the radio segment or television episode (if there is one) in quotation marks, followed by the title of the program, underlined. Next give relevant information about the program's writer ("By"), director ("Dir."), performers ("Perf."), or host ("Host"). Then name the network, the local station (if any), and the date the program was broadcast.

"Monkey Trial." American Experience. PBS. WGBH, Boston. 18 Mar.
　　2003.

"Live in 4A: Konstantin Soukhovetski." Performance Today. Natl. Public
　　Radio. 2 May 2002. 10 May 2002 <http://www.npr.org/programs/
　　pt/features/4a/soukhovetski.02.html>.

If there is a series title, include it after the title of the
program, neither underlined nor in quotation marks.

Mysteries of the Pyramids. On the Inside. Discovery Channel. 7 Feb.
　　2001.

■　**45. RADIO OR TELEVISION INTERVIEW**　Begin with the name
of the person who was interviewed, followed by the word
"Interview." End with the information about the program as
in item 44.

McGovern, George. Interview. Charlie Rose. PBS. WNET, New York. 1
　　Feb. 2001.

■　**46. LIVE PERFORMANCE**　For a live performance of a play,
a ballet, an opera, or a concert, begin with the title of the
work performed. Then name the author or composer of the
work (preceded by the word "By"), followed by as much information about the performance as is available: the director
("Dir."), choreographer ("Chor."), or conductor ("Cond."); the
major performers ("Perf."); the theater, ballet, or opera company; the theater and its city; and the date of the performance.

Art. By Yasmina Reza. Dir. Matthew Warchus. Perf. Philip Franks, Leigh
　　Lawson, and Simon Shephard. Whitehall Theatre, London. 3 Dec.
　　2001.

Cello Concerto No. 2. By Eric Tanguy. Cond. Seiji Ozawa. Perf. Mstislav
  Rostropovich. Boston Symphony Orch. Symphony Hall, Boston. 5
  Apr. 2002.

■ **47. LECTURE OR PUBLIC ADDRESS** Cite the speaker's
name, followed by the title of the lecture (if any), the organization sponsoring the lecture, the location, and the date.

Cohran, Kelan. "Slavery and Astronomy." Adler Planetarium, Chicago.
  21 Feb. 2001.

■ **48. PERSONAL INTERVIEW** To cite an interview that you
conducted, begin with the name of the person interviewed.
Then write "Personal interview," followed by the date of the
interview.

Akufo, Dautey. Personal interview. 11 Aug. 2005.

Other sources (including online versions)

This section includes a variety of traditional print sources
not covered elsewhere. For sources obtained on the Web,
consult the appropriate model in this section and give
whatever information is available for the online source;
then end the citation with the date on which you accessed
the source and the URL. (See the second example under
item 49.)

■ **49. GOVERNMENT PUBLICATION** Treat the government
agency as the author, giving the name of the government
followed by the name of the agency.

United States. Dept. of Labor. America's Dynamic Workforce. Washington: US Dept. of Labor, 2004.

For government documents published online, give as much publication information as is available and end your citation with the date of access and the URL.

United States. Dept. of Transportation. Natl. Highway Traffic Safety
    Administration. <u>An Investigation of the Safety Implications of
    Wireless Communications in Vehicles</u>. Nov. 1999. 20 May 2001
    <http://www.nhtsa.dot.gov/people/injury/research/wireless>.

■ **50. LEGAL SOURCE** For articles of the United States Constitution and laws in the United States Code, no works cited entry is required; instead, simply give an in-text citation (see item 17 on p. 139).

For a legislative act, begin with the name of the act. Then provide the act's Public Law number, its date of enactment, and its Statutes at Large number.

Electronic Freedom of Information Act Amendments of 1996. Pub. L.
    104-418. 2 Oct. 1996. Stat. 3048.

For a court case, name the first plaintiff and first defendant. Then give the case number, the court name, and the date of the decision. In a works cited entry, the name of the case is not underlined.

Utah v. Evans. No. 01-714. Supreme Ct. of the US. 20 June 2002.

■ **51. PAMPHLET** Cite a pamphlet as you would a book.

Commonwealth of Massachusetts. Dept. of Jury Commissioner. <u>A Few
    Facts about Jury Duty</u>. Boston: Commonwealth of Massachusetts,
    2004.

■ **52. DISSERTATION** Begin with the author's name, followed by the dissertation title in quotation marks, the abbreviation "Diss.," the name of the institution, and the year the dissertation was accepted.

Jackson, Shelley. "Writing Whiteness: Contemporary Southern
    Literature in Black and White." Diss. U of Maryland, 2000.

For dissertations that have been published in book form, underline the title. After the title and before the book's publication information, add the abbreviation "Diss.," the name of the institution, and the year the dissertation was accepted.

Damberg, Cheryl L. <u>Healthcare Reform: Distributional Consequences</u>
    <u>of an Employer Mandate for Workers in Small Firms</u>. Diss. Rand
    Graduate School, 1995. Santa Monica: Rand, 1996.

■ **53. ABSTRACT OF A DISSERTATION**   Cite an abstract as you would an unpublished dissertation. After the dissertation date, give the abbreviation *DA* or *DAI* (for *Dissertation Abstracts* or *Dissertation Abstracts International*), followed by the volume number, the date of publication, and the page number.

Chen, Shu-Ling. "Mothers and Daughters in Morrison, Tan, Marshall,
    and Kincaid." Diss. U of Washington, 2000. <u>DAI</u> 61 (2000): 2289.

■ **54. PUBLISHED PROCEEDINGS OF A CONFERENCE**   Cite published conference proceedings as you would a book, adding information about the conference after the title.

Kartiganer, Donald M., and Ann J. Abadie. <u>Faulkner at 100: Retrospect</u>
    <u>and Prospect</u>. Proc. of Faulkner and Yoknapatawpha Conf., 27
    July-1 Aug. 1997, U of Mississippi. Jackson: UP of Mississippi,
    2000.

■ **55. PUBLISHED INTERVIEW** Name the person interviewed, followed by the title of the interview (if there is one). If the interview does not have a title, include the word "Interview" followed by a period after the interviewee's name. Give publication information for the work in which the interview was published.

Armstrong, Lance. "Lance in France." Sports Illustrated 28 June 2004:
    46+.

If the name of the interviewer is relevant, include it after the name of the interviewee, as in the following example.

Prince. Interview with Bilge Ebiri. Yahoo! Internet Life 7.6 (2001):
    82-85.

■ **56. PERSONAL LETTER** To cite a letter that you have received, begin with the writer's name and add the phrase "Letter to the author," followed by the date.

Primak, Shoshana. Letter to the author. 6 May 2005.

MLA information notes (optional)

Researchers who use the MLA system of parenthetical documentation (see pp. 131–41) may also use information notes for one of two purposes:

1. to provide additional material that might interrupt the flow of the paper yet is important enough to include
2. to refer readers to any sources not discussed in the paper

Information notes may be either footnotes or endnotes. Footnotes appear at the foot of the page; endnotes appear on a separate page at the end of the paper, just before the list of works cited. For either style, the notes are numbered consecutively throughout the paper. The text of the paper contains a raised arabic numeral that corresponds to the number of the note.

TEXT

Local governments are more likely than state governments to pass legislation against using a cell phone while driving.[1]

NOTE

[1] For a discussion of local laws banning cell phone use, see Sundeen 8.

MLA manuscript format

In most English and humanities classes, you will be asked to use MLA (Modern Language Association) guidelines for formatting a paper and preparing a list of the works you have cited. The following guidelines are consistent with advice given in the *MLA Handbook for Writers of Research Papers*, 6th ed. (New York: MLA, 2003). For a sample MLA paper, see pp. 178–85.

Formatting the paper

MLA papers should be formatted as follows.

MATERIALS   For papers that you submit as hard copy, use good-quality 8½″ × 11″ white paper. Secure the pages with a paper clip. Unless your instructor suggests otherwise, do not staple or bind the pages.

TITLE AND IDENTIFICATION   MLA does not require a title page. On the first page of your paper, place your name, your instructor's name, the course title, and the date on separate lines against the left margin. Then center your title. (See p. 178 for a sample first page.)

If your instructor requires a title page, ask for guidelines on formatting it. A format similar to the one on page 216 may be acceptable.

PAGINATION Put the page number preceded by your last name in the upper right corner of each page, one-half inch below the top edge. Use arabic numerals (1, 2, 3, and so on).

MARGINS, LINE SPACING, AND PARAGRAPH INDENTS Leave margins of one inch on all sides of the page. Left-align the text.

Double-space throughout the paper. Do not add extra line spaces above or below the title of the paper or between paragraphs.

Indent the first line of each paragraph one-half inch (or five spaces) from the left margin.

LONG QUOTATIONS When a quotation is longer than four typed lines of prose or three lines of verse, set it off from the text by indenting the entire quotation one inch (or ten spaces) from the left margin. Double-space the indented quotation, and don't add extra space above or below it.

Quotation marks are not needed when a quotation has been set off from the text by indenting. See pages 179–80 for an example.

WEB ADDRESSES When a Web address (URL) mentioned in the text of your paper must be divided at the end of a line, do not insert a hyphen (a hyphen could appear to be part of the address). For MLA rules on dividing Web addresses in your list of works cited, see page 177.

HEADINGS MLA neither encourages nor discourages the use of headings and currently provides no guidelines for their use. If you would like to insert headings in a long essay or research paper, check first with your instructor.

A sample MLA paper with headings appears at <http://dianahacker.com/resdoc>.

VISUALS MLA classifies visuals as tables and figures (figures include graphs, charts, maps, photographs, and drawings). Label each table with an arabic numeral (Table 1, Table 2, and so on) and provide a clear caption that identifies the subject. The label and caption should appear on separate lines above the table, flush left. Below the table, give its source in a note like this one:

Source: John M. Violanti, "Cellular Phones and Fatal Traffic Collisions," Accident Analysis and Prevention 30 (1998): 521.

For each figure, place a label and a caption below the figure, flush left. They need not appear on separate lines. The word "Figure" may be abbreviated to "Fig." Include source information following the caption.

Visuals should be placed in the text, as close as possible to the sentences that relate to them unless your instructor prefers them in an appendix. See page 180 for an example of a visual in the text of a paper.

Preparing the list of works cited

Begin the list of works cited on a new page at the end of the paper. Center the title Works Cited about one inch from the top of the page. Double-space throughout. See pages 184–85 for a sample list of works cited.

ALPHABETIZING THE LIST Alphabetize the list by the last names of the authors (or editors); if a work has no author or editor, alphabetize by the first word of the title other than *A, An,* or *The.*

If your list includes two or more works by the same author, use the author's name only for the first entry. For subsequent entries use three hyphens followed by a period. List the titles in alphabetical order. See item 5 on page 146.

INDENTING   Do not indent the first line of each works cited entry, but indent any additional lines one-half inch (or five spaces). This technique highlights the names of the authors, making it easy for readers to scan the alphabetized list.

WEB ADDRESSES   Do not insert a hyphen when dividing a Web address (URL) at the end of a line. Break the line after a slash. Also insert angle brackets around the URL.

For advice about how to cite sources with long URLs, see the note on page 160.

If your word processing program automatically turns Web addresses into hot links (by underlining them and highlighting them in color), turn off this feature.

Sample research paper: MLA style

On the following pages is a research paper on the topic of cell phones and driving, written by Angela Daly, a student in a composition class. Daly's paper is documented with MLA-style in-text citations and list of works cited.

Another student, Paul Levi, has also written a paper on the topic of cell phones and driving; his paper takes the opposite stand from that taken by Angela Daly. His paper is available at *Research and Documentation Online,* <http://dianahacker.com/resdoc>.

Angela Daly
Professor Chavez
English 101
14 March 2001

A Call to Action:

Regulate Use of Cell Phones on the Road

When a cell phone goes off in a classroom or at a concert, we are irritated, but at least our lives are not endangered. When we are on the road, however, irresponsible cell
phone users are more than irritating: They are putting our
lives at risk. Many of us have witnessed drivers so distracted
by dialing and chatting that they resemble drunk drivers,
weaving between lanes, for example, or nearly running down
pedestrians in crosswalks. A number of bills to regulate use of
cell phones on the road have been introduced in state legislatures, and the time has come to push for their passage.
Regulation is needed because drivers using phones are seriously impaired and because laws on negligent and reckless
driving are not sufficient to punish offenders.

No one can deny that cell phones have caused traffic
deaths and injuries. Cell phones were implicated in three fatal
accidents in November 1999 alone. Early in November, two-
year-old Morgan Pena was killed by a driver distracted by his
cell phone. Morgan's mother, Patti Pena, reports that the driver "ran a stop sign at 45 mph, broadsided my vehicle and
killed Morgan as she sat in her car seat." A week later, corrections officer Shannon Smith, who was guarding prisoners
by the side of the road, was killed by a woman distracted by
a phone call (Besthoff). On Thanksgiving weekend that same

Daly 2

month, John and Carole Hall were killed when a Naval
Academy midshipman crashed into their parked car. The driver
said in court that when he looked up from the cell phone he
was dialing, he was three feet from the car and had no time to
stop (Stockwell B8).

Expert testimony, public opinion, and even cartoons
suggest that driving while phoning is dangerous. Frances
Bents, an expert on the relation between cell phones and
accidents, estimates that between 450 and 1,000 crashes a
year have some connection to cell phone use (Layton C9). In
a survey published by Farmers Insurance Group, 87% of those
polled said that cell phones affect a driver's ability, and 40%
reported having close calls with drivers distracted by phones.
Many cartoons have depicted the very real dangers of driving
while distracted (see Fig. 1).

Scientific research confirms the dangers of using phones
while on the road. In 1997 an important study appeared in
the New England Journal of Medicine. The authors, Donald
Redelmeier and Robert Tibshirani, studied 699 volunteers who
made their cell phone bills available in order to confirm the
times when they had placed calls. The participants agreed to
report any nonfatal collision in which they were involved. By
comparing the time of a collision with the phone records, the
researchers assessed the dangers of driving while phoning.
The results are unsettling:

>   We found that using a cellular telephone was asso-
>   ciated with a risk of having a motor vehicle colli-
>   sion that was about about four times as high as
>   that among the same drivers when they were not

Fig. 1. Chan Lowe, cartoon, <u>Washington Post</u> 22 July 2000: A21.

> using their cellular telephones. This relative risk is
> similar to the hazard associated with driving with
> a blood alcohol level at the legal limit. (456)

The news media often exaggerated the latter claim ("similar
to" is not "equal to"); nonetheless, the comparison with drunk
driving suggests the extent to which cell phone use while
driving can impair judgment.

A 1998 study focused on Oklahoma, one of the few
states to keep records on fatal accidents involving cell
phones. Using police records, John M. Violanti of the
Rochester Institute of Technology investigated the relation
between traffic fatalities in Oklahoma and the use or presence of a cell phone. He found a ninefold increase in the risk

Daly 4

of fatality if a phone was being used and a doubled risk simply when a phone was present in a vehicle (522-23). The latter statistic is interesting, for it suggests that those who carry phones in their cars may tend to be more negligent (or prone to distractions of all kinds) than those who do not.

Some groups have argued that state traffic laws make legislation regulating cell phone use unnecessary. Sadly, this is not true. Laws on traffic safety vary from state to state, and drivers distracted by cell phones can get off with light punishment even when they cause fatal accidents. For example, although the midshipman mentioned earlier was charged with vehicular manslaughter for the deaths of John and Carole Hall, the judge was unable to issue a verdict of guilty. Under Maryland law, he could only find the defendant guilty of negligent driving and impose a $500 fine (Layton C1). Such a light sentence is not unusual. The driver who killed Morgan Pena in Pennsylvania received two tickets and a $50 fine-- and retained his driving privileges (Pena). In Georgia, a young woman distracted by her phone ran down and killed a two-year-old; her sentence was ninety days in boot camp and five hundred hours of community service (Ippolito J1). The families of the victims are understandably distressed by laws that lead to such light sentences.

When certain kinds of driver behavior are shown to be especially dangerous, we wisely draft special laws making them illegal and imposing specific punishments. Running red lights, failing to stop for a school bus, and drunk driving are obvious examples; phoning in a moving vehicle should be no exception. Unlike more general laws covering negligent driving, specific laws leave little ambiguity for law officers and for judges and juries imposing punishments. Such laws have another important benefit: They leave no ambiguity for drivers. Currently, drivers can tease themselves into thinking they are using their car phones responsibly because the definition of "negligent driving" is vague.

As of December 2000, twenty countries were restricting use of cell phones in moving vehicles (Sundeen 8). In the United States, it is highly unlikely that legislation could be passed on the national level, since traffic safety is considered a state and local issue. To date, only a few counties and towns have passed traffic laws restricting cell phone use. For example, in Suffolk County, New York, it is illegal for drivers to use a handheld phone for anything but an emergency call while on the road (Haughney A8). The first town to restrict use of handheld phones was Brooklyn, Ohio (Layton C9). Brooklyn, the first community in the country to pass a seat belt law, has once again shown its concern for traffic safety.

Laws passed by counties and towns have had some effect, but it makes more sense to legislate at the state level. Local laws are not likely to have the impact of state laws, and keeping track of a wide variety of local ordinances is confusing for drivers. Even a spokesperson for Verizon Wireless has said that statewide bans are preferable to a "crazy patchwork quilt of ordinances" (qtd. in Haughney A8). Unfortunately, although a number of bills have been introduced in state legislatures, as of early 2001 no state law seriously restricting use of the phones had passed--largely because of effective lobbying from the wireless industry.

Despite the claims of some lobbyists, tough laws regulating phone use can make our roads safer. In Japan, for example, accidents linked to cell phones fell by 75% just a month after the country prohibited using a handheld phone while driving (Haughney A8). Research suggests and common sense tells us that it is not possible to drive an automobile at high speeds, dial numbers, and carry on conversations without significant risks. When such behavior is regulated, obviously our roads will be safer.

Because of mounting public awareness of the dangers of drivers distracted by phones, state legislators must begin to take the problem seriously. "It's definitely an issue that is gaining steam around the country," says Matt Sundeen of the National Conference of State Legislatures (qtd. in Layton C9). Lon Anderson of the American Automobile Association agrees: "There is momentum building," he says, to pass laws (qtd. in Layton C9). The time has come for states to adopt legislation restricting the use of cell phones in moving vehicles.

Works Cited

Besthoff, Len. "Cell Phone Use Increases Risk of Accidents,
    but Users Willing to Take the Risk." <u>WRAL Online</u>. 11
    Nov. 1999. 12 Jan. 2001 <http://www.wral tv.com/
    news/wral/1999/1110-talking-driving>.

Farmers Insurance Group. "New Survey Shows Drivers Have Had
    'Close Calls' with Cell Phone Users." <u>Farmers Insurance
    Group</u>. 8 May 2000. 12 Jan. 2001 <http://
    www.farmersinsurance.com/news_cellphones.html>.

Haughney, Christine. "Taking Phones out of Drivers' Hands."
    <u>Washington Post</u> 5 Nov. 2000: A8.

Ippolito, Milo. "Driver's Sentence Not Justice, Mom Says."
    <u>Atlanta Journal-Constitution</u> 25 Sept. 1999: J1.

Layton, Lyndsey. "Legislators Aiming to Disconnect
    Motorists." <u>Washington Post</u> 10 Dec. 2000: C1+.

Lowe, Chan. Cartoon. <u>Washington Post</u> 22 July 2000: A21.

Pena, Patricia N. "Patti Pena's Letter to Car Talk." <u>Cars.com</u>.
    Car Talk. 10 Jan. 2001 <http://cartalk.cars.com/About/
    Morgan-Pena/letter.html>.

Redelmeier, Donald A., and Robert J. Tibshirani. "Association
    between Cellular-Telephone Calls and Motor Vehicle
    Collisions." <u>New England Journal of Medicine</u> 336
    (1997): 453-58.

Stockwell, Jamie. "Phone Use Faulted in Collision."
    <u>Washington Post</u> 6 Dec. 2000: B1+.

Sundeen, Matt. "Cell Phones and Highway Safety: 2000 State
     Legislative Update." National Conference of State
     Legislatures. Dec. 2000. 9 pp. 27 Feb. 2001
     <http://ncsl.org/programs/esnr/cellphone.pdf>.
Violanti, John M. "Cellular Phones and Fatal Traffic
     Collisions." Accident Analysis and Prevention 30 (1998):
     519-24.

APA Style: The Social Sciences

In most social science classes, you will be asked to use the APA system for documenting sources, which is set forth in the *Publication Manual of the American Psychological Association*, 5th ed. (Washington: APA, 2001). APA recommends in-text citations that refer readers to a list of references.

An in-text citation gives the author of the source (often in a signal phrase), the date of publication, and at times a page number in parentheses. At the end of the paper, a list of references provides publication information about the source; the list is alphabetized by authors' last names (or by titles for works without authors).

IN-TEXT CITATION

Yanovski and Yanovski (2002) reported that "the current state of the treatment for obesity is similar to the state of the treatment of hypertension several decades ago" (p. 600).

ENTRY IN THE LIST OF REFERENCES

Yanovski, S. Z., & Yanovski, J. A. (2002). Drug therapy: Obesity [Electronic version]. *The New England Journal of Medicine, 346*, 591-602.

For a reference list that includes this entry, see pages 227–28.

APA in-text citations

The APA's in-text citations provide at least the author's last name and the date of publication. For direct quotations and some paraphrases, a page number is given as well.

Directory to APA in-text citations

NOTE: APA style requires the use of the past tense or the present perfect tense in signal phrases introducing cited material: *Smith (2005) reported, Smith (2005) has argued.*

■ **1. BASIC FORMAT FOR A QUOTATION** Ordinarily, introduce the quotation with a signal phrase that includes the author's last name followed by the year of publication in parentheses. Put the page number (preceded by "p.") in parentheses after the quotation.

> Critser (2003) noted that despite growing numbers of overweight Americans, many health care providers still "remain either in ignorance or outright denial about the health danger to the poor and the young" (p. 5).

If the author is not named in the signal phrase, place the author's name, the year, and the page number in parentheses after the quotation: (Critser, 2003, p. 5).

NOTE: APA style requires the year of publication in an in-text citation. Do not include a month, even if the source is listed by month and year.

■ **2. BASIC FORMAT FOR A SUMMARY OR A PARAPHRASE** Include the author's last name and the year either in a signal phrase introducing the material or in parentheses following it. A page number or another locator is not required for a summary or a paraphrase, but include one if it would help readers find the passage in a long work.

> According to Carmona (2004), the cost of treating obesity is exceeded only by the cost of treating illnesses from tobacco use (para. 9).

> The cost of treating obesity is exceeded only by the cost of treating illnesses from tobacco use (Carmona, 2004, para. 9).

■ **3. A WORK WITH TWO AUTHORS** Name both authors in the signal phrase or parentheses each time you cite the work. In the parentheses, use "&" between the authors' names; in the signal phrase, use "and."

> According to Sothern and Gordon (2003), "Environmental factors may contribute as much as 80% to the causes of childhood obesity" (p. 104).

> Obese children often engage in less physical activity (Sothern & Gordon, 2003, p. 104).

■ **4. A WORK WITH THREE TO FIVE AUTHORS** Identify all authors in the signal phrase or parentheses the first time you cite the source.

> In 2003, Berkowitz, Wadden, Tershakovec, and Cronquist con-
> cluded, "Sibutramine . . . must be carefully monitored in ado-
> lescents, as in adults, to control increases in [blood pressure]
> and pulse rate" (p. 1811).

In subsequent citations, use the first author's name followed by "et al." in either the signal phrase or the parentheses.

> As Berkowitz et al. (2003) advised, "Until more extensive safety
> and efficacy data are available, . . . weight-loss medications
> should be used only on an experimental basis for adolescents"
> (p. 1811).

■ **5. A WORK WITH SIX OR MORE AUTHORS** Use the first
author's name followed by "et al." in the signal phrase or
the parentheses.

> McDuffie et al. (2002) tested 20 adolescents aged 12-16 over a
> three-month period and found that orlistat, combined with
> behavioral therapy, produced an average weight loss of 4.4 kg, or
> 9.7 pounds (p. 646).

■ **6. UNKNOWN AUTHOR** If the author is unknown, mention
the work's title in the signal phrase or give the first word or
two of the title in the parenthetical citation. Titles of articles
and chapters are put in quotation marks; titles of books
and reports are italicized.

> Children struggling to control their weight must also struggle
> with the pressures of television advertising that, on the one
> hand, encourages the consumption of junk food and, on the
> other, celebrates thin celebrities ("Television," 2002).

NOTE: In the rare case when "Anonymous" is specified as the author, treat it as if it were a real name: (Anonymous, 2001). In the list of references, also use the name Anonymous as author.

■ **7. ORGANIZATION AS AUTHOR** If the author is a government agency or other organization, name the organization in the signal phrase or in the parenthetical citation the first time you cite the source.

> Obesity puts children at risk for a number of medical complications, including type 2 diabetes, hypertension, sleep apnea, and orthopedic problems (Henry J. Kaiser Family Foundation, 2004, p. 1).

If the organization has a familiar abbreviation, you may include it in brackets the first time you cite the source and use the abbreviation alone in later citations.

> **FIRST CITATION** (National Institute of Mental Health [NIMH], 2001)

> **LATER CITATIONS** (NIMH, 2001)

■ **8. TWO OR MORE WORKS IN THE SAME PARENTHESES** When your parenthetical citation names two or more works, put them in the same order that they appear in the reference list, separated by semicolons.

> Researchers have indicated that studies of pharmacological treatments for childhood obesity are inconclusive (Berkowitz et al., 2003; McDuffie et al., 2003).

■ **9. AUTHORS WITH THE SAME LAST NAME**   To avoid confusion, use initials with the last names if your reference list includes two or more authors with the same last name.

> Research by E. Smith (1989) revealed that . . .

■ **10. PERSONAL COMMUNICATION**   Interviews, memos, letters, e-mail, and similar unpublished person-to-person communications should be cited as follows:

> One of Atkinson's colleagues, who has studied the effect of the media on children's eating habits, has contended that advertisers for snack foods will need to design ads responsibly for their younger viewers (F. Johnson, personal communication, October 20, 2004).

Do not include personal communications in your reference list.

■ **11. AN ELECTRONIC DOCUMENT**   When possible, cite an electronic document as you would any other document (using the author-date style).

> Atkinson (2001) found that children who spent at least four hours a day watching TV were less likely to engage in adequate physical activity during the week.

Electronic sources may lack authors' names or dates. In addition, they may lack page numbers (required in some citations). Here are APA's guidelines for handling sources without authors' names, dates, or page numbers.

Unknown author
If no author is named, mention the title of the document in a signal phrase or give the first word or two of the title in

parentheses (see also item 6). (If an organization serves as the author, see item 7.)

> The body's basal metabolic rate, or BMR, is a measure of its at-rest energy requirement ("Exercise," 2003).

Unknown date

When the date is unknown, APA recommends using the abbreviation "n.d." (for "no date").

> Attempts to establish a definitive link between television programming and children's eating habits have been problematic (Magnus, n.d.).

No page numbers

APA ordinarily requires page numbers for quotations, and it recommends them for summaries or paraphrases from long sources. When an electronic source lacks stable numbered pages, your citation should include — if possible — information that will help readers locate the particular passage being cited.

When an electronic document has numbered paragraphs, use the paragraph number preceded by the symbol ¶ or by the abbreviation "para.": (Hall, 2001, ¶ 5) *or* (Hall, 2001, para. 5). If neither a page nor a paragraph number is given and the document contains headings, cite the appropriate heading and indicate which paragraph under that heading you are referring to.

> Hoppin and Taveras (2004) pointed out that several other medications were classified by the Drug Enforcement Administration as having the "potential for abuse" (Weight-Loss Drugs section, para. 6).

NOTE: Electronic files using portable document format (PDF) often have stable page numbers. For such sources, give the page number in the parenthetical citation.

■ **12. INDIRECT SOURCE** If you use a source that was cited in another source (a secondary source), name the original source in your signal phrase. List the secondary source in your reference list and include it in your parenthetical citation, preceded by the words "as cited in." In the following example, Critser is the secondary source.

> Former surgeon general Dr. David Satcher described "a nation of young people seriously at risk of starting out obese and dooming themselves to the difficult task of overcoming a tough illness" (as cited in Critser, 2003, p. 4).

■ **13. TWO OR MORE WORKS BY THE SAME AUTHOR IN THE SAME YEAR** When your list of references includes more than one work by the same author in the same year, use lowercase letters ("a," "b," and so on) with the year to order the entries in the reference list. (See item 6 on p. 196.) Use those same letters with the year in the in-text citation.

> Research by Durgin (2003b) has yielded new findings about the role of counseling in treating childhood obesity.

APA list of references

In APA style, the alphabetical list of works cited, which appears at the end of the paper, is titled "References." Following are models illustrating APA style for entries in the list of references. Observe all details: capitalization, punctuation, use of italics, and so on. For advice on preparing the reference list, see pages 214–15. For a sample reference list, see pages 227–28.

Directory to APA references (bibliographic entries)

General guidelines for listing authors

Alphabetize entries in the list of references by authors' last names; if a work has no author, alphabetize it by its title. The first element of each entry is important because citations in the text of the paper refer to it and readers will be looking for it in the alphabetized list. The date of publication appears immediately after the first element of the citation.

NAME AND DATE CITED IN TEXT

Duncan (2001) has reported that . . .

BEGINNING OF ENTRY IN THE LIST OF REFERENCES

Duncan, B. (2001).

Items 1–4 show how to begin an entry for a work with a single author, multiple authors, an organization as author, and an unknown author. Items 5 and 6 show how to begin an entry when your list includes two or more works by the same author or two or more works by the same author in the same year. What comes after the first element of your citation will depend on the kind of source you are citing (see items 7–31).

■ **1. SINGLE AUTHOR** Begin the entry with the author's last name, followed by a comma and the author's initial(s). Then give the date in parentheses.

Perez, E. (2001).

■ **2. MULTIPLE AUTHORS** List up to six authors by last names followed by initials. Use an ampersand (&) between the names of two authors or, if there are more than two authors, before the name of the last author.

DuNann, D. W., & Koger, S. M. (2004).

Sloan, F. A., Stout, E. M., Whetten-Goldstein, K., & Liang, L. (2000).

If there are more than six authors, list the first six and "et al." (meaning "and others") to indicate that there are others.

■ **3. ORGANIZATION AS AUTHOR** When the author is an organization, begin with the name of the organization.

American Psychiatric Association. (2003).

NOTE: If the organization is also the publisher, see item 28.

■ **4. UNKNOWN AUTHOR** Begin the entry with the work's title. Titles of books are italicized; titles of articles are neither italicized nor put in quotation marks. (For rules on capitalization of titles, see p. 215.)

Oxford essential world atlas. (2001).

Omega-3 fatty acids. (2004, November 23).

■ **5. TWO OR MORE WORKS BY THE SAME AUTHOR** Use the author's name for all entries. List the entries by year, the earliest first.

Schlechty, P. C. (1997).

Schlechty, P. C. (2001).

■ **6. TWO OR MORE WORKS BY THE SAME AUTHOR IN THE SAME YEAR** List the works alphabetically by title. In the parentheses, following the year, add "a," "b," and so on. Use these same letters when giving the year in the in-text citation. (See also p. 214.)

Durgin, P. A. (2003a). At-risk behaviors in children.

Durgin, P. A. (2003b). Treating obesity with psychotherapy.

Articles in periodicals

This section shows how to prepare an entry for an article in a periodical such as a scholarly journal, a magazine, or a newspaper. In addition to consulting the models in this section, you may need to refer to items 1–6 (general guidelines for listing authors).

NOTE: For articles on consecutive pages, provide the range of pages at the end of the citation (see item 7 for an example). When an article does not appear on consecutive pages, give all page numbers: A1, A17.

■ **7. ARTICLE IN A JOURNAL PAGINATED BY VOLUME** Many professional journals continue page numbers throughout the year instead of beginning each issue with page 1; at the end of the year, the issues are collected in a volume. After the italicized title of the journal, give the volume number (also italicized), followed by the page numbers.

Morawski, J. (2000). Social psychology a century ago. *American Psychologist, 55,* 427-431.

■ **8. ARTICLE IN A JOURNAL PAGINATED BY ISSUE** When each issue of a journal begins with page 1, include the issue number in parentheses after the volume number. Italicize the volume number but not the issue number.

Smith, S. (2003). Government and nonprofits in the modern age. *Society, 40*(4), 36-45.

Citation at a glance: Article in a periodical (APA)

To cite an article in a periodical in APA style, include the following elements:

1 Author
2 Date of publication
3 Title of article
4 Name of periodical
5 Volume and issue numbers
6 Page

REFERENCE LIST ENTRY FOR AN ARTICLE IN A PERIODICAL

┌─**1**─┐ ┌─**2**─┐ ┌────**3**────┐ ┌────**4**────┐ ┌**5**┐ ┌**6**┐
Hoxby, C. M. (2002). The power of peers. *Education Next, 2*(2), 57-63.

■ **9. ARTICLE IN A MAGAZINE** In addition to the year of publication, list the month and, for weekly magazines, the day. If there is a volume number, include it (italicized) after the title.

Raloff, J. (2001, May 12). Lead therapy won't help most kids. *Science News, 159,* 292.

■ **10. ARTICLE IN A NEWSPAPER** Begin with the name of the author followed by the exact date of publication. (If the author is unknown, see also item 4.) Page numbers are introduced with "p." (or "pp.").

Lohr, S. (2004, December 3). Health care technology is a promise unfinanced. *The New York Times,* p. C5.

■ **11. LETTER TO THE EDITOR** Letters to the editor appear in journals, magazines, and newspapers. Follow the appropriate model and insert the words "Letter to the editor" in brackets before the name of the periodical.

Carter, R. (2000, July). Shot in the dark? [Letter to the editor]. *Scientific American, 283*(1), 8.

■ **12. REVIEW** Reviews of books and other media appear in a variety of periodicals. Follow the appropriate model for the periodical. For a review of a book, give the title of the review (if there is one), followed by the words "Review of the book" and the title of the book in brackets.

Gleick, E. (2000, December 14). The burdens of genius [Review of the book *The Last Samurai*]. *Time, 156,* 171.

For a film review, write "Review of the motion picture," and for a TV review, write "Review of the television program." Treat other media in a similar way.

Books

In addition to consulting the items in this section, you may need to refer to items 1–6 (general guidelines for listing authors).

■ **13. BASIC FORMAT FOR A BOOK** Begin with the author's name, followed by the date and the book's title. End with the place of publication and the name of the publisher. Take the information about the book from its title page and copyright page. If more than one place of publication is given, use only the first; if more than one date is given, use the most recent one.

Highmore, B. (2001). *Everyday life and cultural theory*. New York: Routledge.

■ **14. BOOK WITH AN EDITOR** For a book with an editor but no author, begin with the name of the editor (or editors) followed by the abbreviation "Ed." (or "Eds.") in parentheses.

Bronfen, E., & Kavka, M. (Eds.). (2001). *Feminist consequences: Theory for a new century*. New York: Columbia University Press.

For a book with an author and an editor, begin with the author's name. Give the editor's name in parentheses after the title of the book, followed by the abbreviation "Ed." (or "Eds.").

Plath, S. (2000). *The unabridged journals* (K. V. Kukil, Ed.). New York: Anchor.

■ **15. TRANSLATION** After the title, name the translator, followed by the abbreviation "Trans.," in parentheses. Add the original date of the work's publication in parentheses at the end of the entry.

Citation at a glance: Book (APA)

To cite a book in APA style, include the following elements:

1 Author
2 Date of publication
3 Title and subtitle
4 City of publication
5 Publisher

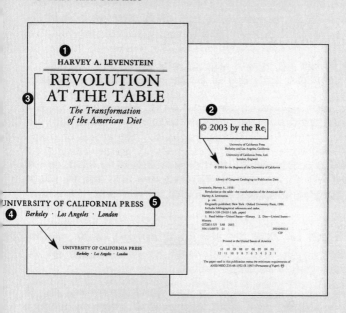

© 2003 by the Re:

University of California Press
Berkeley and Los Angeles, California

University of California Press, Ltd.
London, England

© 2003 by the Regents of the University of California

Library of Congress Cataloging-in-Publication Data

Levenstein, Harvey A., 1938–
Revolution at the table : the transformation of the American diet /
Harvey A. Levenstein.
p. cm.
Originally published: New York : Oxford University Press, 1988.
Includes bibliographical references and index.
ISBN 0-520-23439-1 (alk. paper)
1. Food habits—United States—History. 2. Diet—United States—
History.
GT2853.U5 L48 2003
394.1/2/0973 21   2003040211
                                                              CIP

Printed in the United States of America

11 10 09 08 07 06 05 04 03
12 11 10 9 8 7 6 5 4 3 2 1

The paper used in this publication meets the minimum requirements of
ANSI/NISO Z39.48-1992 (R 1997) (Permanence of Paper). ♾

REFERENCE LIST ENTRY FOR A BOOK

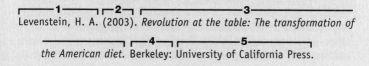

┌────1────┐ ┌─2─┐ ┌──────────────3──────────────
Levenstein, H. A. (2003). *Revolution at the table: The transformation of*

┌──────────┐ ┌─4──┐ ┌──────────5──────────┐
the American diet. Berkeley: University of California Press.

Steinberg, M. D. (2003). *Voices of revolution, 1917.* (M. Schwartz, Trans.). New Haven, CT: Yale University Press. (Original work published 2001)

■ **16. EDITION OTHER THAN THE FIRST**   Include the number of the edition in parentheses after the title.

Helfer, M. E., Keme, R. S., & Drugman, R. D. (1997). *The battered child* (5th ed.). Chicago: University of Chicago Press.

■ **17. ARTICLE OR CHAPTER IN AN EDITED BOOK**   Begin with the author, year of publication, and title of the article or chapter. Then write "In" and give the editor's name, followed by "Ed." in parentheses; the title of the book; and the page numbers of the article or chapter in parentheses. End with the book's publication information.

Luban, D. (2000). The ethics of wrongful obedience. In D. L. Rhode (Ed.), *Ethics in practice: Lawyers' roles, responsibilities, and regulation* (pp. 94-120). New York: Oxford University Press.

■ **18. MULTIVOLUME WORK**   Give the number of volumes after the title.

Luo, J. *Encyclopedia of contemporary Chinese civilization* (Vols. 1-2). Westport, CT: Greenwood Publishing Group.

Electronic sources

This section shows how to prepare reference list entries for a variety of electronic sources, including articles in online periodicals and databases, Web documents, and e-mail.

■ **19. ARTICLE FROM AN ONLINE PERIODICAL** When citing online articles, follow the guidelines for printed articles (see items 7–12), giving whatever information is available in the online source. If the article also appears in a printed journal, a URL is not required; instead, include "Electronic version" in brackets after the title of the article.

Whitmeyer, J. M. (2000). Power through appointment [Electronic version]. *Social Science Research, 29*(4), 535-555.

If there is no print version, include the date you accessed the source and the article's URL.

Ashe, D. D., & McCutcheon, L. E. (2001). Shyness, loneliness, and attitude toward celebrities. *Current Research in Social Psychology, 6*(9). Retrieved July 3, 2001, from http://www.uiowa.edu/ ~grpproc/crisp/crisp.6.9.htm

NOTE: When you have retrieved an article from a newspaper's searchable Web site, give the URL for the site, not for the exact source.

Cary, B. (2001, June 18). Mentors of the mind. *Los Angeles Times*. Retrieved July 5, 2001, from http://www.latimes.com

■ **20. ARTICLE FROM A DATABASE** To cite an article from a library's subscription database, include the publication information from the source (see items 7–12). End the citation with your date of access, the name of the database, and the document number (if applicable).

Holliday, R. E., & Hayes, B. K. (2001). Dissociating automatic and intentional processes in children's eyewitness memory. *Journal of Experimental Child Psychology, 75*(1), 1-5. Retrieved February 21, 2001, from Expanded Academic ASAP database (A59317972).

Citation at a glance: Article from a database (APA)

To cite an article from a database in APA style, include the following elements:

1 Author
2 Date of publication
3 Title of article
4 Name of periodical
5 Volume and issue numbers
6 Page numbers
7 Date of access
8 Name of database
9 Document number

ON-SCREEN VIEW OF DATABASE RECORD

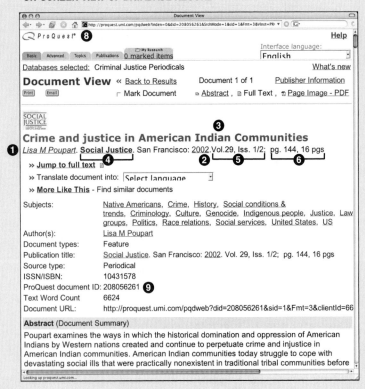

PRINTOUT OF RECORD
AND BEGINNING OF ARTICLE

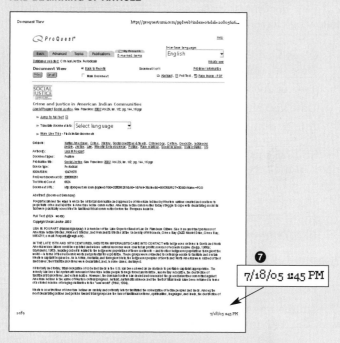

REFERENCE LIST ENTRY FOR AN ARTICLE FROM A DATABASE

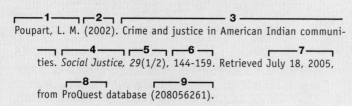

Poupart, L. M. (2002). Crime and justice in American Indian communi-

ties. *Social Justice, 29*(1/2), 144-159. Retrieved July 18, 2005,

from ProQuest database (208056261).

■ **21. NONPERIODICAL WEB DOCUMENT**   To cite a nonperiodical Web document, such as a report, list as many of the following elements as are available.

> Author's name
>
> Date of publication (if there is no date, use "n.d.")
>
> Title of document (in italics)
>
> Date you accessed the source
>
> A URL that will take readers directly to the source

In the first model, the source has both an author and a date; in the second, the source lacks a date.

Cain, A., & Burris, M. (1999, April). *Investigation of the use of mobile phones while driving.* Retrieved January 15, 2000, from http://www.cutr.eng.usf.edu/its/mobile_phone_text.htm

Archer, Z. (n.d.). *Exploring nonverbal communication.* Retrieved July 18, 2001, from http://zzyx.ucsc.edu/~archer

If a source has no author, begin with the title and follow it with the date in parentheses.

NOTE: If you retrieved the source from a university program's Web site, name the program in your retrieval statement.

Cosmides, L., & Tooby, J. (1997). *Evolutionary psychology: A primer.* Retrieved July 5, 2001, from the University of California, Santa Barbara, Center for Evolutionary Psychology Web site: http://www.psych.ucsb.edu/research/cep/primer.html

■ **22. CHAPTER OR SECTION IN A WEB DOCUMENT**   Begin with the author, the year of publication, and the title of the chapter or section. Then write "In" and give the title of the document, followed by identifying information in parentheses. End with your date of access and the URL for the chapter or section.

Heuer, R. J., Jr. (1999). Keeping an open mind. In *Psychology of intelligence analysis* (chap. 6). Retrieved July 7, 2001, from http://www.cia.gov/csi/books/19104/art9.html

■ **23. E-MAIL** E-mail messages and other personal communications are not included in the list of references.

■ **24. ONLINE POSTING** If an online posting cannot be retrieved (because the newsgroup or forum does not maintain archives), cite it as a personal communication in the text of your paper and do not include it in the list of references. If the posting can be retrieved from an archive, treat it as follows, giving as much information as is available.

Eaton, S. (2001, June 12). Online transactions [Msg 2]. Message posted to news://sci.psychology.psychotherapy.moderated

■ **25. COMPUTER PROGRAM** Add the words "Computer software" in brackets after the title of the program.

Kaufmann, W. J., III, & Comins, N. F. (2003). Discovering the universe (Version 6.0) [Computer software]. New York: Freeman.

Other sources

■ **26. DISSERTATION ABSTRACT**

Yoshida, Y. (2001). Essays in urban transportation (Doctoral dissertation, Boston College, 2001). *Dissertation Abstracts International, 62,* 7741A.

Citation at a glance: Document from a Web site (APA)

To cite a document from a Web site in APA style, include the following elements:

1 Author

2 Date of publication or most recent update

3 Title of document on Web site

4 Title of Web site or section of site

5 Date of access

6 URL of document

BROWSER PRINTOUT OF WEB SITE

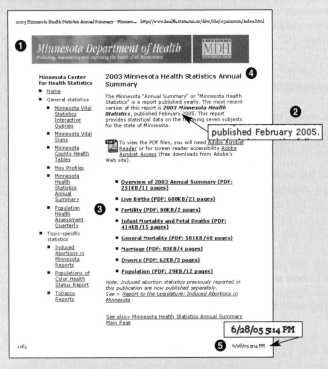

ON-SCREEN VIEW OF DOCUMENT

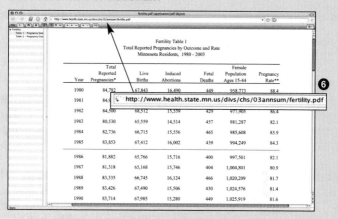

Fertility Table 1
Total Reported Pregnancies by Outcome and Rate
Minnesota Residents, 1980 - 2003

Year	Total Reported Pregnancies*	Live Births	Induced Abortions	Fetal Deaths	Female Population Ages 15-44	Pregnancy Rate**
1980	84,782	67,843	16,490	449	958,773	88.4
1981	84,9					
1982	84,500	68,512	15,559	429	977,905	86.4
1983	80,530	65,559	14,514	457	981,287	82.1
1984	82,736	66,715	15,556	465	985,608	83.9
1985	83,853	67,412	16,002	439	994,249	84.3
1986	81,882	65,766	15,716	400	997,501	82.1
1987	81,318	65,168	15,746	404	1,004,801	80.9
1988	83,335	66,745	16,124	466	1,020,209	81.7
1989	83,426	67,490	15,506	430	1,024,576	81.4
1990	83,714	67,985	15,280	449	1,025,919	81.6

http://www.health.state.mn.us/divs/chs/03annsum/fertility.pdf

REFERENCE LIST ENTRY FOR A DOCUMENT FROM A WEB SITE

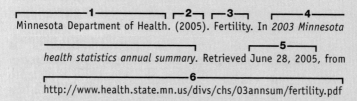

Minnesota Department of Health. (2005). Fertility. In *2003 Minnesota health statistics annual summary*. Retrieved June 28, 2005, from http://www.health.state.mn.us/divs/chs/03annsum/fertility.pdf

■ **27. GOVERNMENT DOCUMENT**

U.S. Census Bureau. (2000). *Statistical abstract of the United States.*
Washington, DC: U.S. Government Printing Office.

■ **28. REPORT FROM A PRIVATE ORGANIZATION**   If the publisher
is the author, give the word "Author" as the publisher. If the
report has an author, begin with the author's name, and
name the publisher at the end.

American Psychiatric Association. (2000). *Practice guidelines for the*
treatment of patients with eating disorders (2nd ed.). Washington,
DC: Author.

■ **29. CONFERENCE PROCEEDINGS**

Stahl, G. (Ed.). (2002). *Proceedings of CSCL '02: Computer support for*
collaborative learning. Hillsdale, NJ: Erlbaum.

■ **30. MOTION PICTURE**   To cite a motion picture (film,
video, or DVD), list the director and the year of the picture's
release. Give the title, followed by "Motion picture" in
brackets, the country where it was made, and the name of
the studio. If the motion picture is difficult to find, include
instead the name and address of its distributor.

Soderbergh, S. (Director). (2000). *Traffic* [Motion picture]. United
States: Gramercy Pictures.

Spurlock, M. (Director). (2004). *Super size me* [Motion picture].
(Available from IDP Films, 1133 Broadway, Suite 926, New York,
NY 10010)

■   **31. TELEVISION PROGRAM**   To cite a television program, list the producer and the date it was aired. Give the title, followed by "Television broadcast" in brackets, the city, and the television network or service.

Pratt, C. (Executive Producer). (2001, December 2). *Face the nation* [Television broadcast]. Washington, DC: CBS News.

For a television series, use the year in which the series was produced, and follow the title with "Television series" in brackets. For an episode in a series, list the writer and director and the year. After the episode title put "Television series episode" in brackets. Follow with information about the series.

Janows, J. (Executive Producer). (2000). *Culture shock* [Television series]. Boston: WGBH.

Loeterman, B. (Writer), & Gale, B. (Director). (2000). Real justice [Television series episode]. In M. Sullivan (Executive Producer), *Frontline*. Boston: WGBH.

APA manuscript format

The American Psychological Association makes a number of recommendations for formatting a paper and preparing a list of references. The following guidelines are consistent with advice given in the *Publication Manual of the American Psychological Association*, 5th ed. (Washington: APA, 2001).

Formatting the paper

APA guidelines for formatting a paper are endorsed by many instructors in the social sciences.

MATERIALS AND TYPEFACE Use good-quality $8\frac{1}{2}'' \times 11''$ white paper. Avoid a typeface that is unusual or hard to read.

TITLE PAGE The APA manual does not provide guidelines for preparing the title page of a college paper, but most instructors will want you to include one. See page 216 for an example.

PAGE NUMBERS AND RUNNING HEAD The title page is numbered as page i; the abstract page, if there is one, is numbered as page ii. Use arabic numerals, beginning with 1, for the rest of the paper. In the upper right-hand corner of each page, type a short version of your title, followed by five spaces and the page number. Number all pages, including the title page.

MARGINS, LINE SPACING, AND PARAGRAPH INDENTS Use margins of one inch on all sides of the page. Left-align the text.

Double-space throughout the paper, but single-space footnotes. Indent the first line of each paragraph one-half inch (or five spaces).

LONG QUOTATIONS AND FOOTNOTES When a quotation is longer than forty words, set it off from the text by indenting it one-half inch (or five spaces) from the left margin. Double-space the quotation. Quotation marks are not needed when a quotation has been set off from the text. See page 225 for an example.

Place each footnote, if any, at the bottom of the page on which the text reference occurs. Double-space between the last line of text on the page and the footnote. Indent the first line of the footnote one-half inch (or five spaces). Begin the note with the superscript arabic numeral that corresponds to the number in the text. See page 218 for an example.

ABSTRACT   If your instructor requires one, include an abstract immediately after the title page. Center the word Abstract one inch from the top of the page; double-space the abstract as you do the body of your paper.

An abstract is a 100-to-120-word paragraph that provides readers with a quick overview of your essay. It should express your main idea and your key points; it might also briefly suggest any implications or applications of the research you discuss in the paper. See page 217 for an example.

HEADINGS   Although headings are not always necessary, their use is encouraged in the social sciences. For most undergraduate papers, one level of heading will usually be sufficient.

In APA style, major headings are centered. Capitalize the first word of the heading, along with all words except articles, short prepositions, and coordinating conjunctions.

VISUALS   The APA classifies visuals as tables and figures (figures include graphs, charts, drawings, and photographs). Keep visuals as simple as possible. Label each table with an arabic numeral (Table 1, Table 2, and so on) and provide a clear title. The label and title should appear on separate lines above the table, flush left and single-spaced. Below the table, give its source in a note. If any data in the table require an explanatory footnote, use a superscript lowercase letter in the body of the table and in a footnote following the source note. Single-space source notes and footnotes and do not indent the first line of each note. See page 221 for an example.

For each figure, place a label and a caption below the figure, flush left and single-spaced. They need not appear on separate lines.

In the text of your paper, discuss the most significant features of each visual. Place the visual as close as possible to the sentences that relate to it unless your instructor prefers it in an appendix.

Preparing the list of references

Begin your list of references on a new page at the end of the paper. Center the title References about one inch from the top of the page. Double-space throughout. For a sample reference list, see pages 227–28.

INDENTING ENTRIES   APA recommends using a hanging indent: Type the first line of an entry flush left and indent any additional lines one-half inch (or five spaces), as shown on pages 227–28.

ALPHABETIZING THE LIST   Alphabetize the reference list by the last names of the authors (or editors); when a work has no author or editor, alphabetize by the first word of the title other than *A, An,* or *The.*

If your list includes two or more works by the same author, arrange the entries by year, the earliest first. If your list includes two or more works by the same author in the same year, arrange them alphabetically by title. Add the letters "a," "b," and so on within the parentheses after the year. Use only the year for articles in journals: (2002a). Use the full date for articles in magazines and newspapers in the reference list: (2001a, July 7). Use only the year in the in-text citation.

AUTHORS' NAMES   Invert all authors' names and use initials instead of first names. With two or more authors, use an ampersand (&) before the last author's name. Separate the names with commas. Include names for the first six authors; if there are additional authors, end the list with "et al." (Latin for "and others").

TITLES OF BOOKS AND ARTICLES Italicize the titles and subtitles of books; capitalize only the first word of the title and subtitle (and all proper nouns). Capitalize names of periodicals as you would capitalize them normally.

ABBREVIATIONS FOR PAGE NUMBERS Abbreviations for "page" and "pages" ("p." and "pp.") are used before page numbers of newspaper articles and articles in edited books (see item 10 on p. 199 and item 17 on p. 202) but not before page numbers of articles appearing in magazines and scholarly journals (see items 7–9 on pp. 197 and 199).

BREAKING A URL When a URL must be divided, break it after a slash or before a period. Do not insert a hyphen.

See pages 227–28 for an example of how to type your list of references. For information about the exact format of each entry in your list, consult the models on pages 195–211.

Sample research paper: APA style

On the following pages is a research paper written by Luisa Mirano, a student in a psychology class. Mirano's assignment was to write a review of the literature paper documented with APA-style citations and references.

Can Medication Cure Obesity in Children?
A Review of the Literature

Luisa Mirano
Psychology 107, Section B
Professor Kang
October 31, 2004

Abstract

In recent years, policymakers and medical experts have expressed alarm about the growing problem of childhood obesity in the United States. While most agree that the issue deserves attention, consensus dissolves around how to respond to the problem. This literature review examines one approach to treating childhood obesity: medication. The paper compares the effectiveness for adolescents of the only two drugs approved by the Food and Drug Administration (FDA) for long-term treatment of obesity, sibutramine and orlistat. This examination of pharmacological treatments for obesity points out the limitations of medication and suggests the need for a comprehensive solution that combines medical, social, behavioral, and political approaches to this complex problem.

Can Medication Cure Obesity in Children?

A Review of the Literature

In March 2004, U.S. Surgeon General Richard Carmona called attention to a health problem in the United States that, until recently, has been overlooked: childhood obesity. Carmona said that the "astounding" 15% child obesity rate constitutes an "epidemic." Since the early 1980s, that rate has "doubled in children and tripled in adolescents." Now more than 9 million children are classified as obese (paras. 3, 6).[1] While the traditional response to a medical epidemic is to hunt for a vaccine or a cure-all pill, childhood obesity has proven more elusive. The lack of success of recent initiatives suggests that medication might not be the answer for the escalating problem. This literature review considers whether the use of medication is a promising approach for solving the childhood obesity problem by responding to the following questions:

1. What are the implications of childhood obesity?
2. Is medication effective at treating childhood obesity?
3. Is medication safe for children?
4. Is medication the best solution?

Understanding the limitations of medical treatments for children highlights the complexity of the childhood obesity

---

[1]Obesity is measured in terms of body-mass index (BMI): weight in kilograms divided by square of height in meters. An adult with a BMI 30 or higher is considered obese. In children and adolescents, obesity is defined in relation to others of the same age and gender. An adolescent with a BMI in the 95th percentile for his or her age and gender is considered obese.

problem in the United States and underscores the need for physicians, advocacy groups, and policymakers to search for other solutions.

What Are the Implications of Childhood Obesity?

Obesity can be a devastating problem from both an individual and a societal perspective. Obesity puts children at risk for a number of medical complications, including type 2 diabetes, hypertension, sleep apnea, and orthopedic problems (Henry J. Kaiser Family Foundation, 2004, p. 1). Researchers Hoppin and Taveras (2004) have noted that obesity is often associated with psychological issues such as depression, anxiety, and binge eating (Table 4).

Obesity also poses serious problems for a society struggling to cope with rising health care costs. The cost of treating obesity currently totals $117 billion per year--a price, according to the surgeon general, "second only to the cost of [treating] tobacco use" (Carmona, 2004, para. 9). And as the number of children who suffer from obesity grows, long-term costs will only increase.

Is Medication Effective at Treating Childhood Obesity?

The widening scope of the obesity problem has prompted medical professionals to rethink old conceptions of the disorder and its causes. As researchers Yanovski and Yanovski (2002) have explained, obesity was once considered "either a moral failing or evidence of underlying psychopathology" (p. 592). But this view has shifted: Many medical professionals now consider obesity a biomedical rather than a moral condition, influenced by both genetic and environmental factors. Yanovski and Yanovski have further noted that the development of weight-loss medications in the early 1990s showed that "obesity should be treated in the same manner as any other chronic disease . . . through the long-term use of medication" (p. 592).

The search for the right long-term medication has been complicated. Many of the drugs authorized by the Food and Drug Administration (FDA) in the early 1990s proved to be a disappointment. Two of the medications--fenfluramine and dexfenfluramine--were withdrawn from the market because of severe side effects (Yanovski & Yanovski, 2002, p. 592), and several others were classified by the Drug Enforcement Administration as having the "potential for abuse" (Hoppin & Taveras, 2004, Weight-Loss Drugs section, para. 6). Currently only two medications have been approved by the FDA for long-term treatment of obesity: sibutramine (marketed as Meridia) and orlistat (marketed as Xenical). This section compares studies on the effectiveness of each.

Sibutramine suppresses appetite by blocking the reuptake of the neurotransmitters serotonin and norepinephrine in the brain. Though the drug won FDA approval in 1998, experiments to test its effectiveness for younger patients came considerably later. In 2003, University of Pennsylvania researchers Berkowitz, Wadden, Tershakovec, and Cronquist released the first double-blind placebo study testing the effect of sibutramine on adolescents, aged 13-17, over a 12-month period. Their findings are summarized in Table 1.

After 6 months, the group receiving medication had lost 4.6 kg (about 10 pounds) more than the control group.

Obesity in Children   4

Table 1

Effectiveness of Sibutramine and Orlistat in Adolescents

Medication	Subjects	Treatment[a]	Side effects	Average weight loss/gain
Sibutra-mine	Control	0-6 mos.: placebo 6-12 mos.: sibutra-mine	Mos. 6-12: increased blood pres-sure; in-creased pulse rate	After 6 mos.: loss of 3.2 kg (7 lb) After 12 mos.: loss of 4.5 kg (9.9 lb)
	Medi-cated	0-12 mos.: sibutra-mine	Increased blood pres-sure; increased pulse rate	After 6 mos.: loss of 7.8 kg (17.2 lb) After 12 mos.: loss of 7.0 kg (15.4 lb)
Orlistat	Control	0-12 mos.: placebo	None	Gain of 0.67 kg (1.5 lb)
	Medi-cated	0-12 mos.: orlistat	Oily spot-ting; flatu-lence; abdominal discomfort	Loss of 1.3 kg (2.9 lb)

Note. The data on sibutramine are adapted from "Behavior Therapy and
Sibutramine for the Treatment of Adolescent Obesity" [Electronic version],
by R. I. Berkowitz, T. A. Wadden, A. M. Tershakovec, & J. L. Cronquist,
2003, *Journal of the American Medical Association, 289,* pp. 1807-1809. The
data on orlistat are adapted from *Xenical (orlistat) Capsules: Complete
Product Information,* by Roche Laboratories, December 2003, retrieved
October 11, 2004, from http://www.rocheusa.com/products/xenical/pi.pdf
[a]The medication and/or placebo were combined with behavioral therapy in
all groups over all time periods.

But during the second half of the study, when both groups received sibutramine, the results were more ambiguous. In months 6-12, the group that continued to take sibutramine gained an average of 0.8 kg, or roughly 2 pounds; the control group, which switched from placebo to sibutramine, lost 1.3 kg, or roughly 3 pounds (p. 1808). Both groups received behavioral therapy covering diet, exercise, and mental health.

These results paint a murky picture of the effectiveness of the medication: While initial data seemed promising, the results after one year raised questions about whether medication-induced weight loss could be sustained over time. As Berkowitz et al. (2003) advised, "Until more extensive safety and efficacy data are available, . . . weight-loss medications should be used only on an experimental basis for adolescents" (p. 1811).

A study testing the effectiveness of orlistat in adolescents showed similarly ambiguous results. The FDA approved orlistat in 1999 but did not authorize it for adolescents until December 2003. Roche Laboratories (2003), maker of orlistat, released results of a one-year study testing the drug on 539 obese adolescents, aged 12-16. The drug, which promotes weight loss by blocking fat absorption in the large intestine, showed some effectiveness in adolescents: an average loss of 1.3 kg, or roughly 3 pounds, for subjects taking orlistat for one year, as opposed to an average gain of 0.67 kg, or 1.5 pounds, for the control group (pp. 8-9). See Table 1.

Short-term studies of orlistat have shown slightly more dramatic results. Researchers at the National Institute of Child Health and Human Development tested 20 adolescents,

aged 12-16, over a three-month period and found that orlistat, combined with behavioral therapy, produced an average
weight loss of 4.4 kg, or 9.7 pounds (McDuffie et al., 2002,
p. 646). The study was not controlled against a placebo
group; therefore, the relative effectiveness of orlistat in this
case remains unclear.

Is Medication Safe for Children?

While modest weight loss has been documented for
both medications, each carries risks of certain side effects.
Sibutramine has been observed to increase blood pressure and
pulse rate. In 2002, a consumer group claimed that the medication was related to the deaths of 19 people and filed a
petition with the Department of Health and Human Services
to ban the medication (Hilts, 2002). The sibutramine study
by Berkowitz et al. (2003) noted elevated blood pressure as a
side effect, and dosages had to be reduced or the medication
discontinued in 19 of the 43 subjects in the first six months
(p. 1809).

The main side effects associated with orlistat were
abdominal discomfort, oily spotting, fecal incontinence, and
nausea (Roche Laboratories, 2003, p. 13). More serious for
long-term health is the concern that orlistat, being a fat-
blocker, would affect absorption of fat-soluble vitamins, such
as vitamin D. However, the study found that this side effect
can be minimized or eliminated if patients take vitamin supplements two hours before or after administration of
orlistat (p. 10). With close monitoring of patients taking the
medication, many of the risks can be reduced.

Is Medication the Best Solution?

The data on the safety and efficacy of pharmacological treatments of childhood obesity raise the question of whether medication is the best solution for the problem. The treatments have clear costs for individual patients, including unpleasant side effects, little information about long-term use, and uncertainty that they will yield significant weight loss.

In purely financial terms, the drugs cost more than $3 a day on average (Duenwald, 2004, paras. 33, 36). In each of the clinical trials, use of medication was accompanied by an expensive regime of behavioral therapies, including counseling, nutritional education, fitness advising, and monitoring. As journalist Greg Critser (2003) noted in his book *Fat Land,* use of weight-loss drugs is unlikely to have an effect without the proper "support system"--one that includes doctors, facilities, time, and money (p. 3). For some, this level of care is prohibitively expensive.

A third complication is that the studies focused on adolescents aged 12-16, but obesity can begin at a much younger age. Little data exist to establish the safety or efficacy of medication for treating very young children.

While the scientific data on the concrete effects of these medications in children remain somewhat unclear, medication is not the only avenue for addressing the crisis. Both medical experts and policymakers recognize that solutions might come not only from a laboratory but also from policy, education, and advocacy. Indeed, a handbook designed to

educate doctors on obesity recommended a notably nonmed-
ical course of action, calling for "major changes in some
aspects of western culture" (Hoppin & Taveras, 2004,
Conclusion section, para. 1). Cultural change may not be the
typical realm of medical professionals, but the handbook urged
doctors to be proactive and "focus [their] energy on public
policies and interventions" (Conclusion section, para. 1).

The solutions proposed by a number of advocacy groups
underscore this interest in political and cultural change. A
report by the Henry J. Kaiser Family Foundation (2004) out-
lined trends that may have contributed to the childhood obesity crisis, including food advertising for children as well as

> a reduction in physical education classes and after-
> school athletic programs, an increase in the availability
> of sodas and snacks in public schools, the growth in
> the number of fast-food outlets . . . , and the
> increasing number of highly processed high-calorie and
> high-fat grocery products. (p. 1)

Addressing each of these areas requires more than a doctor
armed with a prescription pad; it requires a broad mobiliza-
tion not just of doctors and concerned parents but of educators, food industry executives, advertisers, and media representatives.

The barrage of possible approaches to combating childhood obesity--from scientific research to political lobbying--
indicates both the severity and the complexity of the problem.
While none of the medications currently available is a miracle
drug for curing the nation's 9 million obese children, research

has illuminated some of the underlying factors that affect obesity and has shown the need for a comprehensive approach to the problem that includes behavioral, medical, social, and political change.

References

Berkowitz, R. I., Wadden, T. A., Tershakovec, A. M., & Cronquist, J. L. (2003). Behavior therapy and sibutramine for the treatment of adolescent obesity [Electronic version]. *Journal of the American Medical Association, 289*, 1805-1812.

Carmona, R. H. (2004, March 2). *The growing epidemic of childhood obesity*. Testimony before the Subcommittee on Competition, Foreign Commerce, and Infrastructure of the U.S. Senate Committee on Commerce, Science, and Transportation. Retrieved October 10, 2004, from http://www.hhs.gov/asl/testify/t040302.html

Critser, G. (2003). *Fat land: How Americans became the fattest people in the world*. Boston: Houghton Mifflin.

Duenwald, M. (2004, January 6). Slim pickings: Looking beyond ephedra. *The New York Times,* p. F1. Retrieved October 12, 2004, from LexisNexis.

Henry J. Kaiser Family Foundation. (2004, February). *The role of media in childhood obesity*. Retrieved October 10, 2004, from http://www.kff.org/entmedia/7030.cfm

Hilts, P. J. (2002, March 20). Petition asks for removal of diet drug from market. *The New York Times,* p. A26. Retrieved October 12, 2004, from LexisNexis.

Hoppin, A. G., & Taveras, E. M. (2004, June 25). Assessment and management of childhood and adolescent obesity. *Clinical Update*. Retrieved October 12, 2004, from Medscape Web site: http://www.medscape.com/viewarticle/481633

McDuffie, J. R., Calis, K. A., Uwaifo, G. I., Sebring, N. G., Fallon, E. M., Hubbard, V. S., et al. (2003). Three-month tolerability of orlistat in adolescents with obesity-related comorbid conditions [Electronic version]. *Obesity Research, 10,* 642-650.

Roche Laboratories. (2003, December). *Xenical (orlistat) capsules: Complete product information.* Retrieved October 11, 2004, from http://www.rocheusa.com/products/xenical/pi.pdf

Yanovski, S. Z., & Yanovski, J. A. (2002). Drug therapy: Obesity [Electronic version]. *The New England Journal of Medicine, 346,* 591-602.

Chicago Style: History

Most assignments in history and other humanities classes are based to some extent on reading. At times you will be asked to respond to one or two readings, such as essays or historical documents. At other times you may be asked to write a research paper that draws on a wide variety of sources.

Most history instructors and some humanities instructors require you to document sources with footnotes or endnotes based on *The Chicago Manual of Style*, 15th ed. (Chicago: U of Chicago P, 2003).

Chicago documentation style

Professors in history and some humanities courses often require footnotes or endnotes based on *The Chicago Manual of Style.* When you use *Chicago*-style notes, you will usually be asked to include a bibliography at the end of your paper (see p. 250).

TEXT

A Union soldier, Jacob Thomas, claimed to have seen Forrest order the killing, but when asked to describe the six-foot-two general, he called him "a little bit of a man."[13]

FOOTNOTE OR ENDNOTE

13. Brian Steel Wills, *A Battle from the Start: The Life of Nathan Bedford Forrest* (New York: HarperCollins, 1992), 187.

BIBLIOGRAPHY ENTRY

Wills, Brian Steel. *A Battle from the Start: The Life of Nathan Bedford Forrest.* New York: HarperCollins, 1992.

First and subsequent notes for a source

The first time you cite a source, the note should include publishing information for that work as well as the page number on which the passage being cited may be found.

    1. Peter Burchard, *One Gallant Rush: Robert Gould Shaw and His Brave Black Regiment* (New York: St. Martin's, 1965), 85.

For subsequent references to a source you have already cited, you may simply give the author's last name, a short form of the title, and the page or pages cited. A short form of the title of a book is italicized; a short form of the title of an article is put in quotation marks.

    4. Burchard, *One Gallant Rush,* 31.

When you have two consecutive notes from the same source, you may use "Ibid." (meaning "in the same place") and the page number for the second note. Use "Ibid." alone if the page number is the same.

    5. Jack Hurst, *Nathan Bedford Forrest: A Biography* (New York: Knopf, 1993), 8.

    6. Ibid., 174.

Chicago-*style bibliography*

A bibliography, which appears at the end of your paper, lists every work you have cited in your notes; in addition, it may include works that you consulted but did not cite. For advice on constructing the list, see page 243. A sample bibliography appears on page 250.

NOTE: If you include a bibliography, *The Chicago Manual of Style* suggests that you shorten all notes, including the first reference to a source, as described on page 230. Check with your instructor, however, to see whether using an abbreviated note for a first reference to a source is acceptable.

Model notes and bibliography entries

The following models are consistent with guidelines set forth in *The Chicago Manual of Style*, 15th ed. For each type of source, a model note appears first, followed by a model bibliography entry. The model note shows the format you should use when citing a source for the first time. For subsequent citations of a source, use shortened notes (see p. 230).

Directory to *Chicago*-style notes and bibliography entries

Books (print and online)

■ **1. BASIC FORMAT FOR A PRINT BOOK**

1. William H. Rehnquist, *The Supreme Court: A History* (New York: Knopf, 2001), 204.

Rehnquist, William H. *The Supreme Court: A History*. New York: Knopf, 2001.

■ **2. BASIC FORMAT FOR AN ONLINE BOOK**

2. Heinz Kramer, *A Changing Turkey: The Challenge to Europe and the United States* (Washington, DC: Brookings Press, 2000), 85, http://brookings.nap.edu/books/0815750234/html/index.html.

Kramer, Heinz. *A Changing Turkey: The Challenge to Europe and the United States*. Washington, DC: Brookings Press, 2000. http://brookings.nap.edu/books/0815750234/html/index.html.

■ **3. TWO OR THREE AUTHORS**

3. Michael D. Coe and Mark Van Stone, *Reading the Maya Glyphs* (London: Thames and Hudson, 2002), 129-30.

Coe, Michael D., and Mark Van Stone. *Reading the Maya Glyphs.* London: Thames and Hudson, 2002.

■ **4. FOUR OR MORE AUTHORS**

4. Lynn Hunt and others, *The Making of the West: Peoples and Cultures* (Boston: Bedford/St. Martin's, 2001), 541.

Hunt, Lynn, Thomas R. Martin, Barbara H. Rosenwein, R. Po-chia Hsia, and Bonnie G. Smith. *The Making of the West: Peoples and Cultures.* Boston: Bedford/St. Martin's, 2001.

■ **5. UNKNOWN AUTHOR**

5. *The Men's League Handbook on Women's Suffrage* (London, 1912), 23.

The Men's League Handbook on Women's Suffrage. London, 1912.

■ **6. EDITED WORK WITHOUT AN AUTHOR**

6. Jack Beatty, ed., *Colossus: How the Corporation Changed America* (New York: Broadway Books, 2001), 127.

Beatty, Jack, ed. *Colossus: How the Corporation Changed America.* New York: Broadway Books, 2001.

■ **7. EDITED WORK WITH AN AUTHOR**

7. Ted Poston, *A First Draft of History,* ed. Kathleen A. Hauke (Athens: University of Georgia Press, 2000), 46.

Poston, Ted. *A First Draft of History.* Edited by Kathleen A. Hauke. Athens: University of Georgia Press, 2000.

■ **8. TRANSLATED WORK**

8. Tonino Guerra, *Abandoned Places,* trans. Adria Bernardi (Barcelona: Guernica, 1999), 71.

Guerra, Tonino. *Abandoned Places.* Translated by Adria Bernardi. Barcelona: Guernica, 1999.

■ **9. EDITION OTHER THAN THE FIRST**

9. Andrew F. Rolle, *California: A History,* 5th ed. (Wheeling, IL: Harlan Davidson, 1998), 243.

Rolle, Andrew F. *California: A History.* 5th ed. Wheeling, IL: Harlan Davidson, 1998.

■ **10. VOLUME IN A MULTIVOLUME WORK**

10. James M. McPherson, *Ordeal by Fire,* vol. 2, *The Civil War* (New York: McGraw-Hill, 1993), 205.

McPherson, James M. *Ordeal by Fire.* Vol. 2, *The Civil War.* New York: McGraw-Hill, 1993.

■ **11. WORK IN AN ANTHOLOGY**

11. Zora Neale Hurston, "From *Dust Tracks on a Road,*" in *The Norton Book of American Autobiography,* ed. Jay Parini (New York: Norton, 1999), 336.

Hurston, Zora Neale. "From *Dust Tracks on a Road.*" In *The Norton Book of American Autobiography,* edited by Jay Parini, 333-43. New York: Norton, 1999.

■ **12. LETTER IN A PUBLISHED COLLECTION**

12. Thomas Gainsborough to Elizabeth Rasse, 1753, in *The Letters of Thomas Gainsborough,* ed. John Hayes (New Haven: Yale University Press, 2001), 5.

Gainsborough, Thomas. Letter to Elizabeth Rasse, 1753. In *The Letters of Thomas Gainsborough,* edited by John Hayes, 5. New Haven: Yale University Press, 2001.

■   **13. WORK IN A SERIES**

13. R. Keith Schoppa, *The Columbia Guide to Modern Chinese History,* Columbia Guides to Asian History (New York: Columbia University Press, 2000), 256-58.

Schoppa, R. Keith. *The Columbia Guide to Modern Chinese History.* Columbia Guides to Asian History. New York: Columbia University Press, 2000.

■   **14. ENCYCLOPEDIA OR DICTIONARY**

14. *Encyclopaedia Britannica,* 15th ed., s.v. "Monroe Doctrine."

NOTE: The abbreviation "s.v." is for the Latin *sub verbo* ("under the word").

Reference works are usually not included in the bibliography.

■   **15. SACRED TEXT**

15. Matt. 20.4-9 (Revised Standard Version).

15. Qur'an 18:1-3.

The Bible and other sacred texts are usually not included in the bibliography.

Articles in periodicals (print and online)

■   **16. ARTICLE IN A JOURNAL**   For an article in a print journal, include the volume and issue numbers and the date; end the bibliography entry with the page range of the article.

16. Jonathan Zimmerman, "Ethnicity and the History Wars in the 1920s," *Journal of American History* 87, no. 1 (2000): 101.

Zimmerman, Jonathan. "Ethnicity and the History Wars in the 1920s." *Journal of American History* 87, no. 1 (2000): 92-111.

For an article accessed through a database service such as *EBSCOhost* or for an article published online, include a URL. If the article is paginated, give a page number in the note and a page range in the bibliography. For unpaginated articles, page references are not possible, but in your note you may include a "locator," such as a numbered paragraph or a heading from the article, as in the example for an article published online.

Journal article from a database service
16. Eugene F. Provenzo Jr., "Time Exposure," *Educational Studies* 34, no. 2 (2003): 266, http://search.epnet.com.

Provenzo, Eugene F., Jr. "Time Exposure." *Educational Studies* 34, no. 2 (2003): 266-67. http://search.epnet.com.

Journal article published online
16. Linda Belau, "Trauma and the Material Signifier," *Postmodern Culture* 11, no. 2 (2001): par. 6, http://www.iath.virginia.edu/pmc/text-only/issue.101/11.2belau.txt.

Belau, Linda. "Trauma and the Material Signifier." *Postmodern Culture* 11, no. 2 (2001). http://www.iath.virginia.edu/pmc/text-only/issue.101/11.2belau.txt.

■ **17. ARTICLE IN A MAGAZINE** For a print article, provide a page number in the note and a page range in the bibliography.

17. Joy Williams, "One Acre," *Harper's,* February 2001, 62.

Williams, Joy. "One Acre." *Harper's,* February 2001, 58-65.

For an article accessed through a database service such as *FirstSearch* or for an article published online, include a URL. If the article is paginated, give a page number in the note and a page range in the bibliography. For unpaginated articles, page references are not possible.

Magazine article from a database service

17. David Pryce-Jones, "The Great Sorting Out: Postwar Iraq," *National Review,* May 5, 2003, 17, http://newfirstsearch.oclc.org.

Pryce-Jones, David. "The Great Sorting Out: Postwar Iraq." *National Review,* May 5, 2003, 17-18. http://newfirstsearch.oclc.org.

Magazine article published online

17. Fiona Morgan, "Banning the Bullies," *Salon,* March 15, 2001, http://www.salon.com/news/feature/2001/03/15/bullying/index.html.

Morgan, Fiona. "Banning the Bullies." *Salon,* March 15, 2001. http://www.salon.com/news/feature/2001/03/15/bullying/index.html.

■ **18. ARTICLE IN A NEWSPAPER** For newspaper articles — whether in print or online — page numbers are not necessary. A section letter or number, if available, is sufficient.

18. Dan Barry, "A Mill Closes, and a Hamlet Fades to Black," *New York Times,* February 16, 2001, sec. A.

Barry, Dan. "A Mill Closes, and a Hamlet Fades to Black." *New York Times,* February 16, 2001, sec. A.

For an article accessed through a database such as *ProQuest* or for an article published online, include a URL.

Newspaper article from a database service

18. Gina Kolata, "Scientists Debating Future of Hormone Replacement," *New York Times,* October 23, 2002, http://www.proquest.com.

Kolata, Gina. "Scientists Debating Future of Hormone Replacement." *New York Times,* October 23, 2002. http://www.proquest.com.

Newpaper article published online

18. Phil Willon, "Ready or Not," *Los Angeles Times,* December 2, 2001, http://www.latimes.com/news/la-foster-special.special.

Willon, Phil. "Ready or Not." *Los Angeles Times,* December 2, 2001. http://www.latimes.com/news/la-foster-special.special.

■ **19. UNSIGNED ARTICLE** When the author of a periodical article is unknown, treat the periodical itself as the author.

19. *Boston Globe,* "Renewable Energy Rules," August 11, 2003, sec. A.

Boston Globe. "Renewable Energy Rules." August 11, 2003, sec. A.

■ **20. BOOK REVIEW**

20. Nancy Gabin, review of *The Other Feminists: Activists in the Liberal Establishment,* by Susan M. Hartman, *Journal of Women's History* 12, no. 3 (2000): 230.

Gabin, Nancy. Review of *The Other Feminists: Activists in the Liberal Establishment,* by Susan M. Hartman. *Journal of Women's History* 12, no. 3 (2000): 227-34.

Web sites and postings

■ **21. WEB SITE** Include as much of the following information as is available: author, title of the site, sponsor of the site, and the site's URL. When no author is named, treat the sponsor as the author.

21. Kevin Rayburn, *The 1920s,* http://www.louisville.edu/~kprayb01/1920s.html.

Rayburn, Kevin. *The 1920s.* http://www.louisville.edu/~kprayb01/1920s.html.

NOTE: *The Chicago Manual of Style* does not advise including the date you accessed a Web source, but you may provide an access date after the URL if the cited material is time-sensitive: for example, http://www.historychannel.com/today (accessed May 1, 2005).

■ **22. SHORT DOCUMENT FROM A WEB SITE**   Include as many of the following elements as are available: author's name, title of the short work, title of the site, sponsor of the site, and the URL. When no author is named, treat the site's sponsor as the author.

22. Sheila Connor, "Historical Background," *Garden and Forest,* Library of Congress, http://lcweb.loc.gov/preserv/prd/gardfor/historygf.html.

Connor, Sheila. "Historical Background." *Garden and Forest.* Library of Congress. http://lcweb.loc.gov/preserv/prd/gardfor/historygf.html.

22. PBS Online, "Media Giants," *Frontline: The Merchants of Cool,* http://www.pbs.org/wgbh/pages/frontline/shows/cool/giants.

PBS Online. "Media Giants." *Frontline: The Merchants of Cool.* http://www.pbs.org/wgbh/pages/frontline/shows/cool/giants.

■ **23. ONLINE POSTING OR E-MAIL**   If an online posting has been archived, include a URL, as in the following example. E-mails that are not part of an online discussion are treated as personal communications (see item 26). Online postings and e-mails are not included in the bibliography.

23. Janice Klein, posting to State Museum Association discussion list, June 19, 2003, http://listserv.nmmnh-abq.mus.nm.us/scripts/wa.exe?A2=ind0306c&L=sma-l&F=lf&S=&P=81.

Other sources (print, online, multimedia)

■ **24. GOVERNMENT DOCUMENT**

24. U.S. Department of State, *Foreign Relations of the United States: Diplomatic Papers, 1943* (Washington, DC: GPO, 1965), 562.

U.S. Department of State. *Foreign Relations of the United States: Diplomatic Papers, 1943.* Washington, DC: GPO, 1965.

■ **25. UNPUBLISHED DISSERTATION**

25. Stephanie Lynn Budin, "The Origins of Aphrodite (Greece)" (PhD diss., University of Pennsylvania, 2000), 301-2.

Budin, Stephanie Lynn. "The Origins of Aphrodite (Greece)." PhD diss., University of Pennsylvania, 2000.

■ **26. PERSONAL COMMUNICATION**

26. Sara Lehman, e-mail message to author, August 13, 2003.

Personal communications are not included in the bibliography.

■ **27. PUBLISHED OR BROADCAST INTERVIEW**

27. Ron Haviv, interview by Charlie Rose, *The Charlie Rose Show,* PBS, February 12, 2001.

Haviv, Ron. Interview by Charlie Rose. *The Charlie Rose Show,* PBS, February 12, 2001.

■ **28. VIDEO OR DVD**

28. *The Secret of Roan Inish,* DVD, directed by John Sayles (1993; Culver City, CA: Columbia TriStar Home Video, 2000).

The Secret of Roan Inish. DVD. Directed by John Sayles. 1993; Culver City, CA: Columbia TriStar Home Video, 2000.

■ **29. SOUND RECORDING**

29. Gustav Holst, *The Planets,* Royal Philharmonic, André Previn, Telarc compact disc 80133.

Holst, Gustav. *The Planets.* Royal Philharmonic. André Previn. Telarc compact disc 80133.

■ **30. SOURCE QUOTED IN ANOTHER SOURCE**

30. Adam Smith, *The Wealth of Nations* (New York: Random House, 1965), 11, quoted in Mark Skousen, *The Making of Modern Economics: The Lives and the Ideas of the Great Thinkers* (Armonk, NY: M. E. Sharpe, 2001), 15.

Smith, Adam. *The Wealth of Nations,* 11. New York: Random House, 1965. Quoted in Mark Skousen, *The Making of Modern Economics: The Lives and the Ideas of the Great Thinkers* (Armonk, NY: M. E. Sharpe, 2001), 15.

Chicago manuscript format

The following guidelines for formatting a *Chicago* paper and preparing its endnotes and bibliography are based on *The Chicago Manual of Style,* 15th ed. For pages from a sample paper, see pages 245–50.

Formatting the paper

Chicago manuscript guidelines are fairly generic, since they were not created with a specific type of writing in mind.

TITLE PAGE Include the full title of your paper, your name, the course title, the instructor's name, and the date. Do not number the title page but count it in the manuscript numbering; that is, the first page of the text will be numbered 2. See page 245 for a sample title page.

PAGINATION Using arabic numerals, number all pages except the title page in the upper right corner. Depending on your instructor's preference, you may also use a short title or your last name before the page numbers to help identify pages in case they come loose from your manuscript.

MARGINS AND LINE SPACING   Leave margins of at least one inch at the top, bottom, and sides of the page. Double-space the entire manuscript, including long quotations that have been set off from the text. (For line spacing in notes and the bibliography, see p. 243.) Left-align the text.

LONG QUOTATIONS   When a quotation is fairly long, set it off from the text by indenting (see also p. 247). Indent the full quotation one-half inch (five spaces) from the left margin. Quotation marks are not needed when a quotation has been set off from the text.

VISUALS   *The Chicago Manual* classifies visuals as tables and illustrations (illustrations, or figures, include drawings, photographs, maps, and charts). Keep visuals as simple as possible. Label each table with an arabic numeral (Table 1, Table 2, and so on) and provide a clear title that identifies the subject. The label and title should appear on separate lines above the table, flush left. Below the table, give its source in a note like this one:

> *Source:* Edna Bonacich and Richard P. Appelbaum, *Behind the Label* (Berkeley: University of California Press, 2000), 145.

For each figure, place a label and a caption below the figure, flush left. The label and caption need not appear on separate lines. The word "Figure" may be abbreviated to "Fig."

In the text of your paper, discuss the most significant features of each visual. Place visuals as close as possible to the sentences that relate to them unless your instructor prefers them in an appendix.

Preparing the endnotes

Begin the endnotes on a new page at the end of the paper. Center the title Notes about one inch from the top of the page, and number the pages consecutively with the rest of the manuscript. See pages 248–49 for an example.

INDENTING AND NUMBERING Indent the first line of each note one-half inch (or five spaces) from the left margin; do not indent additional lines in the note. Begin the note with the arabic numeral that corresponds to the number in the text. Put a period after the number.

LINE SPACING Single space each note and double-space between notes (unless your instructor prefers double-spacing throughout).

Preparing the bibliography

Typically, the notes in *Chicago*-style papers are followed by a bibliography, an alphabetically arranged list of all the works cited or consulted (see p. 250 for an example). Center the title Bibliography about one inch from the top of the page. Number bibliography pages consecutively with the rest of the paper.

ALPHABETIZING THE LIST Alphabetize the bibliography by the last names of the authors (or editors); when a work has no author or editor, alphabetize it by the first word of the title other than *A, An,* or *The.*

If your list includes two or more works by the same author, use three hyphens instead of the author's name in all entries after the first. You may arrange the entries alphabetically by title or by date; be consistent throughout the bibliography.

INDENTING AND LINE SPACING Begin each entry at the left margin, and indent any additional lines one-half inch (or five spaces). Single-space each entry and double-space between entries (unless your instructor prefers double-spacing throughout).

Sample pages from a research paper: *Chicago* style

Following are sample pages from a research paper by Ned Bishop, a student in a history class. (The complete paper is available at <http://dianahacker.com/resdoc>.) Bishop was asked to document his paper using *Chicago*-style endnotes and a bibliography. In preparing his manuscript, Bishop also followed *Chicago* guidelines.

The Massacre at Fort Pillow:
Holding Nathan Bedford Forrest Accountable

Ned Bishop

History 214
Professor Citro
March 22, 2001

Although Northern newspapers of the time no doubt exaggerated some of the Confederate atrocities at Fort Pillow, most modern sources agree that a massacre of Union troops took place there on April 12, 1864. It seems clear that Union soldiers, particularly black soldiers, were killed after they had stopped fighting or had surrendered or were being held prisoner. Less clear is the role played by Major General Nathan Bedford Forrest in leading his troops. Although we will never know whether Forrest directly ordered the massacre, evidence suggests that he was responsible for it.

What happened at Fort Pillow?

Fort Pillow, Tennessee, which sat on a bluff overlooking the Mississippi River, had been held by the Union for two years. It was garrisoned by 580 men, 292 of them from the Sixth United States Colored Heavy and Light Cavalry, 285 from the white Thirteenth Tennessee Cavalry. Nathan Bedford Forrest's troops numbered about 1,500 men.[1]

The Confederates attacked Fort Pillow on April 12, 1864, and had virtually surrounded the fort by the time Forrest arrived on the battlefield. At 3:30 p.m., Forrest displayed a flag of truce and sent in a demand for unconditional surrender of the sort he had used before: "The conduct of the officers and men garrisoning Fort Pillow has been such as to entitle them to being treated as prisoners of war. . . . Should my demand be refused, I cannot be responsible for the fate of your command."[2] Union Major William Bradford, who had replaced Major Booth, killed earlier by sharpshooters, asked for an hour to consult. Forrest, worried that vessels in the river were bringing in more troops, shortened the time to twenty minutes. Bradford refused to surrender, and Forrest quickly ordered the attack.

The Confederates charged across the short distance between their lines and the fort, helping one another scale the parapet, from which they fired into the fort. Victory came quickly, with the Union forces running toward the river or surrendering. Shelby Foote describes the scene like this:

> Some kept going, right into the river, where a number drowned and the swimmers became targets for marksmen on the bluff. Others, dropping their guns in terror, ran back toward the Confederates with their hands up, and of these some were spared as prisoners, while others were shot down in the act of surrender.[3]

In his own official report, Forrest makes no mention of the massacre. He does make much of the fact that the Union flag was not taken down, saying that if his own men had not taken down the flag, "few if any, would have survived unhurt another volley."[4] However, as Jack Hurst points out and Forrest must have known, in this twenty-minute battle, "Federals running for their lives had little time to concern themselves with a flag."[5]

The federal congressional report on Fort Pillow, which charged the Confederates with appalling atrocities, drew much criticism from Southern writers, and even respected writer Shelby Foote, who does not deny a massacre occurred, says it was largely a "tissue of lies."[6] In an important article, John Cimprich and Robert C. Mainfort Jr. argue that the most trust-

Notes

1. John Cimprich and Robert C. Mainfort Jr., "Fort Pillow Revisited: New Evidence about an Old Controversy," *Civil War History* 28, no. 4 (1982): 293-94.

2. Quoted in Brian Steel Wills, *A Battle from the Start: The Life of Nathan Bedford Forrest* (New York: HarperCollins, 1992), 182.

3. Shelby Foote, *The Civil War, a Narrative: Red River to Appomattox* (New York: Vintage, 1986), 110.

4. Nathan Bedford Forrest, "Report of Maj. Gen. Nathan B. Forrest, C. S. Army, Commanding Cavalry, of the Capture of Fort Pillow," *Shotgun's Home of the American Civil War,* http://www.civilwarhome.com/forrest.htm.

5. Jack Hurst, *Nathan Bedford Forrest: A Biography* (New York: Knopf, 1993), 174.

6. Foote, *Civil War,* 111.

7. Cimprich and Mainfort, "Fort Pillow," 305.

8. Ibid., 299.

9. Foote, *Civil War,* 110.

10. Wills, *Battle from the Start,* 187.

11. Albert Castel, "The Fort Pillow Massacre: A Fresh Examination of the Evidence," *Civil War History* 4, no. 1 (1958): 44-45.

12. Cimprich and Mainfort, "Fort Pillow," 300.

13. Hurst, *Nathan Bedford Forrest,* 177.

14. Ibid.

15. Dudley Taylor Cornish, *The Sable Arm: Black Troops in the Union Army, 1861-1865* (Lawrence, KS: University Press of Kansas, 1987), 175.

16. Foote, *Civil War,* 111.

17. Cimprich and Mainfort, "Fort Pillow," 304.

18. Wills, *Battle from the Start,* 189.

19. Ibid., 215.

20. Hurst, *Nathan Bedford Forrest,* 177.

21. James M. McPherson, *Battle Cry of Freedom: The Civil War Era* (New York: Oxford University Press, 1988), 402.

22. Hurst, *Nathan Bedford Forrest,* 74.

23. Foote, *Civil War,* 106.

Bibliography

Castel, Albert. "The Fort Pillow Massacre: A Fresh Examination of the Evidence." *Civil War History* 4, no. 1 (1958): 37-50.

Cimprich, John, and Robert C. Mainfort Jr. "Fort Pillow Revisited: New Evidence about an Old Controversy." *Civil War History* 28, no. 4 (1982): 293-306.

Cornish, Dudley Taylor. *The Sable Arm: Black Troops in the Union Army, 1861-1865.* Lawrence, KS: University Press of Kansas, 1987.

Foote, Shelby. *The Civil War, a Narrative: Red River to Appomattox.* New York: Vintage, 1986.

Forrest, Nathan Bedford. "Report of Maj. Gen. Nathan B. Forrest, C. S. Army, Commanding Cavalry, of the Capture of Fort Pillow." *Shotgun's Home of the American Civil War.* http://www.civilwarhome.com/forrest.htm.

Hurst, Jack. *Nathan Bedford Forrest: A Biography.* New York: Knopf, 1993.

McPherson, James M. *Battle Cry of Freedom: The Civil War Era.* New York: Oxford University Press, 1988.

Wills, Brian Steel. *A Battle from the Start: The Life of Nathan Bedford Forrest.* New York: HarperCollins, 1992.

CSE Style: Biology and Other Sciences

CSE documentation systems

Though scientific publications document sources in similar ways, the details of presenting source information vary from journal to journal. Often publications provide prospective authors with style sheets that outline formats for presenting sources. Before submitting an article to a scientific publication, you should request its style sheet. If one is not available, examine a copy of the publication to see how sources are documented. When writing for a science course, check with your instructor about how to cite and list your sources.

Most biologists, zoologists, earth scientists, geneticists, and other scientists use one of three systems of documentation specified by the Council of Science Editors in *Scientific Style and Format: The CSE Manual for Authors, Editors, and Publishers* (7th ed., 2006).

In the CSE *name-year* system, the author of the source is named in the text and the date is given in parentheses. The APA documentation section of this booklet (see pp. 186–228) describes an author-date system that is similar to the CSE name-year system.

In the CSE *citation-sequence* system, each source cited in the paper is given a number the first time it appears in the text. Anytime the source is referred to again, the text is marked with the same number. At the end of the paper, a list of references provides full publication information for each numbered source. Entries in the reference list are numbered in the order in which they are mentioned in the paper.

In the CSE *citation-name* system, the list of references is first put in alphabetical order and then the entries are numbered in that order. Those numbers are used in the text to cite the sources from the list.

This section describes formatting of in-text citations and the reference list in all three systems and gives specific models for entries in a citation-sequence reference list.

CSE in-text citations

In the text of a paper using the citation-sequence or citation-name system, the source is referenced by a superscript number.

IN-TEXT CITATION

Scientists are beginning to question the validity of linking genes to a number of human traits and disorders [1].

At the end of the paper, on a page titled References or Cited References, the source is fully identified according to CSE style.

ENTRY IN THE REFERENCE LIST

1. Horgan J. Eugenics revisited. Sci Am. 1993;268(6):122-130.

If the author or publication date of a particular work is important to your discussion, add this information to the sentence.

Smith [11], studying three species of tree frogs in South Carolina, was the first to observe. . . .

This species was not listed in early floras of New York; however, in 1985 it was reported in a botanical survey of Chenango County [13] and has since been verified [14].

In the name-year system, the author's name and the date are given in parentheses in the text of the paper. Alternatively, the author's name can be given in a signal phrase and the date in parentheses.

> This species was not listed in early floras of New York; however, it was reported in a botanical survey of Chenango County (Osiecki and Smith 1985).

> Smith (2003), studying three species of tree frogs in South Carolina, was the first to observe. . . .

Sometimes you will refer to a specific part of a source (such as a figure or a table) or will quote the exact words of a sourse. CSE does not provide guidelines for citing a specific part of a source, but your instructor will probably expect you to include an exact reference. The following style is consistent with CSE's other guidelines.

> My data thus differ markedly from Markam's study on the same species in New York [5](Figs. 2,7).

> Researchers observed an immune response in "19 of 20 people who ate a potato vaccine aimed at the Norwalk virus," according to Langridge [3](p. 68).

CSE reference list

BASIC FORMAT   Center the title References (or Cited References) and then list the works you have cited in the paper; do not include other works you may have read. Double-space throughout.

ORGANIZATION OF THE LIST   In the citation-sequence system, number the entries in the order in which they appear in the text. In the citation-name system, first alphabetize all the entries by authors' last names (or by organization name or by title for a work with no author). Then number the entries in the order in which they appear in the list. In both systems, use the number in the reference list every time you refer to the corresponding source in the paper. Make the entire entry flush with the left margin.

In the name-year system, the entries in the reference list are not numbered. They are alphabetized by authors' last names (or by organization name or by title for a work with no author). The year is placed after the last author's name, followed by a period. To convert the models shown here to the name-year system, omit the number and move the date of publication after the last author's name. CSE provides no guidelines for formatting a reference list in the name-year system in a student paper, but you can use a hanging indent for readability: Type the first line of each entry flush left, and indent any additional lines one-half inch (or five spaces).

AUTHORS' NAMES List authors' names last name first. Use initials for first and middle names, with no periods after the initials and no space between them. Do not use a comma between the last name and the initials. Use all authors' names if a work has up to ten authors; for a work with eleven or more authors, list the first ten names followed by a comma and "et al." (for "and others").

TITLES OF BOOKS AND ARTICLES Capitalize only the first word in the title of a book or article (and all proper nouns). Do not underline or italicize the titles of books; do not place titles of articles in quotation marks.

TITLES OF JOURNALS Abbreviate titles of journals that consist of more than one word. Omit the words *the* and *of*; do not use apostrophes. Capitalize all the words or abbreviated words in the title; do not underline or italicize the title: Science, Sci Am, N Engl J Med, Womens Health.

PAGE RANGES Do not abbreviate page ranges for articles in journals or periodicals and for chapters in edited volumes. When an article appears on discontinuous pages, list all pages or page ranges, separated by commas: 145–149, 162–174. For chapters in edited volumes, use the abbreviation "p." before the numbers (p. 63–90).

Books

■ **1. BASIC FORMAT FOR A BOOK** After the author(s) and title, give the place of publication, the name of the publisher, and the date of publication.

1. Melchias G. Biodiversity and conservation. Enfield (NH): Science; 2001.

■ **2. TWO OR MORE AUTHORS** List the authors in the order in which they appear on the title page. For a work with two to ten authors, list all the authors. For eleven or more authors, list the first ten followed by "et al." (for "and others").

2. Ennos R, Sheffield E. Plant life. Boston: Blackwell Scientific; 2000.

■ **3. EDITION OTHER THAN THE FIRST** Include the number of the edition after the title.

3. Mai J, Paxinos G, Assheuer J. Atlas of the human brain. 2nd ed. Burlington (MA): Elsevier; 2004.

■ **4. ARTICLE OR CHAPTER IN AN EDITED VOLUME** Begin with the name of the author and the title of the article or chapter. Then write "In:" and name the editor or editors, followed by a comma and the word "editor" or "editors." Place the title of the book and publication information next. End with the page numbers on which the article or chapter appears.

4. Underwood AJ, Chapman MG. Intertidal ecosystems. In: Levin SA, editor. Encyclopedia of biodiversity. Vol. 3. San Diego: Academic Press; 2000. p. 485-499.

Articles

■ **5. ARTICLE IN A MAGAZINE** Provide the year, month, and day (for weekly publications), followed by the page numbers of the article.

5. Stevens MH. Heavenly harbingers. Smithsonian. 2001 Nov:20, 22.

■ **6. ARTICLE IN A JOURNAL** After the author(s) and the title of the article, give the journal title, the year, the volume number, the issue number if there is one (in parentheses), and the page numbers on which the article appears.

6. Gulbins E, Lang F. Pathogens, host-cell invasion and disease. Am Sci. 2001;89(5):406-413.

■ **7. ARTICLE IN A NEWSPAPER** After the name of the newspaper, give the edition name in parentheses, the date of publication, the section letter (or number), the page number, and the column number. If the newspaper does not have section designations, use a colon between the date and the page number.

7. O'Neil J. A closer look at medical marijuana. New York Times (National Ed.). 2001 Jul 17;Sect. D:6 (col. 4).

■ **8. ARTICLE WITH MULTIPLE AUTHORS** For a work with up to ten authors, list the names of all authors. For a work with eleven or more authors, list the first ten names followed by a comma and "et al." (for "and others").

8. Longini IM Jr, Halloran ME, Nizam A, Yang Y. Containing pandemic influenza with antiviral agents. Am J Epidemiol. 2004;159(7):623-633.

■ **9. ARTICLE WITH A CORPORATE AUTHOR**   When a work has a corporate author, begin with the authoring organization, followed by the article title, journal title, and all other publication information.

9. International Committee of Medical Journal Editors. Clinical trial registration: a statement from the International Committee of Medical Journal Editors. JAMA. 2004;292(11):1363-1364.

In the name-year system, a familiar abbreviation for an organization is given in brackets at the beginning of the entry: [NCI] National Cancer Institute. 2004. The abbreviation is used in the in-text citation: (NCI 2004).

Electronic sources

CSE guidelines for Web sites and subscription services require publication information as for books: city, publisher, and publication date. This information can usually be found on the home page of a Web site and in a copyright link in a subscription service. Ask a reference librarian if you have trouble locating the information. In addition, include an update date if one is available and your date of access. Do not use a period at the end of a URL unless the URL ends in a slash.

■ **10. HOME PAGE OF A WEB SITE**   Begin with the author, whether an individual or an organization. Include the title of the home page (if it is different from the author's name), followed in brackets by the word "Internet." Provide the place of publication, the publisher (or the site's sponsor), and the date of publication. Include the copyright date if no date of publication is given or if the publication date and the copyright date are different: 2004, c2002. Include in brackets the date the page was last modified or updated and the date you accessed the site: [modified 2005 Mar 14; cited 2005 Nov 3]. Use the phrase "Available from:" followed by the URL.

10. American Society of Gene Therapy [Internet]. Milwaukee (WI): The Society; c2000-2005 [modified 2005 Jun 8; cited 2005 Jun 16]. Available from: http://www.asgt.org/.

■ **11. SHORT WORK FROM A WEB SITE** If the short work does not have an author or if the author is the same as the author of the site, begin the citation as you would for a home page. After the publication information, give the title of the short work, followed by the date of publication or most recent update, if available, and the date of access. Indicate in brackets the number or estimated number of pages, screens, paragraphs, lines, or bytes: about 5 p., about 3 screens, 12 paragraphs, 26 lines, 125K bytes. End the citation with the phrase "Available from:" followed by the URL.

11. Cleveland Clinic. The Cleveland Clinic Health Information Center [Internet]. Cleveland (OH): The Clinic; c2006. Smoking and heart disease; 1 Aug 2006 [cited 2006 Aug 8]; [about 5 screens]. Available from: http://www.clevelandclinic.org/health/health-info/ docs/0300/0384.asp?index=4585

If the short work has an author different from the author of the site, begin with the author and title of the short work, followed by the word "In:" and the home page information as in item 10. End with the URL for the short work.

■ **12. ONLINE BOOK** To cite an online book, follow the instructions for a home page, but include the description "Internet" in brackets following the title.

12. Wilson DE, Reeder DM, editors. Mammal species of the world [Internet]. Washington (DC): Smithsonian Institution Press; c1993 [cited 2005 Jun 16]; [about 200 screens]. Available from: http:// nmnhgoph.si.edu/msw

If you are referring to a specific chapter or section in an online book, begin the citation with the author and the title of the specific part. Follow with the word "In:" and the author, editor, title, and publication information for the entire book. End with access information about the specific part.

12. Olson S. The path to a PhD. In: Jarmul D, editor. Beyond bio 101: the transformation of undergraduate biology education [Internet]. Chevy Chase (MD): Howard Hughes Medical Institute; c2001 [cited 2005 Jun 17]; [about 2 screens]. Available from: http:// www.hhmi.org/beyondbio101/phdpath.htm

■ **13. ARTICLE IN AN ONLINE PERIODICAL** Begin with the name of the author and the title of the article. Include the name of the journal, followed in brackets by the word "Internet." Give the date of publication or the copyright date. Include in brackets the date the article was updated or modified, if any, and the date you accessed it, followed by a semicolon. Then provide the volume, issue, and page numbers. If the article is unpaginated, include in brackets the number or an estimated number of pages, screens, paragraphs, lines, or bytes. Write "Available from:" and the URL.

13. Isaacs FJ, Blake WJ, Collins JJ. Signal processing in single cells. Science [Internet]. 2005 Mar 25 [cited 2005 Jun 17];307(5717):

1886-1888. Available from: http://www.sciencemag.org/cgi/
content/full/307/5717/1886

■   **14. WORK FROM A SUBSCRIPTION SERVICE** CSE does not provide guidelines for an article accessed through a subscription service, such as *InfoTrac* or *EBSCOhost.* The guidelines
presented here are based on CSE's models for an article in
an online periodical and for a complete database.

Begin with information about the online article, as in
item 13. Follow with the name of the database, the place of
publication, the publisher, and the date of publication or the
copyright date. End with the phrase "Available from:" followed by the URL for the database. Include an article or document number, if the database assigns one, after the URL.

14. Cantor RM, Kono N, Duvall JA, Alvarez-Retuerto A, Stone JL,
Alarcon M, Nelson SF, Geschwind DH. Replication of autism linkage:
fine-mapping peak at 17q21. Am J Hum Genet [Internet]. 2005 [cited
2005 Jun 17];76(6):1050-1056. Expanded Academic ASAP. Farmington
Hills (MI): Thomson Gale; c2005. Available from: http://
web4.infotrac.galegroup.com/. Document No.: A133015879.

■   **15. E-MAIL** CSE recommends not including personal
communications such as e-mail in the reference list. A parenthetical note in the text usually suffices: (2006 e-mail to
me; unreferenced).

■   **16. ONLINE POSTING** Online postings include messages to
e-mail discussion lists (often called LISTSERVs), Web
forums, newsgroups, or bulletin boards. CSE does not provide guidelines for including postings in the reference list,
but the following formatting is consistent with other CSE
advice. Begin with the author initiating the message and
the subject line of the message. Next use the word "In:" followed by the name of the host system and in brackets the

phrase "discussion list on the Internet." Give the place where the discussion list is issued and the individual or organization that hosts the discussion list. Provide the date and time the message was posted, the date you accessed it, and the length of the message in screens, paragraphs, lines, or bytes. End with the phrase "Available from:" followed by the e-mail address by which the list can be accessed or the URL at which the list is archived.

16. Buxbaum E. Bradford protein assay in membrane crystals. In: BIOSCI/Bionet: protein-analysis [discussion list on the Internet]. Bloomington: Indiana University; 2005 Jan 26, 10:45 am [cited 2005 Jun 22]; [about 16 lines]. Available from: http://www.bio.net/bionet/mm/proteins/2005-January/000010.html

Other sources (print and electronic)

The advice in this section refers to the print versions of the following sources, but in each case an example is also given for an electronic version.

■ **17. GOVERNMENT REPORT** Begin with the name of the agency and, in parentheses, the country of origin if it is not part of the agency name. Next include the title of the report, a description of the report (if any), the place of publication, the publisher, and the date of publication. Give any relevant identifying information, such as a document number, and then the phrase "Available from:" followed by the name, city, and state of the organization that makes the report available or the URL for an online source.

17. National Institute on Drug Abuse (US). Inhalant abuse. Research Report Series. Bethesda (MD): National Institutes of Health (US); 2005 Mar. NIH Pub. No.: 00-3818. Available from: National Clearinghouse on Alcohol and Drug Information, Rockville, MD 20852.

17. National Institute on Drug Abuse (US). Inhalant abuse [Internet]. Research Report Series. Bethesda (MD): National Institutes of Health (US); 2005 Mar [cited 2005 Jun 23]; [about 13 screens]. NIH Pub. No.: 00-3818. Available from: http://www.drugabuse.gov/ ResearchReports/Inhalants/Inhalants.html

In the name-year system, begin with the abbreviation of the organization, if any, in brackets. (You will use the abbreviation in your in-text citations.) Use the complete name of the organization when you alphabetize the reference list.

[NIDA] National Institute on Drug Abuse (US). 2005 Mar. Inhalant abuse. . . .

■   **18. REPORT FROM A PRIVATE ORGANIZATION**   Begin with the name of the sponsoring organization. Next include the title of the report, a description of the report, the place of publication, the publisher, the year and month of publication, and the product number (if any).

18. American Cancer Society. Cancer facts and figures for African Americans 2005-2006. Report. Atlanta (GA): The Society; 2005.

18. American Cancer Society. Cancer facts and figures for African Americans 2005-2006 [report on the Internet]. Atlanta (GA): The Society; 2005 [cited 2005 Jun 23]; [535K bytes]. Available from: http://www.cancer.org/downloads/STT/CAFF2005AACorrPWSecured.pdf

■   **19. UNPUBLISHED DISSERTATION OR THESIS**   After the author and title of the work, indicate the type of work in brackets. List the city and state of the institution granting the degree, followed by the name of the institution and the date of the degree. Include an availability statement if the work is archived somewhere other than the sponsoring university's library (for example: Available from: University Microfilms, Ann Arbor, MI).

19. Warner DA. Phenotypes and survival of hatchling lizards [master's thesis]. Blacksburg: Virginia Polytechnic Institute and State University; 2001 Jan 16.

19. Warner DA. Phenotypes and survival of hatchling lizards [master's thesis on the Internet]. Blacksburg: Virginia Polytechnic Institute and State University; 2001 Jan 16 [cited 2005 Jun 22]; [125 p.]. Available from: http://scholar.lib.vt.edu/theses/available/ etd-01232001-123230/.

■ **20. CONFERENCE PRESENTATION** Begin with the author and title of the presentation. After the word "In:" give any editors and the name of the conference if it is not included in the title of the publication. Give the dates and location of the conference, followed by publication information and the inclusive page numbers for the presentation. Give an availability statement if appropriate.

20. Pendleton L. The cost of beach water monitoring errors in southern California. In: Proceedings of the 2004 National Beaches Conference; 2004 Oct 13-15; San Diego, CA. Washington (DC): Environmental Protection Agency (US); 2005 Mar. p. 104-110.

20. Pendleton L. The cost of beach water monitoring errors in southern California [conference presentation on the Internet]. In: Proceedings of the 2004 National Beaches Conference [Internet]; 2004 Oct 13-15; San Diego, CA. Washington (DC): Environmental Protection Agency (US); 2005 Mar [cited 2005 Jun 30]. p. 104-110. Available from: http://www.epa.gov/waterscience/beaches/meetings/2004/.

■ **21. MAP** First name the cartographer, if any, followed by the area represented, the title of the map, and, in brackets, the type of map. Provide the place of publication, publisher, and date of publication. If it is relevant, include a brief physical description of the map: the number of sheets, size, color or black and white, and scale.

21. Northeastern United States. West Nile virus: wild bird cases [demographic map]. Washington (DC): Department of the Interior (US); 2001 Jun 1. 1 sheet: color.

21. Northeastern United States. West Nile virus: wild bird cases [demographic map on the Internet]. Washington (DC): Department of the Interior (US); 2001 Jun 1 [cited 2005 Jun 22]; [1 screen]; color. Available from: http://nationalatlas.gov/printable/wnv.html

■ **22. AUDIO OR VIDEO RECORDING** Begin with the title of the work, followed by the medium in brackets. Next include, if available, the author, editor, and producer. Provide the place of publication, the publisher, and the date of publication. Give a brief physical description of the work and, in parentheses, identifying information, if any. End the citation with "Available from:" followed by the name, city, and state of the organization that distributes the work or the URL for an online source.

22. NOVA: cancer warrior [videocassette]. Quade D, editor; WGBH Boston, producer. Boston: WGBH Educational Foundation; 2001 Feb 27. 1 videocassette: 60 min., sound, color. Available from: WGBH Boston Video, Boston, MA.

22. NOVA: cancer warrior [video on the Internet]. Quade D, editor; WGBH Boston, producer. Boston: WGBH Educational Foundation; 2001 Feb 27 [cited 2005 June 22]; 60 min., sound, color. Available from: http://www.pbs.org/wgbh/nova/cancer/program.html

CSE manuscript format

Although the style manual of the Council of Science Editors does not include manuscript guidelines for student papers, most instructors will want you to format your manuscript in ways consistent with common scientific practice. The following guidelines for student writers have been adapted from CSE advice directed to professional authors. When in doubt, check with your instructor. For sample pages of a college biology paper, see pages 268–72.

MATERIALS Use good-quality 8½″ × 11″ white paper. Secure the pages with a paper clip.

TITLE Begin a college paper with an unnumbered title page. Center all information on the page: the title of your paper, your name, the name of the course, and the date. See page 268 for an example.

PAGINATION The title page is counted as page 1, although a number does not appear. Number the first page of the paper as page 2. Type the number in the top right corner of the page. Many instructors will want you to use a shortened form of the title before the page number.

MARGINS, SPACING, AND INDENTATION Leave margins of at least one inch on all sides of the page, and double-space throughout the paper. Indent the first line of each paragraph one-half inch (or five spaces). When a quotation is set off from the text, indent it one-half inch (or five spaces) from the left margin.

ABSTRACT Many science instructors require an abstract, a single paragraph that summarizes your paper. If your paper reports on research you conducted, use the abstract to describe your research methods, findings, and conclusions. Do not include bibliographic references in the abstract.

HEADINGS   CSE encourages the use of headings to help readers follow the organization of a paper. Common headings for papers reporting research are Introduction, Methods (or Methods and Materials), Results, and Discussion. If you use both headings and subheadings for a long paper, make sure to distinguish clearly between them with your choice of typography.

VISUALS   A visual should be placed as close as possible to the text that discusses it. In general, try to place visuals at the top of a page.

APPENDIXES   Appendixes may be used for relevant information that is too long to include in the body of the paper. Label each appendix and give it a title (for example, Appendix 1: Methodologies Used by Previous Researchers).

ACKNOWLEDGMENTS   An acknowledgments section is common in scientific writing because research is often conducted with help from others. For example, you might give credit to colleagues who reviewed your work, to organizations that funded your work, and to writers who allowed you to cite their unpublished work.

LIST OF REFERENCES   For advice on constructing a CSE reference list, see pages 253–56.

Sample pages: CSE style

The following sample pages are based on guidelines set forth in the CSE style manual, *Scientific Style and Format*, 7th ed. (2006).

Hypothermia, the Diving Reflex,
and Survival

Briana Martin

Biology 281
Professor McMillan
April 17, 2002

ABSTRACT

This paper reviews the contributions of hypothermia and the mammalian diving reflex (MDR) to human survival of cold-water immersion incidents. It also examines the relationship between the victim's age and MDR and considers the protective role played by hypothermia. Hypothermia is the result of a reduced metabolic rate and lowered oxygen consumption by body tissues. Although hypothermia may produce fatal cardiac arrhythmias such as ventricular fibrillation, it is also associated with bradycardia and peripheral vasoconstriction, both of which enhance oxygen supply to the heart and brain. The MDR also causes bradycardia and reduced peripheral blood flow as well as laryngospasm, which protects victims against rapid inhalation of water. Studies of drowning and near drowning of children and adults suggest that victim survival depends on the presence of both hypothermia and the MDR, as neither alone can provide adequate cerebral protection during long periods of hypoxia. Future research is suggested to improve patient care.

INTRODUCTION

Drowning and near-drowning incidents are leading causes of mortality and morbidity in both children [1] and adults [2]. Over the past 30 years, there has been considerable interest in cold-water immersion incidents, particularly the reasons for the survival of some victims under seemingly fatal conditions. Research suggests that both hypothermia and a "mammalian diving reflex" (MDR) may account for survival in many near-drowning episodes [3]. However, the extent to which these two processes interact is not fully understood. Controversy also exists regarding the effect of the victim's age on the physiological responses to cold-water immersion. In this paper, I provide an overview of recent research on the protective value of hypothermia and the MDR in cold-water immersions. I also examine hypotheses concerning the effects of age on these processes and conclude with suggestions about future lines of research that may lead to improved patient care.

Hypoxia during drowning and near-drowning incidents

The major physiological problem facing drowning victims is hypoxia, or lack of adequate oxygen perfusion to body cells [1,4]. Hypoxia results in damage to many organs, including the heart, lungs, kidneys, liver, and intestines [4]. Generally, the length of time the body has been deprived of oxygen is closely related to patient prognosis. Only 6-7 s of hypoxia may cause unconsciousness; if hypoxia lasts longer than 5 min at relatively warm temperatures, death or irreversible brain damage may result [5]. However, some victims of cold-water immersion have survived after periods of oxygen deprivation lasting up to 2 h [4]. . . .

[*The student goes on to highlight the major controversies and to add interpretation and analysis.*]

CONCLUSIONS

Recent research on cold-water immersion incidents has provided a better understanding of the physiological processes occurring during drowning and near-drowning accidents. Current findings suggest that the cooperative effect of the MDR and hypothermia plays a critical role in patient survival during a cold-water immersion incident [3]. However, the relationship between the two processes is still unclear. Because it is impossible to provide an exact reproduction of a particular drowning incident within the laboratory, research is hampered by the lack of complete details. Consequently, it is difficult to draw comparisons among published case studies.

More complete and accurate documentation of cold-water immersion incidents--including time of submersion; time of recovery; and a profile of the victim including age, sex, and physical condition--will facilitate easier comparison of individual situations and lead to a more complete knowledge of the processes affecting long-term survival rates for drowning victims. Once we have a clearer understanding of the relationship between hypothermia and the MDR--and of the effect of such factors as the age of the victim--physicians and rescue personnel can take steps to improve patient care at the scene and in the hospital.

ACKNOWLEDGMENTS

I would like to thank V. McMillan and D. Huerta for their support and suggestions throughout the research and writing of this paper. I am also grateful to my classmates in Biology 281 for their thoughtful comments during writing workshops. Finally, I thank Colgate University's interlibrary loan staff for help securing the sources I needed for this review.

CITED REFERENCES

1. Kallas HJ, O'Rourke PP. Drowning and immersion injuries in children. Curr Opin Pediatr. 1993;5(3):295-302.

2. Keatinge WR. Accidental immersion hypothermia and drowning. Practitioner 1997;219(1310):183-187.

3. Gooden BA. Why some people do not drown--hypothermia versus the diving response. Med J Aust. 1992;157(9):629-632.

4. Biggart MJ, Bohn DJ. Effect of hypothermia and cardiac arrest on outcome of near-drowning accidents in children. J Pediatr. 1999;117(2 Pt 1):179-183.

5. Gooden BA. Drowning and the diving reflex in man. Med J Aust. 1972;2(11):583-587.

6. Bierens JJ, van der Velde EA. Submersion in the Netherlands: prognostic indicators and the results of resuscitation. Ann Emerg Med. 1999;19(12):1390-1395.

7. Ramey CA, Ramey DN, Hayward JS. Dive response of children in relation to cold-water near drowning. J Appl Physiol. 1987;62(2):665-688.

List of Style Manuals

Research and Documentation describes four commonly used systems of documentation: MLA, used in English and the humanities (see pp. 129–85); APA, used in psychology and the social sciences (see pp. 186–228); *Chicago*, used in history and some humanities (see pp. 229–50); and CSE, used in biology and other sciences (see pp. 251–72). Following is a list of style manuals used in a variety of disciplines.

BIOLOGY (See pp. 251–72.)
Council of Science Editors. *Scientific Style and Format: The CSE Manual for Authors, Editors, and Publishers.* 7th ed. Reston: Council of Science Eds., 2006.

BUSINESS
American Management Association. *The AMA Style Guide for Business Writing.* New York: AMACOM, 1996.

CHEMISTRY
Dodd, Janet S., ed. *The ACS Style Guide: A Manual for Authors and Editors.* 2nd ed. Washington: Amer. Chemical Soc., 1997.

ENGINEERING
Institute of Electrical and Electronics Engineers. *IEEE Standards Style Manual.* Rev. ed. New York: IEEE, 2005 <http://standards.ieee.org/guides/style/2005Style.pdf>.

ENGLISH AND THE HUMANITIES (See pp. 129–85.)
Gibaldi, Joseph. *MLA Handbook for Writers of Research Papers.* 6th ed. New York: MLA, 2003.

GEOLOGY
Bates, Robert L., Rex Buchanan, and Marla Adkins-Heljeson, eds. *Geowriting: A Guide to Writing, Editing, and Printing*

in *Earth Science*. 5th ed. Alexandria: Amer. Geological
Inst., 1995.

GOVERNMENT DOCUMENTS

Garner, Diane L. *The Complete Guide to Citing Government
Information Resources: A Manual for Social Science and
Business Research*. 3rd ed. Bethesda: Congressional
Information Service, 2002.

United States Government Printing Office. *Style Manual*.
Washington: GPO, 2000.

HISTORY (See pp. 229–50.)

The Chicago Manual of Style. 15th ed. Chicago: U of Chicago
P, 2003.

JOURNALISM

Goldstein, Norm, ed. *Associated Press Stylebook and Briefing
on Media Law*. Rev. ed. New York: Associated Press,
2005.

LAW

Harvard Law Review et al. *The Bluebook: A Uniform System of
Citation*. 18th ed. Cambridge: Harvard Law Rev. Assn.,
2005.

LINGUISTICS

Linguistic Society of America. "LSA Style Sheet." Published
annually in the December issue of the *LSA Bulletin*.

MATHEMATICS

American Mathematical Society. Author Resource Center
<http://www.ams.org/authors>.

MEDICINE

Iverson, Cheryl, et al. *American Medical Association Manual of
Style: A Guide for Authors and Editors*. 9th ed. Baltimore:
Williams, 1998.

MUSIC

Holoman, D. Kern, ed. *Writing about Music: A Style Sheet from the Editors of* 19th-Century Music. Berkeley: U of California P, 1988.

PHYSICS

American Institute of Physics. *Style Manual: Instructions to Authors and Volume Editors for the Preparation of AIP Book Manuscripts.* 5th ed. New York: AIP, 1995.

POLITICAL SCIENCE

American Political Science Association. *Style Manual for Political Science.* Rev. ed. Washington: APSA, 2001.

PSYCHOLOGY AND OTHER SOCIAL SCIENCES (See pp. 186–228.)

American Psychological Association. *Publication Manual of the American Psychological Association.* 5th ed. Washington: APA, 2001.

SCIENCE AND TECHNICAL WRITING

American National Standards Institute. *American National Standard for the Preparation of Scientific Papers for Written or Oral Presentation.* New York: ANSI, 1979.

Microsoft Corporation. *Microsoft Manual of Style for Technical Publications.* 3rd ed. Redmond: Microsoft, 2004.

Rubens, Philip, ed. *Science and Technical Writing: A Manual of Style.* 2nd ed. New York: Routledge, 2001.

SOCIAL WORK

National Association of Social Workers. *Writing for the NASW Press: Information for Authors* <http://naswpress.org/resources/tools/01-write/guidelines_toc.htm>.

PART V. GLOSSARY OF RESEARCH TERMS

abstract A summary of an article. An abstract usually appears at the beginning of a scholarly or technical article. Databases and indexes often contain abstracts that can help you decide whether an article is relevant for your purposes.

annotated bibliography A list of sources that gives the publication information and a short description — or annotation — for each source. In some bibliographies the annotation merely describes the content and scope of the source; in others the annotation also evaluates the source's quality and usefulness.

anthology A collection of writings compiled into a book.

bibliography (1) A list of sources, usually appearing at the end of a research paper, an article, a book, or a chapter in a book. The list documents evidence used in the work and points out sources that might be useful for further research. Each entry provides publication information for each source so that an interested reader can track down the source. (2) A list of recommended readings on a given topic, usually sorted into subcategories.

Boolean operators The words *and, or,* and *not* used in databases or search engines to relate the contents of two or more sets of data in different ways. When search terms are combined with *and,* the search results contain only those items that include all the terms. When *or* is used, the results include items that contain any one of the terms. *Not* is used to exclude items containing a term.

call number The letter and number combination that indicates where a book is kept on a library's shelves. Call numbers are assigned using a system that locates books on the same subject next to one another for easy browsing. Most academic libraries use the Library of Congress (LC) system; public libraries typically use the Dewey decimal system.

catalog A database containing information about the materials owned by a library and their location. Most catalogs are online, though a library may have all or part of its catalog on cards. Catalogs usually can be searched by author, title, subject heading, or keyword; search results provide a basic description of the item (book, journal title, video, or other) and a call number.

citation A reference to a book, article, Web page, or other source that provides enough information to allow a reader to retrieve the source. Citations in a paper must be given in a standard format (such as MLA, APA, *Chicago,* or CSE), depending on the discipline in which the paper is written.

citation management software Computer programs that store bibliographic references and notes in a personal database and that can automatically format bibliographies, reference pages, or lists of works cited in the appropriate style (MLA, APA, *Chicago,* CSE).

citation trail The network of citations formed when a reference work refers to sources that in turn refer to additional sources. The process used by researchers to track down additional sources on a topic is sometimes referred to as following the path of a "citation trail" or "citation network."

cite (1) As a verb, to provide a reference to a source. (2) As a noun, a shortened form of *citation.* (*Note:* This term is frequently misused when referring to Web *sites.*)

corporate author An organization, an agency, an institution, or a corporation identified as an author of a work.

database A collection of data organized for retrieval. In libraries, databases usually contain references to sources retrievable by a variety of means. Databases may contain bibliographic citations, descriptive abstracts, full-text documents, or a combination.

descriptors Terms assigned by compilers of a database to describe the subject content of a document. Descriptors are chosen so that all of the work on a particular topic can be found with a single word or phrase, even though there may be many different ways of expressing the same idea. For example, the *PsycINFO* database uses *academic achievement* as a descriptor to help researchers locate texts on the subject of scholastic achievement or grade-point average. *See also* **subject heading.**

discipline An academic field of study such as history, psychology, or biology. Often books and articles published by members of a discipline and intended for other scholars are called *the literature of the discipline* — referring not to literary expression but to research publications in the field.

field (1) An area of study within an academic discipline. (2) A particular area in a database in which the same type of information is regularly recorded. One field in an article database may contain the titles of articles, for example, while another field may contain the names of journals the articles are in. Some search engines allow a user to limit a search to one or more specific fields.

full text A complete document contained in a database or on a Web site. (*Note:* Illustrations and diagrams may be omitted from a full-text document.) Some databases search full-text documents; others search only the citation or abstract. In some cases researchers can set their own preferences.

hits (1) The list of results called up by a search of a database, a Web site, or the Internet. (2) The number of times a Web site has been visited. Web site owners track hits as a measure of the popularity of a site.

holdings The exact items a library owns. The term most typically refers to the specific issues of a magazine or journal in a library. This information is often listed in a library's catalog as a *holdings statement.*

index (1) In a book, the alphabetical listing of topics and the pages on which information about them can be found. The index is located at the back of the book. (2) A publication that lists articles or other publications by topic. (3) An alphabetical listing of elements that can be found in a database.

journal A type of periodical usually sold by subscription and containing articles written for specialized or scholarly audiences.

keyword A word used to search a library database, a Web site, or the Internet. Keyword searches locate results by matching the search word to an item in the medium being searched. Keyword searches often search very broadly through many database fields. However, researchers who perform a keyword search using terms that are different from those used in the database may not retrieve all of the information in the database related to their topic. For example, a search using the keyword *third world* will find items containing that term but may not include related items using the term *developing countries*. *See also* **descriptors.**

library catalog. *See* **catalog.**

licensed database. *See* **subscription database.**

literature review A survey of published research on a particular topic. The purpose of a literature review (sometimes called a *review article*) is to select the most important publications on the topic, sort them into categories, and comment on them so that a researcher can gain a quick overview of the state of the art in that area. Published articles often include a literature review section to place their research in the context of other work in the field.

magazine A type of periodical containing articles that are usually written for general and popular audiences. Magazines are sold on newsstands or by subscription and earn a part of their revenue through advertising.

microform A process that reproduces texts in greatly reduced size on plastic film called *microfilm*. Flat sheets of microfilm are called *microfiche*. Both forms must be read on special machines that magnify the text.

online catalog. *See* **catalog.**

OPAC (online public access catalog). *See* **catalog.**

peer review A process during which a group of experts examine a document to determine whether it is worthy of publication. Journals and other publications use a peer review process — usually arranged so that reviewers do not know who the author of the document is — to filter articles for quality and relevance. *See also* **refereed publication.**

periodical A publication issued at regular intervals. Periodicals may be magazines, journals, newspapers, or newsletters.

periodical index A list of all the articles that have been published in a magazine, journal, newspaper, or newsletter or in a set of periodicals. Many periodical indexes are available as online databases, though many online versions are limited to articles published in the last ten or twenty years. Print indexes often include all years of a periodical's publication.

plagiarism The unattributed use of a source of information that is not considered common knowledge. Forms of plagiarism are failure to cite quotations and borrowed ideas, failure to enclose borrowed language in quotation marks, failure to put summaries and paraphrases in your own words, and submission of someone else's work as your own.

primary source An original source, such as a speech, diary, novel, legislative bill, laboratory study, field research report, or eyewitness account. While not necessarily more reliable than a secondary source, a primary source has the advantage of being closely related to the information it conveys and as such is often considered essential for research, particularly in history.

professional journal A journal containing scholarly articles addressed to a particular professional audience such as doctors, lawyers, teachers, engineers, or accountants. Professional journals differ from trade publications, which usually do not include in-depth research articles. *See also* **scholarly journal** and **trade publications.**

record Each item included in a database. Records contain the information about the books, articles, or other sources that users can search for in a database.

refereed publication A publication for which every submission is screened through a peer review process. Refereed publications are considered authoritative because unbiased experts have reviewed the material in advance of publication to determine its quality. *See also* **peer review.**

reference (1) A source used in research and mentioned by a researcher in a paper or an article. (2) In libraries, a part of the library's collection that includes encyclopedias, handbooks, directories, and other publications that are useful for finding overviews of information and facts. (*Note*: *Reference* may also indicate a desk or counter where librarians provide assistance to researchers.)

review article *See* **literature review.**

scholarly journal A journal that is primarily addressed to scholars, often focusing on a particular discipline. Scholarly journals tend to be refereed publications and for some purposes may be considered more authoritative than magazines. Scholarly journals tend to have articles that are substantial in length, use specialized language, contain footnotes or endnotes, and are written by academic researchers rather than by journalists. *See also* **refereed publication** and **magazine.**

search engine (1) A program that allows users to search for material on the Internet or on a Web site. (2) The search function of a database.

secondary source A source that comments on, analyzes, or otherwise relies on primary sources. An article in a newspaper that reports on a scientific discovery or a book that analyzes a writer's work is a secondary source.

serial A term used in libraries to encompass all publications that appear in a series: magazines, journals, newspapers, and books that are published regularly (such as annual reviews).

subject heading A word or phrase assigned to an item in a database to describe the item's content. This content information can help a researcher evaluate whether a book or an article is worth further examination. Subject headings also suggest alternative terms or phrases to use in a search. Most academic library catalogs use the *Library of Congress Subject Headings* to describe the subjects of books in the catalog. Other databases create their own list, or thesaurus, of accepted descriptive terms. In some databases, subject headings are called *descriptors*. *See* **descriptors.**

subscription database A database that can be accessed only by paying a fee. Most of the online materials that libraries provide free to their patrons are paid for by the library through a subscription. Often the material provided in a subscription database is more selective and quality controlled than sources that are freely available on the Web. Because these databases are often provided through a license agreement, they are sometimes referred to as *licensed databases.*

thesaurus A list of the subject headings or descriptors that are used in a particular catalog or database to describe the subject matter of each item. A thesaurus is useful to researchers because it identifies which term among a variety of available synonyms has been used by the database compilers to describe a topic. Some databases provide a searchable thesaurus that helps researchers choose the most effective search terms before they start searching.

trade publications Periodical publications, such as magazines or newsletters, covering specialized news and information for members of a particular profession or industry. Unlike scholarly journals, trade publications do not include in-depth research articles.

truncation A shortened version of a search term. In some search engines and databases, the root of a word plus a wild card symbol (such as an asterisk or a question mark) can be used to search all possible variations of the word. *See also* **wild card.**

URL (uniform resource locator) An Internet address. Most URLs consist of a protocol type (such as *http* or *telnet*), a domain name (such as *dianahacker.com*), and an extension of letters and/or numbers to identify an exact resource or page within the domain.

wild card A symbol used to substitute any letter or combination of letters in a search word or phrase. A wild card may replace a single letter (as in *wom*n,* to search for *women* or *woman* in one search) or any number of letters (as in *psycholog** to search for *psychology, psychologist,* and *psychological*). Typical wild card symbols are asterisks, question marks, and exclamation points. *See also* **truncation.**

Authors' names   Reverse the order of all authors' names. Use initials for first and middle names. Use an ampersand (&) for "and."

> Goodglass, H., & Blumstein, S.

When the author is an organization or government agency, provide the group's name.

> American Psychiatric Association.

Titles   Capitalize the first word and proper nouns for books, articles, and other short works. Capitalize all major words for journals. Italicize the titles of books, journals, and short works from Web sites. Do not put article titles in quotation marks.

- *Book:*
  The lost children of Wilder: The epic struggle to change foster care.

- *Article in a periodical:*
  Lead therapy won't help most kids. *Science News,*

- *Article from an online periodical or subscription service:*
  Comprehension skills of language-competent apes [Electronic version]. *Language and Communication,*

- *Short work from a Web site:*
  Exploring nonverbal communication.

Publication and retrieval information

- *Book:* Follow the author's name with the publication date. Follow the title with the publisher's location and name in brief form. (Spell out "University Press.")
  Bernstein, N. (2001). *The lost children of Wilder: The epic struggle to change foster care.* New York: Pantheon.

- *Article in a periodical:* Follow the author's name with the year, month, and day of publication (if any). Include the volume number after the periodical title, in italics.
  Roloff, J. (2001, May 12). Lead therapy won't help most kids. *Science News, 159,* 292.

- *Article from an online periodical:* For an online article with a print counterpart, no URL is needed; instead, include [Electronic version] following the title. For an online article without a print counterpart, include the retrieval date and the URL.
  Ashe, D. D., & McCutcheon, L. E. (2001). Shyness, loneliness, and attitude toward celebrities. *Current Research in Social Psychology, 6*(9). Retrieved July 3, 2001, from http://www.uiowa.edu/~grpproc/crisp/crisp.6.9.htm

- *Article retrieved from a subscription service:* Include the retrieval date, name of the database, and the document number (if available).
  Holliday, R. E., & Hayes, B. K. (2001). Dissociating automatic and intentional processes in children's eyewitness memory. *Journal of Experimental Child Psychology, 75*(1), 1-5. Retrieved February 21, 2001, from Expanded Academic ASAP database (A59317972).

Page numbers   If *consecutive,* provide range (e.g., 310-330). If *nonconsecutive,* list all pages (e.g., 7-10, 210-222). If *no page numbers in online sources,* provide paragraph numbers.

Authors' names Reverse the order of the first author's name. Use first and last names and middle initials.

> Riordon, William L., and Anne Gund.

When the author is an organization or government agency, provide the group's name.

> U.S. Department of State.

When the author cannot be determined, begin with the work's title.

Titles Capitalize all major words. Italicize titles of books, periodicals, and Web sites. Place titles of articles or short works from Web sites in quotation marks (followed by the title of the periodical or Web site).

- *Book:*
  > A First Draft of History.

- *Article in a periodical:*
  > "Radiation in Russia." *U.S. News and World Report,*

- *Article from an online periodical or subscription service:*
  > "Democracy Held Hostage." *Salon,*

- *Short work from a Web site:*
  > "Historical Background." *Garden and Forest.*

Publication and retrieval information

- *Book:* Give the publisher's location and name followed by the date.
  > New York: Knopf, 2005.
  > New Haven: Yale University Press, 2004.

- *Article in a periodical:* Follow the title or volume number with the publication date.
  > *National Review,* May 5, 2003,
  > *Educational Studies* 34, no. 2 (2003):

- *Article from an online periodical:* Follow the title of the periodical with the date of publication and the URL.
  > *Salon,* September 29, 2001. http://www.salon.com/news/feature/
  > 2001/09/20/democracy.index.html.

- *Article from a database service:* Follow the periodical title with as much publication information as is available, followed by the URL.
  > *Educational Studies* 34, no. 2 (2003): 266-67. http://search.epnet.com.

Page numbers Provide the range of pages (e.g., 210-43; 399-401).

Authors' names   Reverse the order of all authors' names. Use initials for first and middle names, with no periods or spaces.

Spier RE, Griffiths JB.

When the author is an organization or government agency, provide the group's name.

National Vaccine Advisory Committee (US).

Titles   Capitalize only the first word and proper nouns for books, articles in periodicals, and Web sites. Do not underline, italicize, or place titles in quotation marks. Abbreviate journal titles of more than one word.

- *Book:*

  Biodiversity and conservation.

- *Article in a periodical:*

  Apgar score imprecision. J Pediatr.

- *Article from an online periodical or subscription service:*

  A gene that heals. Popular Sci [Internet].

- *Short work from a Web site:*

  Rhinoviruses [report on the Internet].

Publication and retrieval information

- *Book:* Give the publisher's location, its name, and the publication date.

  Cambridge (MA): Harvard University Press; 2005.

- *Article in a periodical:* Follow the periodical title with the publication date.

  Discover. 2005 Aug;

- *Article in an online periodical:* Follow the periodical title with "Internet" in brackets. Provide the publication date; the retrieval date; volume, issue, and page numbers; and the URL. No period follows the URL unless the URL ends in a slash.

  Science [Internet]. 2005 Mar 25 [cited 2005 Jun 17];307(5717):1886-1888. Available from: http://www.sciencemag.org/cgi/content/full/307/5717/1886

- *Article retrieved from a subscription service:* Give print publication information, with the word "Internet" in brackets after the periodical title and the date of access in brackets after the publication date. Provide publication information for the database publisher, including the copyright date. End with the URL of the database and the document number, if any.

  Popular Sci [Internet]. 2001 [cited 2001 Sep 20];259(3):41. Health Source: Consumer Education. Ipswich (MA): EBSCO; c1984-. Available from: http://ehostweb17.epnet17.epnet.com/. Document No.: 4928058.

Page numbers   If *consecutive*, provide the range (e.g., 310-330, 22-24). If *nonconsecutive*, list all pages (e.g., 7, 8-12). If *no page numbers*, estimate the number of pages, screens, paragraphs, lines, or bytes, in brackets (e.g., [about 10 p.]).